ENVIRONMENTS FOR LEARNING

For TIMOTHY AND GENEVIEVE – may their environments always be conducive to learning

ENVIRONMENTS
FOR
LEARNING

Edited by Kevin Marjoribanks

NFER Publishing Company Ltd.

Published by the NFER Publishing Company Ltd.,
Book Division, 2 Jennings Buildings, Thames Avenue,
Windsor, Berks., SL4 1QS
Registered Office, The Mere, Upton Park, Slough, Berks., SL1 2DQ
First Published 1974
© Kevin Marjoribanks 1974
85633 040 X

Printed in Great Britain by
King, Thorne & Stace Ltd., School Road, Hove, Sussex, BN3 5JE
Distributed in the USA by Humanities Press Inc.
Hillary House-Fernhill House,
Atlantic Highlands, New Jersey 07716, USA

Contents

Acknowledgements

THE EDITOR wishes to thank the authors and journals concerned for their kind permission to reproduce the following articles, details of which are included in the introductions to the relevent sections.

Preface

A WIDELY-QUOTED – but seldom read – book of mine summarized a great deal of longitudinal evidence on the development of human characteristics. One set of generalizations about the rapid early development of selected characteristics was taken up by educators, politicians, and journalists to emphasize the importance of early childhood education and the need for further research on human development.

A second set of generalizations about the importance of the environment was given relatively little attention. It is this set of ideas which is the subject of the present book. We are all indebted to Kevin Marjoribanks for bringing together some of the critical papers and research approaches to the more sophisticated study of environments and their effects on human characteristics.

In this earlier work of mine, I attempted to emphasize the importance of the environment in accounting for changes in physical, cognitive, and emotional characteristics of humans. This was expressed in the formula $C_2 = C_1 + f(E_{1-2})$. That is, the measurement of an individual *characteristic* at time 2 (C_2) is accounted for by the measurement of the same characteristic at time 1 (C_1) plus some function of the *Environment* between times 1 and 2 (E_{1-2}). In our research, using longitudinal methods, we found that when the time between the two measurements of a characteristic is relatively small or when the characteristic has reached a stable condition, the relation between the two measurements approaches unity (if the measurements are perfectly reliable). However, in periods of rapid growth of a characteristic and in measurements of a characteristic separated by long time intervals, the environment has a large role to play. My students and I made this formula into a central hypothesis and search model to guide our further research.

My faculty colleagues had, over many years, taught me about the importance of social class and socioeconomic status, especially as it influences child rearing and educational achievement. When we applied indices of social class or socioeconomic status in our formula, we found that these environmental measures added little to the earlier measure of the characteristic (C_1) in predicting the later measure of the characteristic (C_2). We concluded that while a status measure such as social class or socioeconomic status was useful for some purposes, it was too general and too static a measure to serve as the environmental measure for such specific human characteristics as physical growth, verbal ability, intelligence, school learning, and selected personality characteristics.

My graduate students then proceeded to teach me how to attack the problem of environmental measurement for selected human characteristics. Instead of viewing the environment as a single entity, they conceived of a single physical environment as made up of a number of subenvironments, each of which operates to influence the development of a specific characteristic – stature, verbal ability, need achievement, etc.

Through a review of previous research and theory and from an analysis of the characteristic under investigation, they attempted to make a list of the environmental process most likely to have a direct influence on the development of the specific characteristic. They reasoned that it is what parents, teachers, or others in the environment *do* in their interactions with the individual that is likely to influence the development of the specific characteristic rather than the more static or status attributes of the parents, teachers, etc.

They then searched for ways in which to gather evidence on these process variables through interviews, observations, or other procedures. They also developed ways of summarizing the evidence in terms of the hypothesized variables. Finally, they related these separable as well as combined variables to the measurement of the characteristic under question. In these procedures, they typically found that a large proportion of the hypothesized variables were related to the characteristic, but that some of the variables were redundant while others departed greatly from the initial hypotheses. In many of the studies they attempted to replicate the research to determine whether the variables finally selected held up under cross-validation procedures.

In most of these studies, they found the environmental process measures to account for a quarter to two-thirds of the variance of the selected characteristic. Where they used longitudinal methods, they typically found the multiple correlation between the earlier measure of a characteristic plus the environmental measure to predict the later measure of the characteristic with correlations in the range of $+\cdot90$ to $+\cdot95$ (when corrected for the unreliability of the measurements). In general, our basic formula has been found to represent a good approximation of the data when the appropriate environmental measures are combined with good measures of the characteristics. There have been some major exceptions, especially with personality and attitudinal characteristics. We still have much to learn about how to measure some environments – and some characteristics.

While it has not been difficult to improve our predictions of particular characteristics through the use of environmental process measures, my students were not satisfied with a predictive approach to human characteristics. They held the view that environmental measurement when well done should enable us to explain why characteristics develop in a particular way. Where the prior theoretical work was supported by clear evidence for the environmental variables, they believed that this constituted strong evidence for the causal significance of these environmental variables for the development of particular human characteristics. In some cases, their views have been supported by later research which attempted *experimentally to alter* particular variables in the home or school and to determine, with appropriate experimental designs, the effects of these alterations. In general, I believe these students are on sound ground and that there is an accumulating body of evidence on the causal relations between environments and characteristics.

If further research supports these views, then we will better understand what it is that parents, teachers, and others do that influences the development of particular human characteristics. There is much to be learned about these processes. In this first stage of this research we have been primarily concerned about how adults influence the young. There is a strong likelihood that the young also influence the behaviours of the adults. Increasingly we must study the interactions of the young with adults and others in the environment.

It is my hope that this collection of readings on environmental measurement and research will prompt many researchers to make investigations in this area. But, more important, it is to be hoped that serious investigators in the social sciences and education will be alerted to the role of environmental processes in accounting for many aspects of human development and learning.

BENJAMIN S. BLOOM
PROFESSOR OF EDUCATION
UNIVERSITY OF CHICAGO

Introduction

A NEW and distinctive area of research, which is concerned with the investigation of the social-psychological environments of individuals, has started to emerge in the social sciences. Within this new field of inquiry, which may be labelled 'environmental social psychology', attempts are being made to increase our understanding of the relations between environments and human behaviour. Instead of defining environments in terms of global static indicators, such as social status and ethnic groups, the environmental social-psychological approach assesses environments in terms of sets of dynamic process variables. In educational research the new environmental approach has been used in investigations of the relationships between environments and the cognitive and affective characteristics of students. The purpose of presenting the following set of readings is to provide an evaluation of how successful this research has been in increasing our understanding of the environmental correlates of the cognitive and affective behaviour of individuals.

Much of the impetus for the environmental social-psychological approach has been supplied by the work of Bloom (1964), who proposed that the environment may be regarded as providing a network of forces and factors which surround, engulf and play on the individual. It is also suggested (e.g. see Dave, 1963; Wolf, 1964; Weiss, 1969) that the development of any particular human characteristic is related to a subset, or subenvironment, of the total set of environmental forces. For example, if in the following diagram ABCD represents the total set of environmental forces, then EFGH may represent a subenvironment of forces which is related to the development of verbal ability, while JKLM may represent another subenvironment related, say, to the development of achievement motivation. Thus the task of the researcher investigating the relation between the environment and a particular human characteristic becomes one of isolating, and then measuring, the pertinent subenvironment from the total set of environmental forces.

Once a subenvironment has been defined, it is necessary to consider the possibility that it may be present in a variety of situations, such as the home, community and school. Therefore, if an understanding of the relations between the social-psychological environment and cognitive and affective characteristics is to be

FIGURE 1

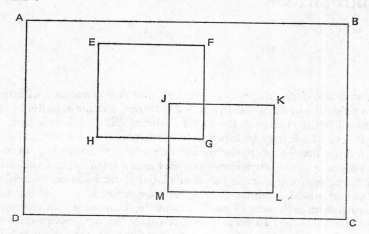

obtained, a model of environmental influences, such as that presented in the above diagram, is necessary as a guide for research. And in the following text the model has been used to assist in the presentation of the readings. That is, the readings have been presented so that they (a) reflect a transition from the use of global environmental indicators to social-psychological variables; (b) indicate the influence of the environment in a number of different ecological settings; and (c) assess the simultaneous influence on cognitive and affective characteristics of environments from different settings.

The readings have also been selected so that they bring together an analysis of the most recent theoretical, methodological and statistical developments in the study of environmental social psychology. The text is arranged into five interrelated sections. A theoretical, methodological and statistical overview is provided in the first part. Then the environmental influences on cognitive and affective characteristics of the community; the home; classroom; and college are examined in the following three sections. In the final part studies are presented which have investigated the simultaneous influences of environments from a number of settings.

In the overview, two readings have been presented. The first, by Walberg, indicates that educational research has not, in general, been guided by paradigms that could be expressed in mathematical form, and then subjected to statistical examination. In order to understand the process of learning, Walberg suggests that measures

FIGURE 2

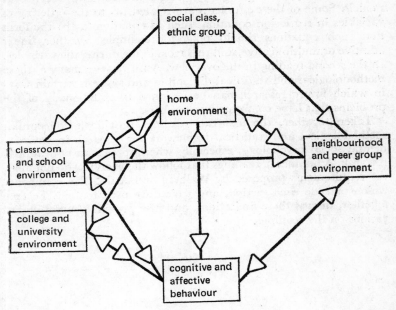

of the environment must be integrated into paradigms that also include assessments of student aptitude and types of instruction. Models of the form:

$$L_L = b_1 (A_i), b_2 (E_j), b_3 (I_k), \tag{1}$$

are suggested which state that learning (L_L) is a function (b) of aptitude (A_i), environment (E_j), and instruction (I_k).

From the paradigm a multiplicative model of learning is proposed in which:

$$L_L = b_1(A_i) + b_2(E_j) + b_3(I_k) + b_4(A_iE_j) + b_5(A_iI_k) + b_6(E_jI_k) \tag{2}$$

That is, a model which assumes that environment, aptitude and instruction interact with one another to afford a better prediction of learning than the first three terms alone. In order to predict learning outcomes, research using the paradigm would derive empirical weights (through regression analysis, for example) for each term in equation 2. Then particular values for each term would be multiplied by the corresponding weights and the final values summed together.

However, much of the research in environmental social psychology has been difficult to interpret owing to the many problems associated with deriving empirical weights from multiple regression models. Some of these problems are related (a) to the ordering of variables in regression equations such as equation 2, (b) the form that such equations should take, for example, whether linear additive or multiplicative, and (c) errors in measuring the variables. In the second reading in the overview, Astin reviews many of these methodological and statistical difficulties and suggests certain ways in which future research can be designed to avoid many of the problems that have confronted researchers.

Taken together, the first two readings provide a conceptual, methodological and statistical framework for research in environmental social psychology, especially when applied to educational research. A number of readings that follow the overview do not meet the requirements proposed by Walberg and Astin. The comments which precede each section, and which are used to link the text together, discuss these limitations, and also provide general observations on the readings.

PART ONE

The Overview

Readings

WALBERG, H. J. (1971). 'Models for optimizing and individualizing school learning', *Interchange*, 3, 15–27.
ASTIN, A. W. (1970). 'The methodology of research on college impact, part one', *Sociology of Education*, 43, 223–54.

1. Models for Optimizing and Individualizing School Learning

HERBERT J. WALBERG

In his paper, 'Twenty-five Years of Educational Research', Bloom (1966) called for a mapping of educational research and proceeded to sketch a global map of the present field. The original intent in preparing the present paper was to construct a territorial map of school learning using three of Bloom's land-form descriptors: (1) predictability of human characteristics, (2) effects of the environment, and (3) instructional strategies. The map was to be neither as global as Bloom's nor as detailed as an ordinary review of research. Consequently the working elements of the proposed map were to become the gross features or landmarks of more detailed reviews, particularly Bloom's (1964) massive summary and analysis of work on human characteristics and environments and Stephens' (1968) review of research on instruction. However, preliminary sketches revealed that even after a half-century of research, the area is much more like the old Northwest Territory than the streets of New York; explorers have blazed a few trails that may lead to the Continental Divide, but many of the wagon trains are moving on well-worn ruts that apparently lead in circles. At this point no satisfactory map can be drawn, but a description of the trails and ruts does seem possible. To get out of the wilderness, perhaps a few trails can be identified on the basis of how far they lead in optimizing and individualizing school learning.

Three Traditions in Educational Research
Individual Differences and Learning Variables
Historically, two substantive and methodological traditions in psychology have greatly influenced research in education. The first, 'experimental', originated in the work of Wundt and Pavlov and developed methodologically in the variance analysis of Fisher. The experimental tradition in educational research has generated hypotheses on how conditions and processes of instruction, particularly immediate stimulus variables, can be employed to optimize learning. The second tradition, 'correlational', had origins in the approaches

of Galton and Spearman and became grounded in the covariance techniques of Pearson and Thurstone. The correlational tradition in educational research has focused on individual differences, their interrelationships, and structure. Findings from this tradition have provided data and schemes for the accurate prediction of learning and selection for instruction.

In the last two decades, Cronbach (1957), Lindquist (1953), and others have reminded us that these two traditions must eventually be brought together and that in general psychology, stimulus and organismic variables must be investigated simultaneously. This position suggests that in educational research, the interactions of individual differences and instructional variables must be analysed. Indeed, 'individualizing' instruction (under one definition) depends on finding instructional treatments that are differentially effective for different learners.

Environmentalism

In the last decade, a third tradition has been emerging (or re-emerging) in social science research, i.e. 'environmentalism', the focus on the context of behaviour, particularly the social-psychological aspects. With origins in Darwin, it was applied to the study of society by Herbert Spencer and was incorporated into the mainstreams of sociology and psychology by George Herbert Mead and John Dewey. It became known as 'social' or 'symbolic interactionism' in sociology and 'Chicago functionalism' in psychology during the 1920s. More recently, the psychological study of the context of behaviour has had its advocates in Egon Brunswick and Kurt Lewin.

Bloom (1964) made a strong case for environmental research in education. Reviewing and consolidating work on growth rates and environmental effects, Bloom pointed to the development of measures of environment as crucial for accurate prediction and effective manipulation of learning. The work of Dave (1963) and Wolf (1964) on home environments and Pace and Stern (1958) and others on college environments have confirmed the powerful effects of contextual variables on learning (see Bloom, 1964).

Since 1966, a series of studies has demonstrated that student perceptions of the classroom learning environment can be measured reliably and that environmental measures are valid predictors of cognitive, effective, and behavioural measures of learning (Walberg, 1969b). Environmental variables themselves can be manipulated (Anderson, Walberg and Welch, 1969) and predicted from the class size, the biographical characteristics of its members, mean intelligence, prior interest and achievement, and instructional variables

(Walberg and Ahlgren, 1970). Moreover, powerful interactions have been identified between environment and both instructional variables (Walberg, 1969a) and individual differences in aptitudes and personality (Anderson, 1968; Bar-Yam, 1969).

Toward Integration

Thus the problem now requiring solution is the integration of the three traditions, particularly the incorporation of individual differences and environmental factors into experimental designs for instructional research. The three traditions are separately able to answer such questions as: Which students are most likely to succeed in a given instruction sequence? Which instructional method optimizes learning for students in general? Which environments stimulate learning of most students? Research based on an integration of the three traditions, however, would answer the same questions and these in addition: Which instruction (content, media, method) individualizes (is specifically best) for a student with a given aptitude? Which environment individualizes for students with given characteristics? Which environment is best for a given method of instruction?

When these questions are answered by research carried out in the laboratory or preferably in classroom settings, it will be possible to select the best instructional method or medium for each student or to place the student in the most appropriate stage in the sequence of instruction. Also, many other instructional management decisions for personally tailored education could be made on the basis of the research such that individuals in target populations will be learning under instruction and in environments optimally suited to their individual aptitudes. Theories of individualized instruction (discussed below) hold that learning would proceed farther and faster under these conditions.

Prediction: The Basis for Integration

A recently proposed model for research on school learning attempts to bring the three traditions to bear on school learning by hypothesizing that learning is a function of aptitude, environment, and instruction (Walberg, 1969a). Table 1 shows some rough estimates of the amount of variance in learning (school achievement) predicted by each of the three explanatory components of the general model. Measured intelligence is included as both an explanatory and criterion variable because it is the most pervasive aptitude (i.e. the most general predictor of school achievement).

Predicting Aptitudes

Consider first the factors associated with intelligence. Estimates of

TABLE 1: *Variance in intelligence and achievement associated with several factors*

	COMMON VARIANCE (PER CENT)	
Explanatory factor	*Measured intelligence*	*School achievement*
Heredity		
Burks (1928)	66	
Burt (1958)	77–88	
Jensen (1969)	81	
Leahy (1935)	78	
Newman, Freeman and Holzinger (1937)	65–80	
Woodworth (1941)	60	
Measured intelligence		40–60
Environment		
Social class (Bloom, 1964)	16 or less	25 or less
Home environment (Wolf, 1964; Dave, 1963)	58	64
School class—before (and after) removing aptitude variance		
Elementary school (Anthony, 1968)		58 (29)
High School (Walberg, 1969b)		37 (16)
College environment (Astin, 1968)—before (and after) removing aptitude variance		10–20 (3–6)
Instruction		
Individual studies (Schutz, 1966)		
Comparisons of two groups		5*
Comparisons of three groups		17*
Replication across studies		
(Stephens, 1968; see also Table 2)		near 0

* These figures have a strong upward bias; see text.

variance in measured intelligence associated with (or accounted for by) heredity range from ·60 (Woodworth, 1941) to ·81 (Jensen, 1969) with a mean of ·73. When crude measures of the child's environment are estimated by measures of socioeconomic status (such as parental education, income, or occupation), they typically account for less than 16 per cent of the variance in intelligence. On the other hand, when the home environment is measured more validly (on the basis of the number of books, the complexity of parental language, and similar indices), an estimated 58 per cent of the variance in intelligence can be predicted (Wolf, 1964). Now it is well known that genetic and environmental factors overlap and interact: e.g. bright parents stimulate their children; and bright children may make their own environments more stimulating. It would not be fruitful here to enter the nature-nurture controversy, which has a long history of complex, value-laden arguments, exceedingly difficult to resolve with present theory and research methods. It is important to note, however, that by school age, much of the variance in measured intelligence and other aptitudes in children and hence their school achievement is already predictable by factors beyond the reach of schools as they are presently organized (Bloom, 1964). For this reason, any model for research on school instruction, intended to guide the prediction (and eventual control) of learning, must take as one of its major components, the assessment of aptitudes.

Predicting Learning

Let us turn to the predictability of school achievement. It can be noted in Table 1 (and in literally hundreds of studies predicting grades and achievement test scores) that about 40–60 per cent of the variance in learning can be accounted for by measures of intelligence. With respect to environment, it can be noted, again, crude measures, social class indices, predict relatively little variance (25 per cent or less), but precise measures of the home environment (Dave, 1963) predict a major fraction of the variance (64 per cent) in school learning. More immediate but less pervasive measures, observer ratings of elementary school class environments (Anthony, 1968) and student ratings of high school class environments (Walberg, 1969b) account for a sizeable fraction of variance (58 per cent and 37 per cent, respectively) in school achievement (Table 1). These fractions are reduced considerably (though not below statistical significance or practical levels), however, after partialing out the effect of aptitude from learning criteria (see Table 1). It seems ironic that in educational research enormous efforts have gone into the measurement of aptitude that cannot be manipulated very effectively after school age (except in the sense of selecting students for instruction), while few studies have been made of environment that can be manipulated (Anderson, Walberg and Welch, 1969; Walberg and Ahlgren, 1970). In recognition of its potential, environment should also be included in models for research on instruction.

Instructional Variables

Thus measures of aptitude and environment must be considered because they predict learning. Instructional variables, however, must be included in the model by definition, not because they account for variance in learning criteria. This conclusion is supported by Schutz's (1966) tabulation of variance accounted for in learning criteria by experimental factors in instructional research reported in all issues of the *Journal of Educational Psychology* and the *American Educational Research Journal* for 1964. As shown in Table 1, the median variance accounted for in 38 studies of two-group comparisons (using T tests) was 17 per cent, and the median for 21 studies of three or more groups (using F tests) was five per cent. As Schutz points out, these figures are strongly biased upward since editors of these journals reject about 80 per cent of the manuscripts submitted, and those rejected tend to be statistically nonsignificant studies that account for little or no variance in learning criteria. Glass and Hakstian (1969) have reservations about the method used by Schutz, but it is accurate enough to show that instructional variables (as they have been recently investigated) typically make little difference in learning.

If the published results of instructional research tend to occur by chance, we should expect to find many conflicting or nonreplicated studies in the literature. This is exactly what Stephens (1968) concluded in his review of a half-century of instructional research. The main conclusions of Stephens and others (summarized in Table 2) suggest that the things commonly believed to promote learning actually make little or no difference at all. Summaries of research on teaching, for example, reveal that such modern techniques as group-centred versus traditional teacher-centred approaches or discussion opposed to lecturing produce essentially the same levels of student achievement. Similar conclusions apply to television and regular instruction, team and traditional teaching, instruction in large and small classes, homogeneous and heterogeneous groups, core and traditional curricula, and large and small schools. Now it might be hypothesized that while these factors have no effect singly, they would have powerful effects in concert provided funds were available. Astin (1968) has subjected this hypothesis to a rough test at the college level by attempting to predict scores on graduate school admission tests (Graduate Record Examination subscores) from such things as number of books in the library, percentage of faculty with PhD degrees, and per student expenditure for education (which ranged from $660 to $4,280 in his sample of colleges). After controlling for freshman aptitude (as measured on the Scholastic Aptitude Test) however, no significant impact of expenditures and instructional variables singly or as a group could be detected.

Why Instruction Apparently Makes No Difference

It should be made clear that the foregoing analysis applied to methods of instruction, not its content. Obviously when students are exposed to a given content, they are more likely than other students to learn it. A special instance is the baneful banality of curriculum evaluation: 'Students in a new course score higher on tests based on the new content, while students in traditional courses score higher on traditional tests'. The important question here, however, is why

TABLE 2: *Instructional factors and student achievement: a summary of review papers*

FACTOR	RESULTS
Time Attendance 　Finch and Nemzek (1940)	'While research at the moment is not conclusive, what there is tends to refute the common assumption that absence results in a harmful effect on scholarship as expressed by marks' (p. 920).
Stephens (1968)	Essentially no effect of attendance on achievement; accounts for one to four per cent of the variance.
Time spent in study 　(Strang, 1937)	In six studies reviewed, no significant correlation between time allowed or taken for instruction and achievement.
Units of Instruction Ability grouping 　(Ekstrom, 1961)	In 30 studies, no identifiable advantage or disadvantage of homogeneous grouping.
Class Size 　(Marklund, 1963)	Of 281 comparisons, 37 favoured large classes; 22, small classes; 222 were non-significant.
School Size 　(Hoyt, 1959)	Of 18 studies, six favoured large schools; three, medium-sized; three, smaller; six studies were non-significant.
Methods of Instruction Discussion vs. lecture 　(Wallen and Travers, 1963)	In a review of 16 studies: 'With respect to immediate mastery of factual information, most studies find no significant differences between lecture and discussion methods' (p. 481). Of three studies of long-term retention, two favoured discussion; one, lecture.
Teacher vs. group-centred techniques 　(Stephens, 1968)	A summary of three reviews of studies revealed a very slight and inconsistent favouring of teacher-centred methods.
Tutoring 　(Stephens, 1968)	Of three studies, one favoured tutoring, two favoured control groups.
Counselling 　(Callis, 1963)	Of four studies, one favoured counselled students; one had mixed results; and two were non-significant.
Televison 　(Schramm, 1962)	Of 393 studies, 83 favoured television; 55, regular classroom instruction; 255 were non-significant.
Programmed instruction 　(Stephens, 1968)	'Much to suggest that this device is about on par with other methods of individual study . . . overall superiority to classroom teaching is by no means apparent' (p. 82).

different methods of instruction fail to make detectable, replicable differences in learning.

Comparatively Weak Effects

In the first place, as noted above, heredity and pre-school environment are such potent forces that the effects of instructional methods are miniscule by comparison. Even after school entrance, learning environments outside school, such as the home and community, are more long-lasting, continuous, and pervasive than typical sequences of instruction. Moreover, replicated studies of social environments of classrooms suggest that they have an effect on learning that far outshadows instruction (see Table 1). These studies suggest that measures of learning environments must be included in classroom research to increase statistical control and precision. (Laboratory studies of pair-associates learning and 'brass instrument' psychology often fail to replicate in schools precisely because environmental variables obscure and confound stimulus variables in the classroom; in the laboratory, environmental variations, particularly the social aspects, are effectively eliminated or experimentally controlled.)

Research Methods and Manipulation

A second reason why research on instruction fails to detect differences in learning is inadequate research methods. It would be pointless to try to summarize the copious literature on methodology. What is needed now is examples of proven methods in substantive research in classrooms rather than more studies and criticism of methods as such. Yet it seems necessary to mention one methodological point related to the present argument. Methods of instruction may fail to make a difference because they are relatively homogeneous, e.g. a small change in class size or student participation is unlikely to have a great effect when a host of other variables are allowed to vary in natural settings (even when true experiments are carried out). In order to detect differences in learning, fairly radical changes must be brought about. (These, of course, are difficult to carry out in school experiments; and, for this reason, the International Study of Educational Achievement may prove to be extremely significant even though it is correlational. While instruction may vary little within countries, it varies enormously across countries as does achievement.)

Operationalism and Validity

Third, researchers have failed to define, specify, administer, and monitor both independent and dependent variables uniformly and validly across studies. One researcher's 'group-centred teaching' is another's 'inquiry learning'; one man's 'understanding' is another's 'comprehension'. Rigorous operational definitions, if not taxonomies of instruction and learning, will be required for generalization and replication. Moreover, researchers have generally chosen criteria of learning that can be measured precisely (reliably) rather than those that have relevance to important goals beyond themselves (predictive validity). While school boards, curriculum guides, parents, teachers, and students espouse holistic social, moral, and affective goals, the criteria of learning continue to be tests that tap random elements of factual knowledge and isolated cognitive skills. This tradition seems to insist that what cannot be precisely measured does not exist or is not important and, further, that what is most measurable is most important. Now it must be admitted that prior achievement test scores and grades predict scores and grades in subsequent levels of education and that reaching successive levels permits entry into higher levels in occupational hierarchies; in this sense, these measures are valid predictors. However, for groups of students who have attained a given level of education, course grades and achievement tests have almost no relationship to occupational success (Hoyt, 1965). (Hoyt's excellent but apparently little-known review of this subject surveyed studies of scientific researchers, school teachers, physicians, businessmen, and engineers employing criteria such as professional reputation, income, employer ratings, and on-the-job observations.)

Cost-Effectiveness and Evaluation
If the results of instructional research with conventionally measured learning criteria were to be combined with cost-effectiveness analysis, the results would suggest enormous 'efficiencies' by reducing expenditures for education while maintaining current 'benefits'. Happily, however, Congress and the general public have viewed education as too important to leave to dust bowl empiricists, and expenditures are likely to continue even though their benefits have not been 'scientifically' documented.

Clearly the industrial research model has not been (and perhaps cannot be) effectively applied to the broad field of education. A number of writers have specified stages of this model as they might be applied to educational innovation:
1. Idea (or analogy from outside education);
2. Research (basic disciplinary research and applied educational research);
3. Development (and 'formative' analyses for improvement);
4. Evaluation ('summative' comparisons with alternatives); and
5. Dissemination.
In point of fact, many innovations leap from the first or second stage

to the fifth. Glass (1968) documented three extraordinary cases of what he called the 'Piltdown syndrome'; the tendency for a few researchers to produce startling, ill-described findings that fail to replicate and yet are widely accepted and disseminated. Current candidates of the syndrome are 'teacher expectancies', 'sensitivity training', and 'discovery learning'. Even the well-funded first-generation 'new science' courses since Sputnik did not undergo thorough evaluation. In the past, Gestalt, psychoanalytic, and stimulus-response theories of learning and school-organization concepts of non-graded, individualized instruction such as the Winnetka and Dalton Plans were neither evaluated nor disseminated widely (Walberg, 1968; Anderson and Ritcher, 1969). But today, departmental, team, non-graded, and ability-group organizations are gaining acceptance despite contradictory research and evaluation findings (Heathers, 1969). There are obviously great needs and opportunities for Research and Development Centres and Regional Laboratories to carry out formative and summative evaluation of these forms of organization before they are released for widespread use.

Normal Science

Until this century, inquiry in education had its main origins in philosophy and social criticism. Since the 1920s, psychology and, to a lesser extent, sociology have been the major influences. In the last decade, anthropology, economics, political science, and systems analysis have had their advocates in education. However, if educational research continues to borrow uncritically from other fields either on grounds of authority or analogy, it is likely to remain underdeveloped and pre-paradigmatic. Kuhn (1962) defined paradigms as 'universally recognized scientific achievements that for a time provide model problems and solutions to a community of practitioners'. In distinguishing pre-paradigmatic and 'normal' science, Kuhn writes (p. 17):

'No natural history can be interpreted in the absence of at least some implicit body of intertwined theoretical and methodological belief that permits selection, evaluation, and criticism. If that body of belief is not already implicitly in the collection of facts – in which case more than "mere facts" are at hand – it must be externally supplied, perhaps by a current metaphysic, by another science, or by personal or historical accident. No wonder, then, that in the early stages of development of any science different men confronting the same particular phenomena, describe and interpret them in different ways.'

Thus, to become a part of normal science, educational researchers must develop their own paradigms or models, however crude and preliminary. And to that end, the remainder of this paper is devoted to the analysis of some proposed models for optimizing and individualizing learning.

An Analysis of Models

The discussion above analysed the contribution of three groups of variables to the prediction of learning; Table 3 contains working definitions of the three domains and depicts their conceptual relationships to one another and to the criterion, learning. The general model for research on school learning specifies four terms: two measures of the individual, learning (or achievement) and aptitude, and two measures of contextual variation, instruction and environment. Although the definitions distinguish achievement from aptitude and instruction from environment, the differences are relative rather than absolute. Instruction and goals of learning are more specific, intended, and temporary while aptitudes and environment tend to be more general, implicit, and enduring. (In a given experimental design, operational distinctions must be made between the terms – for instance, the best aptitude measure, i.e. predictor of achievement, is often prior achievement rather than conventional aptitude tests, e.g. measures of intelligence.) The general model states that learning (L_h) is a function (b) of aptitude (A_i), environment (E_j), and instruction (I_k) as in equation 1.

$$L_h = b_1(A_i),\ b_2(E_j),\ b_3(I_k) \qquad (1)$$

Before the general model (or special models) can be comprehensively and specifically applied to problems of prediction (and possible manipulation) of learning, three related questions must be answered. (1) How many elements are in each domain and how are they related? (2) How are the domains of aptitude, environment, and instruction related to learning? (3) How do the elements within each domain develop and how can they be manipulated? Since there is little consistency in the research bearing on each of the three

TABLE 3: *Definitions of, and relations between, four domains*

Locus	RELATIVE CHARACTERISTICS	
	Specific, Intended, Temporary	*General, Implicit, Enduring*
Person	*Learning* (or *Achievement*) – a change in (or state of) thought, feeling, behaviour.	*Aptitude* – a characteristic of the individual that predicts learning.
Context	*Instruction* – a stimulus intended to bring about learning.	*Environment* – a stimulus, aside from instruction, that predicts learning.

questions (except the aptitude-learning relation), we examine several models, identify their assumptions, and propose the assumptions as hypotheses for empirical research.

The most parsimonious model for research on school learning is additive and assumes that aptitude, environment, and instruction do not interact, e.g. no particular instruction is more suitable for individuals with given aptitudes. Research based on this general model would simply derive empirical weights (through regression analysis, for example) for each term in equation 2,

$$L_h = b_1(A_i) + b_2(E_j) + b_3(I_k) \qquad (2)$$

from classroom settings. To make predictions, particular values for each term would be multiplied by the corresponding weights, and the three products would be summed. The research reviewed earlier (and shown in Table 1) suggests two general hypotheses concerning the magnitudes of the weights. Aptitude will be the best predictor, and instruction the worst, in natural settings of learning; therefore, aptitude will have the biggest weight, and instruction the smallest (or $b_1 > b_2 > b_3$). In fact, the null hypothesis for instruction will often be the most likely, that is, $b_3 = 0$. The studies reviewed in Table 1 suggest that the aptitude term typically accounts for 40–60 per cent of the variance in learning and that environment accounts for another 16 per cent or 29 per cent (from secondary and elementary school estimates, respectively). This leaves only from 11 per cent to 33 per cent to be accounted for by instruction, interaction terms, and error of measurement of the criterion. On grounds of parsimony, then, aptitude and environment might be entered in regression models first, and instructional variables might be entered last to determine if they account for additional variance.

The Interaction Model

The multiplicative model assumes that aptitude, environment, and instruction interact with one another to afford a better prediction of learning than the first three terms alone.

$$L_h = b_1(A_i) + b_2(E_j) + b_3(I_k) + b_4(A_iE_j) + b_5(A_iI_k) + b_6(E_jI_k)$$
$$+ b_7(A_iE_jI_k) \qquad (3)$$

For example, $b_4(A_iE_j)$ states that environmental characteristics individualize student learning. Anderson (1968) and Bar-Yam (1969), in hypothesis-testing research, found that students with a given level of intelligence, personality, or other characteristics differ sharply in their learning performance in different environments. Walberg (1969a) has found evidence for $b_6(E_jI_k)$, the tendency for environmental variables to suboptimize different kinds of instruction; more specifically, student performance levels were considerably lower in traditional physics courses when the class environment was less suitable, while students in a new course did fairly well under almost all environmental conditions.

Models Assumed in Instruction

Selection, Enrichment, and Acceleration

Consider $b_5(A_iI_k)$, the interaction of student characteristics with instructional methods. Perhaps more educational research bears upon this than any of the other interactions, and the major models for individualizing learning are depicted in Figures 3 and 4. Three models in Figure 3 have been traditionally proposed: Selection, Enrichment, and Acceleration. Selection has two variants, Eugenic, originally proposed by Plato, and Selection for instruction, most commonly used in higher education especially in Europe, wherein the 'unfit' are simply not accepted. Both variants are potent enough, but for many educators, who do not wish to reject the unborn or born, they are essentially conservative, defeatist doctrines.

Enrichment and Acceleration are presently the most common methods for individualizing learning. In both models, there are a series of activity units and tests and generally a post-test criterion, e.g. a final examination (see Figure 3). Students move through the same course of instruction in the same sequence. In Enrichment programmes, which are most common, students all spend the same amount of time in learning, and individual variability is evidenced in normally distributed test scores on unit and post-test criteria that would be correlated with aptitude and environment measures. In sharp contrast, Acceleration (currently termed by some as 'mastery learning') ideally means that the criterion is fixed and, as a consequence, time spent by each student varies. However, Strang's (1937) and Stephens' (1968) reviews of classroom research surprisingly conclude that there is little relation between time spent in instruction and achievement. It might be difficult to find pure types of either Acceleration or Enrichment models in ordinary classroom settings; and it should be noted that in both cases the student generally must repeat the entire course of instruction if he is judged a failure.

In contrast, two recent methods for individualizing learning employ diagnostic pre-tests (see Figure 3) to assess entry behaviours before beginning instruction. The Hierarchical model assumes that it is necessary to learn the content of one unit of instruction (say A, in Figure 3) before going on to the next (B and C) and that some students have already mastered some units of instruction before beginning. Therefore, the pre-test serves to place the student at the most appropriate point in the sequence of instruction. His progress is measured after each unit, and he is recycled through a unit if he fails before proceeding on to the next. An example of this model is the preliminary form of Developing Mathematical Process (Romberg and Harvey, 1969), which, in addition to unit tests, also makes use of continuous monitoring of student performance.

The Random model assumes that the elements of learning need not be presented in a particular sequence, e.g. some students will need instruction in units A and C but not B (see Figure 3). Diagnostic pre-tests are given before instruction to determine which units to assign to the students. An example of this model is the Wisconsin Prototypic System of Reading Skill Development (Otto, 1969), which employs criterion-referenced tests to diagnose specific reading difficulties to permit appropriate assignment of units of instruction to particular students.

Multi-modal and Multi-valent Models
The models presented in Figure 3 require only one basic course of instruction, although there are variants in its use. Figure 4 shows two models that require multiple courses of instruction. In the first, Multi-modal, there are several courses of instruction all leading to the same achievement goal. Students are administered a pre-test to determine their level of aptitude, and each is assigned to the course of instruction best suited to his aptitude, e.g. prior achievement, learning styles, and preferences. Or students might be left to select their own. This model assumes that aptitudes interact with educational treatments – $b_5(A_iI_k)$ in equation 3. Led by Lee J. Cronbach and Richard E. Snow at Stanford, much research in the last few years has been directed toward 'aptitude-treatment interactions'. Unfortunately, they have been difficult to find. Bar-Yam (1969), in a 231-item review, found some replicated evidence that bright, flexible, and assertive students perform better than their counterparts when instructional methods are flexible and require independence. Compared to the main effects of aptitude and environment, however, aptitude-instruction interactions appear to account for little variance in achievement; and it is likely that, if they are powerful, they would have been uncovered by now. It is important that the search continues, however, since much theorizing about individualization seems to be based on their premise. Bracht and Glass (1968) cautioned against searching in conventional courses since they are complex and contain many instructional elements.

An example of a course that in theory might make use of the

FIGURE 3: *Some models for individualizing instruction*

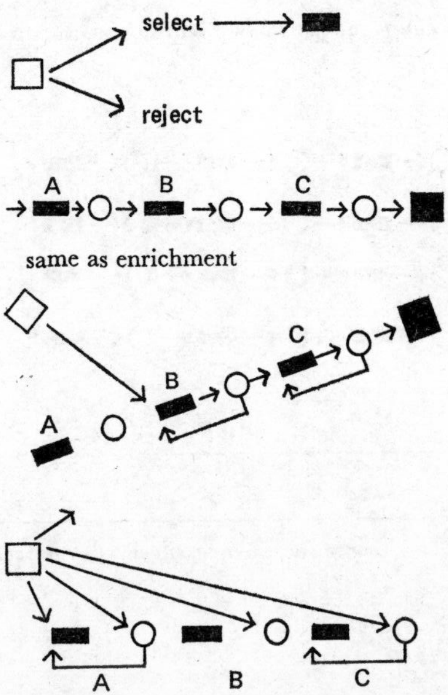

MODEL	COURSE OF INSTRUCTION	CHARACTERISTICS: Time spent in learning	Post-test Criterion	Aptitude–Criterion relation	Environment–Criterion relation
Traditional					
Selection					
Eugenic	select / reject				
For instruction					
Enrichment	A → B → C	Fixed	Variable	Positive	Positive
Acceleration	same as enrichment	Variable	Fixed	Zero	Positive
Diagnostic					
Hierarchical	A, B, C	Variable	Fixed	Zero	Positive
Random	A, B, C	Variable	Fixed	Zero	Positive

Key: Pre-test □ Post-test criterion ■ Unit of instruction ▬
Unit test ○

FIGURE 4: *Additional models for individualizing instruction*

COURSE OF INSTRUCTION

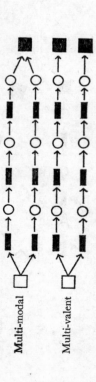

Multi-modal

Multi-valent

Note: The Courses of Instruction may have variants of any of those shown in Figure 3.

Multi-modal model is the Biological Sciences Curriculum Study (Grobman, 1969). Although there is no predetermined system for student assignment, there are different sequences of instruction for reaching the same general goals; the blue version represents the molecular approach; the yellow version, the systematic, taxonomic approach; the green represents the ecological approach. There are also special sequences for bright and dull students. The use of interest and ability pre-tests would permit appropriate assignments to sequences if aptitude-instruction interactions are found.

The other model in Figure 4 is termed 'Multi-valent'. This model assumes (or is based on the value judgment) that not only should there be different sequences of instruction but that they should lead to different goals for different students. Harvard Project Physics (described by Welch, Walberg, and Watson, 1970) was deliberately based on these premises since it was felt that different teachers and students might elect to pursue different goals in physics, e.g. mathematical mastery or understanding the nature and history of scientific methods. Teacher and student guides describe the course organization, various objectives, and alternative instructional activities to permit co-operative planning.

Management and Grouping for Instruction

Still another way to examine models for optimization and individualization lies in their organization for grouping students.

TABLE 4: *Grouping for instruction*

GROUPING	ASSUMPTION ABOUT STUDENT	ANALOGUE IN INDUSTRY	PER UNIT COST	MANAGEMENT SOPHISTICATION
Individual	Particular – each learns according to his own aptitude (rate, style).	Unit production – crafts, cottage industries, prototypes	High	Low
Small Group	Generalization – sub-groups of students sharing the same levels of aptitude can be identified.	Mass production – batch production. differentiated assembly lines.	Medium	Medium
Large Group	Universal – all students share the same levels of aptitude.	Process production – intermittent chemical production in multi-purpose plant, continuous flow production of liquids, gases.	Low	High

Table 4 shows an analysis of individual, small-group, and large-group organizations for instruction and their industrial analogues. It can be noted that each organization makes a different assumption about the nature of the learners or our knowledge about them. To use Gordon Allport's terms, is the psychological science of man 'idiographic' wherein the individual is *sui generis* or 'nomothetic' wherein generalizations may be made about groups of men or universal statements may be made about all men? History shows that industry has progressively moved from expensive unit production with primitive management to mass and process production with sophisticated management and lower costs per unit (Rackham, 1968).

It should be noted that the Acceleration, Random, Hierarchical, and Multi-modal models require a large data base and rapid feedback for assigning students to instruction. Thus, they would depend on reliable, valid, and efficient testing or monitoring as well as an effective system for quick summarization of the data for decision-making. Indeed, the continuing pervasiveness of Enrichment models in contemporary schools, despite other alternatives that are advocated by some theorists, may be attributable to the lack of well-developed management systems for instruction. Such a management system is almost sure to require an extensive data processing system to be feasible in education.

Whether such a system can or should be introduced in education is an open question. 'Mass methods' such as increasing class and school size or employing large lectures and television may reduce per student costs and apparently do not impair achievement (see Table 1); however, Walberg and Ahlgren (1970) found large classes inhibit the development of classroom social environments conducive to affective and voluntary behavioural learning.

In addition, caution is necessary in considering the counsel of educational technologists, behavioural engineers, and others who are now designing and advocating automated 'behavioural-training systems', which appear to be based on Acceleration, Random, and Hierarchical models. The reservations of schoolmen and parents should not be gratuitously dismissed; the pleas of students who do not want to be 'processed' or 'monitored' should not be ignored. Nor must early basic-skill training for children of the poor (or the young or beginners in general) be accepted without more critical research and evaluation. Whitehead (1929) warned against the dangers of overemphasis on early training as opposed to early liberal (what is termed here as 'Multi-valent' and 'Multi-modal') education (p. 96):

'The result (of training) is that qualities essential at a later stage of a career are apt to be stamped out at an earlier stage. This is only an instance of a more general fact, that necessary technical excellence can only be acquired by training which is apt to damage those energies of mind which should direct the technical skill. This is a key fact of education, and the reason for most of its difficulties.'

Summary and Implications

In conclusion, it may be helpful to attempt to draw together the strands of the foregoing discussion as implications for research on optimizing and individualizing learning. As noted earlier, there are no maps and certainly no highways, but perhaps a few converging trails have been uncovered.

The three substantive-methodological traditions in educational research – aptitude correlates, instructional experiments, and environmental studies – must be brought to bear simultaneously on real problems in school learning. Findings from the three traditions might be best organized using theoretical models and paradigms that characterize normal science. These might encourage parsimonious conceptualization and explicit operationalizing of key constructs in the three traditions, help to develop educational research into a more mature, autonomous discipline, and separate empirical facts and testable hypotheses from value judgments, opinions, and educational evangelism.

Based upon prediction and optimization of learning outcomes, a general additive model is proposed here that includes three construct domains – aptitudes, instruction, and environment – reflecting the three traditions of educational research. A general review of research in the three domains suggests the irony that much research concerns aptitudes (which make for relatively large differences in learning but cannot be manipulated very effectively) and instructional methods (which can be manipulated but apparently make little difference), while the little extant research on classroom environments shows both their manipulability and validity in predicting cognitive and affective learning outcomes.

A second model, the multiplicative, points to the possibilities of individualization through the study of interactions between student aptitudes, instructional variables, and environments. There is some limited evidence that different classroom environments are optimal for students with given levels of aptitudes; however, most research bearing on individualization has concerned the aptitude-instruction interaction. Although much of theory and practice of individualized instruction appears to be premised on the presence of strong aptitude-instruction interactions, they must be taken on faith or authority, since they have not been uncovered empirically in classroom research with any consistency, even in experiments deliberately contrived to detect them. For example, advocates of Multi-modal instruction assume that one type of instruction is best for students with one kind of aptitude, while another type is best for students with a different aptitude. Acceleration theorists assume that increased time for instruction can raise slow students (those with less than optimal aptitudes) to given criterion levels, while fast students may finish quickly. Though admittedly subject to much methodological criticism, research in classroom settings on these plausible assumptions has failed to support them. Moreover, a number of tacit assumptions concerning learning implicit in other theories and programmes of individualized instruction and its management are identified here.

Thus, a number of important practical questions concerning optimizing and individualizing instruction are raised. The models for research on instruction proposed here, however crude and tentative, appear to sharpen some theoretical issues and assumptions implicit in current programmes of instruction as well as in prototypic programmes and management systems now being developed. Since there are as yet no strong research findings bearing upon many of these issues, instructional activities might best continue to be a pluralistic mix of the various models based upon the raw experience and values of the practising educator, his constituency, and students. However, educational researchers might contribute much by evaluating fairly pure forms of the models using classic experimental designs (e.g. random sampling and assignment) and the advanced research methods that have been emerging in the educational research community. To make his work conceptually and methodologically rigorous as well as educationally important should offer a continuing challenge to the research worker's ingenuity and energy.

2. The Methodology of Research on College Impact, Part One

ALEXANDER W. ASTIN

In their recent comprehensive review of research on college impact, Feldman and Newcomb (1969) summarize more than 1,000 empirical studies in which investigators have attempted to learn how students are affected by their college experience. For the most part, the findings from these studies are very difficult to interpret, primarily because of problems in research design and methodology. In view of the burgeoning state of current research on college impact, it may be useful to review these methodological difficulties and to suggest certain ways in which future research can be designed to avoid some of those which have plagued most of the studies reviewed by Feldman and Newcomb.

Among the problems that will be covered in this first of two papers on studying college impact are the following: single-institution versus multi-institution studies, longitudinal versus cross-sectional data, alternative statistical designs, the effects of measurement error, and methods for detecting student-environment interaction effects. Throughout the paper, however, the discussion will focus on problems of inferring causation: that is, of determining if and how the student is affected by his college experience.

A Conceptual Model

For purposes of discussion, we shall utilize a model of student development in higher education that has characterized much recent multi-institutional research. In this model, the college can be seen as comprising three conceptually distinct components: student outputs, student inputs, and the college environment.

Student outputs refer to those aspects of the student's development that the college either does influence or attempts to influence. Although these outputs can be expressed at very high levels of abstraction (for example, 'the ultimate welfare and happiness of the individual'), research usually is concerned with those relatively immediate outputs that can be operationalized. Specifically, then, the term outputs refers to measures of the student's achievements, knowledge, skills, values, attitudes, aspirations, interests, and daily activities. Adequate measures of relevant student outputs are, clearly, the *sine qua non* of meaningful research on college impact.

Remarkably, only a handful of the studies reviewed by Feldman and Newcomb were concerned with the impact of colleges on cognitive outcomes. There are, to be sure, many hundreds of studies of academic achievement (Feldman and Newcomb did not review these), but such studies usually are concerned with predicting college grade point averages rather than with measuring growth or change in cognitive skills or with assessing college impact on such skills. Considering that the development of the student's cognitive skills probably is the most common educational objective of both students and colleges, this lack of research is unfortunate. Probably it can be explained by the logistical problems involved in measuring cognitive outcomes (the necessity for proctoring and the high costs of achievement testing, for example), problems much more formidable than those encountered in measuring attitudinal outcomes (which can be assessed with relatively inexpensive, self-administered questionnaires).

Student inputs are the talents, skills, aspirations, and other potentials for growth and learning that the new student brings with him to college. These inputs are, in a sense, the raw materials with which the institution has to deal. Many inputs can be viewed simply as 'pre-test's on certain outputs (career choice and personal values, for example), whereas others (sex and race, for example) are static personal attributes. Inputs can affect outputs either directly or by interaction with environmental variables.

The college environment refers to those aspects of the higher educational institution that are capable of affecting the student. Broadly speaking, they include administrative policies and practices, curriculum, physical plant and facilities, teaching practices, peer associations, and other characteristics of the college environment.

The relationships among these three components of the model are shown schematically in Figure 5. The principal concern of research on college impact is to assess relationship 'B', the effects of the college environment on relevant student outputs. Relationship 'C' refers to the fact that outputs also are affected by inputs, and relationship 'A' to the fact that college environments are affected by the kinds of students who enroll.

In addition to the 'main' effects of college environments on student outputs (B), the investigator also may be interested in certain interaction effects involving student inputs and college environments. The diagram suggests that there are two types of interaction effects: those in which the effect of input on output is

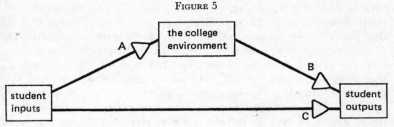

FIGURE 5

different in different college environments (AC), and those in which the effect of the college environment is different for different types of students (AB). Research on college impact ordinarily is concerned more with the second type.

Problems of Design

Although the ideal study of college impact would incorporate information on all three components of the model – student inputs, environments, and student outputs – most of the studies covered by Feldman and Newcomb lacked data on at least one of these components. In this section, we shall review some of the inferential problems that characterize such studies.

Following the conventions of statistical inference, we can assume that studies of college impact should be designed to minimize two kinds of inferential error:

Type I errors (rejection of the null hypothesis when it is true) occur when there is no college effect, but the investigator concludes that there is.

Type II errors (acceptance of the null hypothesis when it is false) occur when there is a significant college effect, but the investigator concludes that there is not.

The special problems inherent in the design of college effects studies indicate that there is still a third type of inferential error which we shall call Type III errors. These occur when there is a significant college effect, but the investigator concludes that the opposite effect occurs. In a sense, a Type III error combines both Type I and Type II errors, since it involves simultaneously the rejection of a null hypothesis which is true and (implicitly) the acceptance of a null hypothesis which is false. (A convenient mnemonic device for defining Type III errors is that $1 + 2 = 3$.)

Some of the controversy over the design of college impact studies stems not so much from basic disagreements over design strategy as from differences in the relative values assigned to Type I and Type II errors. Investigatiors who are concerned primarily with minimizing Type I errors, for example, fear that the highly non-random distribution of students among institutions will lead educators and students to conclude that certain college 'effects' exist when, in fact, they do not. Thus, they regard adequate control of differential student inputs as an essential feature in their design. Researchers who are more concerned about Type II errors, on the other hand, fear that too much control over student inputs will reduce the chances of finding environmental effects. These two somewhat opposed emphases are, in part, historical. That is, the earliest investigators of college impact exerted virtually no control over students inputs; as a consequence, the very substantial institutional differences in student outputs which were found they attributed to the environmental influences of the colleges. When another group of investigators subsequently re-examined this early work, they discovered that differences in institutional outputs could be attributed largely to differences in inputs and that the relative 'impacts' of colleges diminished markedly once these differential student inputs were taken into account. Most recently, however, some investigators have been disturbed by the possibility that a design which controls for student inputs may tend to underestimate the differential impact of colleges, or, in some cases, to obscure particular environmental effects.

We shall discuss these and other possible effects of various designs on both types of error in the section on multi-institution Longitudinal Studies (below). It should be pointed out here, however, that very large differences in student inputs at various institutions – a prominent characteristic of higher education in the United States (Astin, 1965b) – are almost sure to make for large differences in student outputs, regardless of the actual effects of institutions. As a result, failure to take into account these differences in input when studying college effects virtually guarantees that the investigator will commit some Type I errors. More important, ignoring differential student inputs maximizes the investigator's chances of committing Type II errors.

Studies of 'Growth' or 'Change' at Individual Colleges
Perhaps the prototypical study reviewed by Feldman and Newcomb involves the testing and retesting of students at a single institution. Characteristically, the students complete an attitudinal questionnaire or inventory when they first enter college and take it again one year later, four years later, or in a few cases, many years after graduation. Measures of 'change' or 'growth' are obtained by comparing the student's input scores from the initial administration with his output scores from the follow-up administration. (These comparative measures usually are simple difference scores, although residual gain

scores are used occasionally.) In subsequently interpreting these scores, the investigator typically assumes that any observed changes are due to the students' experiences in college. In other words, he equates 'change' with 'impact'.

This type of design has the advantage of focusing attention on the longitudinal nature of student change and development in that it views the student's output performance in relation to his input characteristics. Its glaring weakness, however, is that it really produces no information that bears directly on the question of environmental impact. Would the same changes have occurred if the student had attended a different kind of college or had not gone to college at all? In the context of our conceptual model, this type of study yields information on student inputs and outputs but not on the environment. Thus, the college environment is not a variable but a constant. (The situation here is identical to the one encountered in experimentation when no control group is used.)

The very practical danger in assuming that change equals impact can be illustrated with an anecdote. I recently overheard a colleague from a highly selective small college complaining that nearly a third of his undergraduates who start out majoring in science shift to a nonscience field before graduation. He interpreted this decline in science interest (change) as somehow resulting from the science curriculum of the college (impact). As a consequence, he and other members of a committee on curriculum reform were seriously considering major changes in the science curriculum of the college in the hope of reducing the number of students who withdraw from science fields. As it happened, this colleague's institution was one of several hundred colleges participating in a longitudinal study of institutional impact on career choice (Astin and Panos, 1969). What he did not know was that the longitudinal analyses had revealed that the dropout rate from science actually was lower at his college than at almost any other college in the sample. Thus, his college was exerting a relatively positive rather than a negative influence on the student's interest in science. Under these circumstances, major changes in the existing science curriculum very well could increase rather than decrease the student dropout rate from science at the college.

Many investigators use a variation of this basic design: instead of collecting longitudinal information, they simply compare groups of freshmen and upper-class men simultaneously on some measure. This method is so full of pitfalls (many of which are discussed at length by Feldman and Newcomb), that one wonders if there is the slightest justification for supposing that the observed 'changes' are related in any way to the college experience. In addition to the problems already mentioned, this method carries with it potentially serious deficiencies in sampling. It rests on the assumptions that (a) upper-class men are a representative sample – at least insofar as the output variable is concerned – of the total cohort of freshmen from which they were drawn, and (b) this original cohort was drawn from the same population as the current freshmen who are being compared with the upper-class men.

The tenuousness of these assumptions is obvious when one realizes that any sample of upper-class men necessarily excludes dropouts and includes transfers – two groups that are very likely to differ from the students who entered as freshmen and continued on without a break in their undergraduate progress. Moreover, changes in the nature of successive entering freshman classes may occur as a result either of modifications in either the applicant pool or admissions practices or of changes in the college student population itself. That such population shifts are indeed possible – even over a brief period of time – is revealed by the ACE's annual surveys of entering freshmen. (See Astin, Panos and Creager, 1966; Panos, Astin and Creager, 1967; Creager, Astin, Bayer and Boruch, 1968; and Creager, Astin, Bayer, Boruch and Drew, 1969). For example, during the four most recent years – 1966, 1967, 1968 and 1969 – the percentage of entering freshmen who checked 'none' as their present religious preference has gone up consistently: 6·9, 7·9, 9·6 and 13·2. These trends held true for both men and women and for students at most types of institutions. Thus, even if no students had dropped out or changed their religious preferences since entering college, a comparison of the current (1969–1970) freshmen with the current senior classes at many colleges would lead to the conclusion that nearly half of the students who initially reported that they had no religious preference 'changed' to some other choice after entering college.

The dangers in assuming that change is equivalent to 'college impact' suggest that changes in students during college should be viewed as comprising two components: change resulting from the impact of the college and change resulting from other influences (maturation, non-college environmental effects, etc.). Note that the college may (a) bring about changes which otherwise would not occur, (b) exaggerate or accelerate changes resulting from other sources, or (c) impede or counteract changes resulting from other sources (as in the example, cited above, where the college's dropout rate from science was much lower than average).

Studies of Environments and Student Outputs
One alternative to the single-institution studies that are so common

in research on college impact is the multi-institution study, in which the student outputs of several institutions are compared. It was a frequent practice during the 1950s, for example, to compare instutions on such output measures as the percentage of graduates obtaining PhD degrees or the number of alumni listed in *Who's Who*. While such studies have the advantage of permitting the investigator to study variations in college environments, the empirical findings that result tend to be highly ambiguous because the student input has been disregarded.

The importance of student input data in multi-institution studies is illustrated aptly by the history of research on 'PhD productivity'. The earliest of these studies indicated that the graduates of certain colleges and universities were much more likely than were the graduates of other institutions to win fellowships for graduate study and to go on to obtain the PhD degree (Knapp and Goodrich, 1952; Knapp and Greenbaum, 1953). More important, the environments of the 'highly productive' institutions, when compared with those of the less productive ones, were found to have higher faculty-student ratios, larger libraries, more funds for scholarships and research, and similar resources usually assumed to indicate institutional 'excellence' and eminence. In short, the causal inferences drawn from these early studies were that such institutional resources are conducive to the development of the student's motivation to seek advanced training. Among other things, this research evidence seemed to confirm the folklore about what makes for 'quality' in higher education. Taken at face value, and assuming that the output measure under study (motivation to seek advanced training) was relevant to the goals of the institution, these findings offered empirical support to the administrator in his attempts to increase the size of his faculty, library, and so forth.

But the validity of these earlier studies came to be doubted when it was shown that institutions differ widely in their student inputs: highly productive institutions, for example, enroll greater proportions of academically able students than do less productive institutions (Holland, 1957). Intellectually advantaged students are, of course, more likely than are average students both to win graduate fellowships and to be interested in pursuing the doctorate even if their institution exerts no special influence during the undergraduate years. These doubts subsequently were confirmed by a series of studies (Astin, 1962, 1963a, 1963b) in which differential undergraduate student inputs to diverse institutions were controlled. Thus, when the abilities, career plans, and socioeconomic backgrounds of the entering students were taken into account, an institution's output of PhDs was revealed to be largely a function of the characteristics of its entering students rather than of its resources. Moreover, certain types of institutions that were earlier described as 'highly productive' of PhDs turned out to be underproductive in relation to their student inputs. In addition, the apparent 'effects' of library size, faculty-student ratio, and other similar indicators of institutional quality disappeared.

Multi-Institution Longitudinal Studies

The inferential problems inherent in single-institution studies and in those multi-institution studies that do not utilize student input data indicate that an adequately designed study of college impact requires information concerning all three components of our model: student inputs, college environments, and student outputs. Merely collecting such data, however, does not assure that true college effects will be identified and spurious college effects will not. The avoidance of such inferential errors depends on a number of factors, including the nature of the student input data obtained and the statistical method used to analyse the data. Since there is no way to guarantee that the non-random distribution of students among institutions will be compensated for completely, the investigator's task in collecting data and in selecting a statistical method is simply to reduce the chances that his inferences will be wrong.

Student Input Data

'Relevant' student input data are those which affect the student's choice of a college or the student output variable under study or both. To reduce the chances of committing Type I errors, however, it is not necessary to collect both types of data: as Figure 5 indicates, an unbiased estimate of the environment-output effect (B) can be obtained if either A (input-environment) or C (input-output) is controlled. If both relationships are controlled, however, a more sensitive test of environment-output effects will result, thus reducing the probability of committing Type II errors.

The designs that result when student input data are controlled in different ways can be depicted by a simple 2×2 table (Figure 6). (For purposes of illustration, we have used the terminology of linear multiple regression to label the different designs, although the basic logic of the designs does not require that linear regression be the method used.)

The lower right-hand box in Figure 6 represents the multi-institutional design in which no student input data are used (see previous section for examples). The upper left-hand box represents the partial correlational design in which the effects of student inputs on both output and environment are controlled. As we have already indicated, this design provides the most sensitive test of environmental effects.

Part Correlation II (lower left box of Figure 6) involves control over the input-output relationship but not over the input-environment relationship. Since the total output variance is likely to be dependent more on input than on environment, this design probably is the second most sensitive of the four. An interesting application of this design in multi-institution studies is first to solve the regression equations using all students, and then to aggregate the residual output scores of students within an institution, thereby producing a mean residual output score for the institution. This mean residual can provide a useful quantitative measure of institutional 'impact'. For example, in a recent multi-institution longitudinal study (Astin and Panos, 1969), one of the output measures was whether or not the student had dropped out during the four years after entering college (scored as a dichotomy: 1=stayed in college for four years; 0=dropped out). The mean college residuals on this measure, which varied among the 246 colleges from −30 per cent to +16 per cent, thus provided a measure of the extent to which each college's retention rate was either above or below what would have been expected from the characteristics of its entering students.

The fourth design shown in Figure 6 – Part Correlation I – involves control over the input-output relationship. Although this method has seldom been used, it yields an estimate of the efficiency of a particular environmental variable (or combination of environmental variables). By 'efficiency' we mean the extent to which the total variation in student performance on the output measure can be attributed solely to the operation of environmental variables.

A final question relating to student input data concerns the data which actually are used. Investigators who are used to thinking in

FIGURE 6: *Four types of multi-institution designs for studying the relationship between college environments and student outputs*

| | | Input Partialled Out of Output? | |
		Yes	No
Input Partialled Out of Environment?	Yes	Partial Correlation	Part Correlation I
	No	Part Correlation II	Zero-Order Correlation Between Environment and Output

terms of experimental rather than correlational models run the risk
of utilizing only a single student input measure, a 'pre-test' measure
or 'covariate'. (Investigators who regard research on college impact
as simply a matter of 'change' will be tempted similarly to rely on a
single input measure.) The problem with single input measures is
that they are almost sure to be inadequate, since the distribution of
student inputs among institutions is biased with respect not just to
one but to many student attributes (Astin, 1965b; Holland, 1959).
Because the factors influencing college choice often are difficult to
identify, probably the best protection for the researcher here is to
measure and control all student attributes that are likely to affect
the output measures under study.

That using only a single 'pre-test' measure in studying college
impact can bias the conclusions seriously, is illustrated by a recent
study in which the three Area Tests on the Graduate Record
Examination (GRE) were used as output measures (Astin, 1968b). In
all three analyses, the student's initial ('pre-test') aptitude entered
as the first variable in the stepwise regression. In two of the three
analyses, however, the student's sex entered with a large weight at
the second step. The sex ratio in the student body, it should be
noted, also is strongly related to environmental attributes such as
Co-operativeness, Cohesiveness, and Femininity (Astin, 1968a).
Clearly, if initial aptitude had been the only student input variable
considered, the findings might have shown – incorrectly – that the
student's learning and achievement are affected significantly by the
degree of co-operativeness, cohesiveness, or femininity of the college
environment.

Statistical Alternatives
Three basically different statistical methods have been used to
analyse input, output, and environmental data: matching, actuarial
tables, and linear multiple regression analysis.

Matching
Perhaps the least desirable statistical approach is to match students
entering different colleges in terms of their input characteristics.
Not only are many subjects lost, but also the sub-samples of students
selected for study are unrepresentative of their institutions; thus,
potentially serious regression artifacts are introduced into the data.
These and other problems with matching designs have been discussed at length elsewhere. (See, for example, Campbell and
Stanley, 1963.) Briefly, the major inferential problem is that the
analysis is likely to yield artifactual 'effects' which are in reality the
result of errors of measurement in the input variables. (These and

other problems associated with measurement errors will be discussed in the next section.)

It is not generally recognized that research on interaction effects ordinarily employs a kind of matching design and therefore is liable to the same deficiencies. That is, if one sorts out his students in terms of attributes such as ability, sex, race, and so forth, his findings on the effects of college variables are likely to be biased by errors of measurement in these student attributes. For example, if students are stratified by ability level (in order to detect possible interaction effects between ability and some college characteristic), the students in any given ability category will include representative sub-samples of students from some colleges and highly non-representative sub-samples from others. Since the error of measurement in any student's ability test performance is likely to be correlated with the extent to which his score deviates from the mean score of his classmates (i.e. students with relatively high scores being more likely to have positive errors of measurement than students with relatively low scores), the 'superior' students from the least selective colleges are more likely to have spuriously high ability test scores (i.e. positive measurement errors) than are the 'superior' students from the most selective colleges. Thus, such studies may find that college selectivity, or some variable correlated with selectivity, 'affects' highly able students, when in fact there is no effect. (For a fuller description of this phenomenon, see the next section.)

Even interaction studies that use highly objective student input characteristics, such as race and sex, are not free from these artifacts, since the measurement of these attributes, too, is likely to contain some error: a few women probably will be mis-classified as men, a few non-whites mis-classified as whites, and so forth. The bias occurs because such errors are not equally probable in all types of institutions. Thus, there is likely to be more error of measurement in classifying students as 'white' (i.e. more non-whites) among those attending predominantly Negro colleges than among those attending predominantly white colleges. Similarly, the chances probably are greater that students classified as 'female' really are male if they are attending a technological institution than if they are attending a teachers college.

Actuarial Tables

The second basic type of design involves the use of actuarial tables for controlling differential student inputs. Actuarial tables are especially helpful when the input variables are qualitative rather than quantitative in nature (Astin, 1962, 1963a). Briefly, what the investigator does is to sort his total pool of subjects into discrete cells on the basis of their input attributes (by sex, by race, by family SES, and so forth). Cells need not, of course, be balanced (e.g. one might form separate sex cells for one race but not for another). The purpose of the sorting procedure is to generate new cells in such a way that the between-cell variance in the ouput measure is maximized and within-cell variance is minimized. The actuarial approach is similar in some ways to multiple group discriminant analysis, except that the roles of the independent and dependent variables are reversed. In discriminant analysis, the groups define the dependent variable and the independent variables are used to form a metric which maximally discriminates the groups. Conversely, in actuarial analysis, the metric is a given (the dependent variable), and the independent variables are used to form groups which maximally discriminate this metric.

At the point where it is no longer possible to form further groups which significantly discriminate with respect to the output variable, the 'predicted' or 'expected' output score for each student becomes the mean output score of all students occupying the cell where he is located. (One refinement, which might be desirable for use with relatively small samples, is to exclude a given subject in computing the mean for his cell.) The difference between the expected value and the student's actual score on the output measure thus becomes the dependent variable for analysis of college impact. Students can be sorted into their respective colleges, and the mean discrepancy score computed separately for each college. At this stage, one has a situation similar to that described above for Part Correlation II (Figure 6).

The principal advantages of the actuarial table are that it is probably much easier to understand than standard regression techniques (below) and that it permits the investigator to take into account interaction effects among student input variables as well as nonlinear effect of input variables. Its principal disadvantage is that there is no generally accepted analysis method for determining how the cells should be formed; the number of possible cells increases exponentially as the number of input variables increases. Moreover, to use the method effectively, one must have a very large sample of subjects. Nevertheless, it has been shown (Astin, 1962, 1963a) that actuarial tables can produce wide separations on student output measures and that, given large enough samples, the cell means prove to be highly stable on cross-validation. While the actuarial approach does not easily accommodate variables that are continuous (rather than qualitative), it is possible, under certain conditions, to combine actuarial tables with regression analyses (see below).

Linear Multiple Regression

The statistical method used most frequently in recent multi-institution longitudinal studies is linear multiple regression. This technique can be applied in three basically different ways. The first, and perhaps the most straightforward, approach is the 'full model' described by Bottenberg and Ward (1963), in which the output measure is regressed on both input and enironmental variables, with the student used as the unit of analysis.

The second application is identical to the first, except that the institution rather than the student is used as the unit in the analyses both of environmental effects and of input effects. Mean scores on each input variable are calculated separately for each institution. Then the output variable is regressed on these mean input variables, after which the environmental variables are permitted to enter the analysis. Although the much smaller number of units involved (institutions versus students) makes this method computationally much simpler than the first, it should be used with caution because it greatly increases the probability of Type II errors. The major problem here is that the method treats peer group effects as input, rather than environmental, effects. That is, many potentially important environmental variables are a reflection of (or at least highly correlated with) the aggregate or mean score on particular student input characteristics (the mean ability level of the student body, for example). If the magnitude of a particular environmental effect is proportional to the institution's mean score on a particular input variable, this method may partial out the environmental effect along with any input variable effects.

The third application of regression analysis, which was alluded to in the previous discussion of acturial tables, combines the first two uses. The output variables first are regressed on input variables using the student as the unit of analysis. Mean residuals are then computed separately by college, and the effects of environmental variables assessed using the institution as the unit of analysis. This application is useful when the magnitude of the effects of particular colleges is being investigated. Moreover, in cases where the output measurement has a meaningful zero point (the percentage of students who are affected in some way, for example), the third method offers some interesting possibilities for further analyses of the mean residuals. For example, one might conduct a series of analyses using several different outcome criteria, each of which has been scored dichotomously so that the mean residual indicates the percentage of students at a given college who were differentially affected by that college. An empirical typology of colleges then could be developed by factoring the covariances (rather than the correlations) among the mean residuals obtained on the several different output variables. The resulting typology thus would give greatest weight to those environmental influences that affect the largest percentage of students (i.e. to those output variables whose mean residuals show the greatest interinstitutional variance).

A similar two-stage analysis can be carried out using the first two regression methods. Student input variables first are permitted to enter the regression equation, after which environmental measures are permitted to enter. Some investigators object that such a two-stage analysis biases the findings in favour of student input, as opposed to environmental variables, but this supposed 'rivalry' between the two types of variables is something of a straw man. Student input variables are controlled prior to the assessment of environmental effects for two reasons. First, there is the practical problem of reducing Type I and Type III errors. Unless some control over differential student inputs is exerted prior to the assessment of environmental effects, the investigator maximizes his chances of committing both of these types of inferential errors. Second, there is the logical question of the temporal sequence of student input and environmental variables. While the college environment clearly can be influenced by the nature of the student input, it is illogical to assume that the student's input characteristics have been affected by the environment of his college. That is, the student's sex, race, SES, initial aptitude, and other input variables are set before he has any opportunity to be exposed to the college environment. It is true, of course, that the entering student's plans or attitudes already may have been influenced by his expectations about the college or by his having been accepted by the college for admission, but we are concerned here with the 'environmental effects' that occur only after he matriculates.

One way of regarding the problem of what percentage of the total output variance can be attributed to input or environmental variables is to conceive of the predictable variance in any output measure as comprising three conceptually and statistically separate components:

R^2 part (IE): the percentage of output variance uniquely attributable to student input variables. This quantity refers to Part Correlation II (Figure 6) and is the squared multiple correlation between the output measure and the residual input variables (i.e. input independent of environmental variables).

R^2 part (EI): the percentage of ouput variance uniquely attributable to college environmental variables. This quantity refers to Part Correlation I (Figure 6) and is the squared multiple correlation between the output measure and the residual environmental variables (i.e. environmental indedendent of input variables).

R^2–R^2 part (IE) – R^2 part (EI): the percentage of confounded output variance, or output variance which is jointly attributable to input and environment.

The first two coefficients provide 'lower-bounds' estimates of the total output variance that can be attributed, respectively, to input and environmental sources. An alternate method of computing 'lower-bounds' estimates would be simply to determine how much R^2 increases when one set of variables is added to the other. This latter approach, however, may give too high an estimate because it would assign all 'suppressor' effects between the two sets of variables to the second set (i.e. the set being added to the equation).

'Upper-bounds' estimates can be obtained simply by adding the lower-bounds estimates to the confounded variance. An alternative method would be simply to leave out one set in computing R^2. This alternate 'upper-bounds' estimate, however, may be too low because it does not capitalize on any possible suppressor effects between environmental and input variables.

During the past several years, some discussion has appeared in the literature concerning the most appropriate use of multivariate analysis in analysing student input, environmental, and student output information. Some writers (Werts and Watley, 1969) prefer to pool all input and environmental variables in a single analysis rather than to use the two-stage input-environment analysis. The resulting regression coefficients, according to these writers, would reflect the 'independent contribution' of various input and environmental variables in accounting for variation in the ouput variable. One interpretive difficulty with this method is that the various input and environmental variables are not independent. Under such conditions, some writers have concluded that 'the notion of "independent contribution to variance" has no meaning when predictor variables are intercorrelated (Darlington, 1968:169)'. The problem here is essentially one of what happens to the confounded variance. Since this variance must be reflected in the regression coefficients, there is no way to determine merely from these coefficients just how much of the confounded versus unique variance has been allotted to any independent variable or class of variables. Another problem is that the regression coefficients do not show whether a particular variable is acting directly on the output variable or whether it is operating primarily as a suppressor variable by accounting for extraneous variance in other independent variables.

A possible solution to these problems associated with regression weights would be to compute 'lower-bounds' estimates of the unique influence of a particular variable or class of variables by means of squared part correlations and then to compute 'upper-bounds' estimates by adding the confounded variance to the squared part correlations. (It should be noted, however, that even these part correlations are not independent. See Creager, 1970; Creager and Boruch, 1970.) The investigator then could evaluate these two estimates in terms of the various risks that he is willing to take of incurring Type I and Type II errors. Obviously, the greater the discrepancy between the upper- and lower-bounds estimates, the greater the risks.

A variation in the use of regression analysis proposed by some authors is causal path analysis (Duncan, 1966). Perhaps its major advantage over ordinary linear regression analysis is that it forces the investigator to specify the known or hypothesized relationships among his input, environmental, and output variables and aids him in differentiating 'direct' from 'indirect' influences on output variables. Path diagramming can also be a useful way of helping the investigator to see possible connections among his variables that he had not considered previously (Werts, 1968). Perhaps the major limitation of this method is that it can be unwieldy or even un-workable when the number of independent variables is large or when their temporal sequencing is not know. Since path analysis is more useful for testing specific causal hypotheses than for an open-ended exploration of college impact, its use probably should be confined to situations where the number of independent variables is relatively small, and where their inter-relationships are relatively well understood.

Causal analyses of input, output, and environmental data by means of multiple regression techniques as a general approach to studying college impact has been critized by Richards (1966), who is also cited at length by Feldman and Newcomb (Appendix F) on the grounds that residual values are 'notoriously unreliable and subject to errors of various sorts'. But residual values are no less 'reliable' than difference scores or even the change scores which Richards himself recommends as alternatives. Richards also objects to the regression approach because it can 'obscure true college effects'. In this regard, it is important to note that the first and third uses of regression analysis described earlier (i.e. the ones where inputs are controlled using the student as the unit of analysis) will not 'obscure' even very small environmental effects, except in the special case where there is total confounding of input and environmental variables. (It would be difficult, for example, to compare the effects of men's colleges and women's colleges on some output variable that is related to sex.) Under these circumstances, there is no within-college variance in input, so that the environmental and input variables are completely confounded. However, so long as there is some overlap between institutions in student input characteristics, the application of regression analysis described above will not obscure any college effects, no matter how small.

Detecting Interaction Effects

In presenting our three-component model of college impact, we indicated that at least two kinds of student-college interaction effects can occur: those in which the effect of input on output is different in different college environments and those in which the effect of the environment is different for different types of students.

In certain respects, the problem of interaction effects between student and college characteristics has more practical significance for administrative policy than the problem of the main effects of college environmental variables. A knowledge of environmental main effects is useful only when it is possible to modify existing colleges or to design new colleges in ways which will maximize the desired main effects. A knowledge of interaction effects, however, can be useful if there is no realistic possibility of making significant changes in existing college environments, since such knowledge permits one to maximize desired educational objectives by re-distributing students among existing institutions in the most efficacious way. Such knowledge is of obvious value to large city or state systems comprising several institutions; it also can be useful to individual private colleges in selecting students who are likely to benefit most from the particular programme offered by the institution.

Knowledge concerning interaction effects also can be applied within individual institutions. It can be used, for instance, as a basis for selecting those students most likely to profit from counselling and guidance in situations where resources for these services are limited, or for assigning students to various schools and colleges within an institution. Even if the final decision is left to the individual student, information about interaction effects can help him to make the most appropriate choice.

Assessing interaction effects presents many methodological problems, primarily because the number of possible student-environmental interaction effects is so large. Simply to 'shotgun' the study of interaction effects by generating all possible combinations is usually unrealistic either because of the large loss in degrees of freedom or because of limits on the number of variables that can be accommodated in a given analysis.

Perhaps the most common approach is to generate only those interaction terms suggested by a particular theory. However, the paucity of comprehensive theory in this field greatly limits the range of interaction terms that one can explore in this manner.

Another approach is to select a limited number of student input variables on the basis of their intrinsic importance (sex, race, SES, or ability, for example) and to determine which are most likely to interact with environmental variables across a wide range of student outcomes. Future studies of college impact then routinely could examine interaction effects involving such variables.

There are many possible methods for assessing interaction effects in the multivariate model. The simplest (and probably most expensive) is to perform separate analyses on subgroups of students (all men, for example) defined in terms of the student characteristics that might interact with environmental variables. Another approach is to perform only one analysis, but to 'score' the interaction terms (student ability × college size, for example) as a separate variable. This method has the advantage of computational simplicity, provided that the number of interaction terms is not excessively large. If the investigator wishes to assess such interaction terms using a very large number of environmental variables, the former method of separate analyses by subgroups probably is preferable.

Whatever method the investigator uses, he cannot be sure he has identified significant interaction effects until he first has controlled for the main effects of the variables that make up the interaction term. (The problem here is similar to the one encountered in analysis of variance designs, where the main effects of the independent variables must first be removed before the interaction effects can be studied.)

Many investigators who study college impact fail to recognize the need for controlling main effects before examining interaction effects. Take, for example, studies of the 'congruence' between the student and his college, which are designed to test the assumption that the student's success and his satisfaction with college will be related to the degree of similarity between certain of his own characteristics and some comparable measure of the college environment. In some cases, the student's personality is compared with the typical personality of his fellow students; in others, his expectations about the college environment are compared with some 'objective' measure of that environment. Whatever the measure used, such studies do not yield evidence on the importance of congruence unless one first examines how the student input and the environmental variables directly affect the output under consideration. In the single-institution study, of course, the main effects of the environmental variables cannot be tested since the environment is essentially a constant rather than a variable. Even in multi-institution studies, however, the main effects of the student input and the environmental characteristics in question first have to be controlled.

The stepwise linear regression model provides a convenient way of examining such interaction effects. This method allows the investigator to score his interaction terms as separate variates, omitting them from the stepwise analysis until the significant main effects of the input and environmental variables are controlled.

A similar multi-stage regression analysis can be used to assess other kinds of interaction effects. For example, if the investigator wished to analyse possible interaction effects among input variables or among environmental variables as well as those between input and environmental variables, his analysis would involve separate stages in which the various effects would be controlled in the following sequence: main effects of input variables, interactions among input variables, main effects of environmental variables, interaction effects among environmental variables, and interactions between input and environmental variables.

The assessment of interaction effects by repeated analyses of different subgroups rather than by the multi-stage analysis just described presents certain problems for the investigator in determining when he actually had identified a significant 'interaction' effect. Some investigators are tempted to conclude that they have done so in cases where a particular environmental variable is found to have a significant effect in one subgroup but not in another. It would be more definitive to test the significance of difference between environment-output correlations rather than simply to ascertain that one correlation is significant but not the other. Even under these conditions, however, difference in the sizes of the samples or in the variances of either environmental or output variables can affect differences between environment-output correlations. The method of separate analyses by subgroups also presents the problems discussed in the previous section in connection with matching designs.

Error of Measurement

We already have indicated that one major difficulty with matching designs is the bias caused by error of measurement in the matching variables. What happens is that in order to match subjects on an attribute like, say, academic ability, unrepresentative sub-samples of students must be selected from each institution. If the institutions under study differ markedly in selectivity, the investigator must select the less able students from the highly selective institutions and the most able students from the least selective. Since the latter are above average in ability in comparison with their classmates, their scores are likely to contain more positive than negative errors of measurement. By contrast, the students from the highly selective colleges, being below average in ability relative to their classmates, are likely to have more negative than positive errors of measurement in their scores. Under these conditions, in each matched pair of students, the one from the highly selective college will more often than not have a higher 'true' score than the one from the least selective college. Another way of demonstrating this effect is to give all members of each matched pair a second, independent test. Students from the highly selective colleges will tend to score slightly higher than they did on the first test, whereas students from the least selective colleges will tend to score slightly lower than previously. Multivariate analyses avoid such errors by making it possible to utilize all subjects from all institutions, so that within-institution errors of measurement in the input variable sum to zero.

Measurement error can introduce the opposite kind of bias if the fallible input measure is used also as a basis for selecting students for admission. Under these circumstances, students in the highly selective institutions will tend to have more positive than negative errors of measurement in their test scores, whereas the rejects from these colleges, who enter less selective institutions, will tend to have more negative than positive errors in their scores. Unless the investigator can estimate precisely the extent to which a particular measure is relied upon in the admissions process, he would do well to avoid using the measure altogether in his longitudinal analyses of college impact.

An even subtler and potentially more serious consequence of measurement error – one that arises not only in matching designs but also in designs that use correlational methods – is attenuation in the observed correlation between input and output variables. It is a well-known statistical fact that error of measurement in either of a pair of correlated variables lowers their observed correlation. To the extent that such attenuation results from error in the input variables, a serious bias is introduced into the analysis if the input variable also is correlated with environmental variables.

The way in which this bias operates can be indicated by means of a hypothetical example. Assume that we are interested in determining how the student's achievement is affected by the 'quality' of his college. Furthermore, we have longitudinal data on students attending a variety of colleges of differing degrees of quality. Our output measure of achievement is the student's composite performance on the Graduate Record Examination (GRE), and our environmental measure of quality is the percentage of faculty members holding PhDs. For the sake of simplicity, let us assume that there is only one relevant input measure: the student's composite score on the National Merit Scholarship Qualifying Test

(NMSQT). To complete our hypothetical picture, we can make the following additional assumptions: (a) the NMSQT was not used in making admissions decisions; (b) the NMSQT is positively correlated with the GRE; and (c) NMSQT scores are positively correlated with college quality. This last assumption states simply that bright students are more likely to attend relatively high-quality colleges.

Our analyses of these three measures might involve only computing the partial correlation between college quality and GRE performance, holding constant the effects of NMSQT scores. Or perhaps we might want to compute residual GRE scores (regressed on NMSQT scores) and plot the mean residuals for each college against the college quality measure (this latter type of analysis would permit us to see any non-linear effects of quality and also to identify individual institutions that might have very large mean residuals). No matter which approach is used, however, we are likely to find that college quality has a positive 'effect' on achievement, even if there is in fact no effect. The reason for this is that error of measurement in the NMSQT causes us to underestimate the correlations of NMSQT with college quality and GRE scores, and thereby to 'undercorrect' for initial NMSQT performance. Thus, even though we have equated the student bodies entering each college statistically in terms of their mean observed NMSQT scores, we have not equated them in terms of their mean true NMSQT scores: since the adjusted 'true' score still is positively correlated both with college quality and GRE scores, we still should expect to find a positive correlation between quality and GRE performance.

Perhaps these artifacts can be illustrated better in terms of regression analysis. In simple linear regression, the slope of the regression line (regression coefficient) is a direct function of the correlation coefficient:

$$b_{yx} = \frac{r_{xy}s_y}{s_x}$$

(b and r, of course, will be identical if the two variances are equated). Thus, if r is attenuated by error of measurement in x (NMSQT scores), then b_{yx} also will be attenuated. The net effect of error of measurement in our example, then, is to flatten the slope of the regression of GRE on NMSQT scores. Figure 7 shows the consequences of this phenomenon: if one flattens the slope of the regression line (dotted line), he will tend to underestimate GRE for high values of NMSQT and to overestimate GRE for low values of NMSQT. Therefore, if we attempt, statistically, to equate students entering different colleges by partialling out the effects of their initial ability (NMSQT scores) on the GRE performance, the residuals for students with above-average NMSQT scores will be too large and those for below-average students too small. Similarly, the mean residuals for students attending high-quality colleges will be spuriously large (because there are more high-ability than low-ability students at these institutions) and the mean residuals for students attending low-quality colleges will be spuriously small. The magnitude of these spuriously large residuals is a direct function of the amount of measurement error in the NMSQT.

The same problem occurs, of course, if we compute residual college 'quality' scores: the residual environmental scores for students at high-quality colleges are spuriously high and those for students at low-quality colleges spuriously low. In short, the net result of error of measurement in the NMSQT is that we under-correct for initial differences in ability, thereby creating a spurious positive partial or part correlation between college quality and GRE performance.

A real danger in spurious 'effects' of this sort is that they are likely to be believed by educators and policy-makers because they confirm existing theories about college impact. For example, it is widely held that students get a 'better education' in the 'good' colleges. Indeed, this is one of the beliefs that attracts the brightest students to such colleges. Moreover, since most highly selective colleges manifest other traditional signs of prestige or quality (large libraries, distinguished faculty, competitive atmosphere, and so forth), the expectation that the student's intellectual development will prosper more in a high-quality college than in one of low quality is reinforced.

The same 'believability' of results may be created by errors of measurement in many other types of input variables. Thus, we would expect students to become relatively more 'liberal' if they attend colleges where the students already are highly liberal. We would expect a student with strong science interests to maintain these interests during college if he attends an institution where a high proportion of his fellow students also have strong science interests. The notion that students tend to change in the direction of their fellow students' dominant characteristics has been stated by Astin (1965a) and Astin and Panos (1969) as the theory of 'progressive conformity' and by Feldman and Newcomb (1969) as the theory of 'accentuation of initial differences'. The point here is that even if such theories are wrong, they will tend to be confirmed by virtue of error of measurement in the student input variables.

The fundamental importance of measurement error bias in studies of college impact indicates that some statistical proof of the

FIGURE 7: *True and observed regression of GRE scores on NMSQT scores*

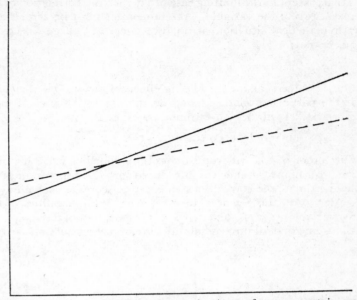

- - - - Observed regression (error of measurements in NMSQT)
———————— True regression (no error of measurements in NMSQT)

bias be presented. For this purpose we can use the example of the study of the effects of college selectivity on GRE performance. The three basic variables can be designated with subscripts as follows:

$$0 = \text{GRE score}$$
$$1 = \text{NMSQT score}$$
$$2 = \text{College quality.}$$

Let us begin by assuming that (a) the correlations among these three variables are all non-zero and positive (which happens to be the case), but (b) there is no true effect of College Quality on GRE performance. In other words, let us assume that if it were possible to obtain error-free measurements of all three variables, the partial correlation between GRE and College Quality, holding constant the effects of NMSQT scores, would be zero. Using the familiar formula for a first-order partial correlation coefficient, the true partial correlation between quality and GRE performance thus would be:

$$(1) \quad \text{(true scores)} \quad r_{02 \cdot 1} = \frac{r_{02} - r_{01} r_{12}}{\sqrt{(1 - r_{01}^2)\ (1 - r_{12}^2)}} = 0.$$

Since the denominator of this formula is always non-zero and positive (except in the limiting case of a zero-order correlation of $1 \cdot 0$ between two of the variables), the numerator must be zero. Thus, our hypothetical situation of no true effect of college selectivity requires that:

(2) (true scores) $r_{02} - r_{01}r_{12} = 0$.

Our hypothesis about the biasing effects of measurement error is that the partial correlation based on the observed scores of these three variables will be non-zero and positive:

(3) (observed scores) $r_{02} - r_{01}r_{12} > 0$.

Our proof of (3) will consist simply of showing what happens when error of measurement is introduced into (2). First we must be able to estimate the correlations among true scores as shown in (2). In order to do this we need to know what the reliabilities of the three variables (r_{00}, r_{11}, and r_{22}) are. For purposes of discussion we shall assume that all three reliabilities are imperfect but non-zero:

(4) $0 < r_{00} < 1$
(5) $0 < r_{11} < 1$
(6) $0 < r_{22} < 1$.

Since the true correlation between two variables is equal to the ratio between their observed correlation and the geometric mean of their reliabilities, formula (2) can now be expressed in terms of correlations among observed scores as follows:

(7) (observed scores) $\dfrac{r_{02}}{\sqrt{r_{00}} \ \sqrt{r_{22}}} - \dfrac{r_{01}r_{12}}{\sqrt{r_{00}} \ \sqrt{r_{22} \cdot r_{11}}} = 0$

or, (8) $\dfrac{1}{\sqrt{r_{00}} \ \sqrt{r_{22}}} \left(r_{02} - \dfrac{r_{01} \ \ r_{12}}{r_{11}} \right) = 0$.

Note that, in order for the left side of the equation to equal zero, the two terms within the parenthesis must be an equality, i.e.:

(9) $r_{02} = \dfrac{r_{01}r_{12}}{r_{11}}$

Now if we compute the partial correlation between GRE and College Quality using observed scores but make no correction for unreliability in our measures, only the right-side of (9) is affected, i.e. we omit the correction for unreliability and the denominator becomes $1 \cdot 0$. (Making no correction for unreliability is equivalent to assuming that there are no measurement errors and that the reliability of the variable is $1 \cdot 0$.) Since $r_{11} < 1 \cdot 0$ from (5):

$$(10) \quad r_{01}r_{12} < \frac{r_{01}r_{12}}{r_{11}}$$

and $(11) \quad r_{02} > r_{01}r_{12} > 0.$

Consequently, when no correction is made, the parenthetical term in (8) becomes non-zero and positive. Since the two reliabilities, r_{00} and r_{22}, also are non-zero and positive, the entire left side of equation (8) and, hence, the observed partial correlation between GRE and college selectivity becomes non-zero and positive. In short, failure to adjust for error of measurement in the NMSQT will lead to the conclusion that achievement is favourably affected by college quality when there is no true effect.

Several additional interesting conclusions can be deduced from formula (8):

1. The principal source of bias results from measurement error in the partialled variable (variable number 1 in equation 8). Failure to adjust for such bias can:
   (a) Create spurious 'effects' when there are no true effects;
   (b) Exaggerate the magnitude of true effects;
   (c) Reverse the sign of the true effect.

2. The direction (sign) of the bias resulting from errors of measurement in the partialled variable depends on the signs of its correlations with the other variables (r_{01} and r_{12}).

3. Failure to adjust for measurement error in either the independent or dependent variable only will attenuate the observed partial correlation between the independent and dependent variables.

Several remedies can be employed to compensate for error of measurement in the input variables when multivariate techniques are used to evaluate college impact. A remedy for the two variable case (input and output) has been proposed by Tucker, Damerin and Messick (1966). An appropriate generalization of their approach to the multivariate case would be to compute correlation matrices using the variance in the 'true' (rather than observed) scores of all independent variables (student input as well as environmental). Since the true variance in a set of scores is simply the product of the observed variance and the reliability of the measure, it would be relatively simple to make such corrections if the reliabilities of all of the input and environmental variables were known. Estimates of reliability usually are available for psychometric devices, though not for the demographic and other types of questionnaire data that characterize so much of the research on college impact. Recognizing

the need for this information, the research staff of ACE currently is
engaged in an extensive empirical study to obtain estimates of error
of measurement in questionnaire data (Boruch, 1970).

Resolving some Inferential Dilemmas

No matter how elegant his design, the investigator can never be
absolutely sure that he has isolated 'true' college effects. But, there
are certain situations in which he can have a good deal of confidence
that his data are indeed revealing environmental influences.

One situation which justifies a high degree of confidence is that in
which the environmental variable is uncorrelated with the input
variables. For example, one college environmental characteristic
that has no relationship, or only a very low one, with most student
input variables is institutional size (Astin, 1965b). In other words,
students who go to large institutions differ very little from those who
go to small ones. Consequently, the observed effect of size on some
student output measure is almost certainly not just an artifact of the
researcher's failure to control input differences.

A related situation arises when the correlation between environment and output is substantially higher than the correlation between
environment and input. Ideally, one would like to see the correlation
between environment and output increase as differential inputs are
controlled. (The more usual situation, of course, is that the
environment-output relationship shrinks consistently as input
variables are controlled successively.) Thus, if the environment-
output correlation increases, or at least holds its own, as input
variables are controlled, the investigator can be reasonably con-
fident that his observed environmental effect is a true one. However,
if the correlation between environment and output diminishes
consistently as input variables are controlled until only a small
relationship remains, there is a very real possibility that if one or two
other input variables had been included in the analyses, the relationship would have disappeared altogether.

Perhaps the strongest evidence for true causation exists when the
direction (sign) of a particular environmental effect is the opposite
of the zero-order correlation between that environmental variable
and the output measure. Although rare, this reversal in sign has
been observed in at least one study (Astin and Panos, 1969). In this
study, cohesiveness, an ICA environmental measure reflecting
primarily the proportion of students who report having many close
friends among their fellow students, was shown to have a positive
effect on the student's chances of staying in college. However, the
zero-order correlation between cohesiveness and the percentage of
students remaining in college for four years was negative ($r = -\cdot13$).

When differential student input variables were controlled, this partial correlation reversed sign (to $+\cdot25$). The explanation of this apparent paradox is that students who go to highly cohesive institutions are, on the average, more dropout-prone than are the students who go to the less cohesive institutions. Consequently, the positive relationship between the dropout-proneness of entering freshman classes and the cohesiveness of institutional environments masks the negative effect of cohesiveness on the individual student's chances of dropping out.

Research data that reveal significant interaction effects represent another situation where causal inferences can be made with more than usual confidence. Consider, for example, a situation where a measure of, say, the peer environment is found to have a significant main effect on some outcome. If this apparent effect is, indeed, a true one rather than an artifact, then we would expect to find that the effect is stronger among resident students – who would have more contact with their fellow students and thus would be more affected by their characteristics – than among commuters. Therefore, if it can be shown that there is a significant interaction effect involving resident-commuter status and the particular peer environmental measure in question, then the conclusion that the environmental attribute is related causally to the outcome is strengthened. By the same reasoning, we should not expect to find such interactions with measures of, say, the classroom environment, since both residents and commuters presumably have equal exposure to such environmental factors by virtue of attending classes.

Similar checks on the validity of causal inferences can be made by examining many other types of interaction effects. For example, extroverts or gregarious students presumably are more susceptible to the effects of peer factors than are introverted or shy students. To take another example, the magnitude of a particular effect should increase the longer the student is at the college. The point is that for many of the apparent environmental effects that may be observed in longitudinal studies, it is possible to hypothesize the existence of certain interaction effects which, if subsequently confirmed by additional analyses, would lend support to the assumption that the relationship is, indeed, a causal one.

Summary

The purpose of this paper has been to review some of the major methodological problems in the design of studies of college impact.

To facilitate the discussion of design problems, one may view the question of college impact in terms of three components: student outputs, student inputs, and environmental characteristics. Any

c

problem in the design of college impact studies can be seen in terms of the relationships between these three components.

The major goal of college impact studies is to minimize three kinds of inferential error: Type I and Type II errors (the traditional inferential errors of experimental design), and Type III errors, which are defined as inferential statements which simultaneously involve both Type I and Type II errors. Type III errors are possible in college impact research primarily because of the highly non-random distribution of students among institutions.

Much of the previous research on college impact has resulted in ambiguous findings primarily because at least one of the three informational components was missing. The single-institution study, through input and output information, indicates how the student changes during college, but it provides no information bearing directly on environmental impact. The multi-institution cross-sectional study provides information on the relationship between environments and outputs, but it is highly susceptible to Type I and Type III errors unless student input data also are collected.

The most definitive information about college impact is obtained from multi-institution longitudinal studies in which data on student inputs, student outputs, and environmental characteristics are obtained. Such data can be analysed by a variety of 'quasi-experimental' designs (path analysis, for example), although step-wise linear multiple regression analysis is perhaps the most flexible and versatile method, particularly if the regression is carried out in separate 'stages' dictated by the logic of the college impact process.

The variance in student output in the multi-institution studies can be assigned to four sources: error, variance uniquely attributable to input variables, variance uniquely attributable to environmental variables, and confounded variance. Variance uniquely attributable to input variables can be defined as the squared multiple part correlation between the output measure and the residual input measure. Variance uniquely attributable to environmental sources can be defined as the squared multiple part correlation between the output measure and the residual environmental measures. Confounded variance is defined as the remainder of the total predictable output variance (that is, the final R^2 minus the two squared part correlations). The two-part correlations can be used as 'lower-bounds' estimates of the total output variance attributable to a particular source, whereas the part correlation plus the confounded variance can be used as an 'upper-bounds' estimate. Additional part correlations and confounded variance estimates can be obtained for interaction effects, if desired.

One of the most serious sources of potential bias in college effects studies, regardless of the method of analysis used, are errors of measurement in the input variables. Unless corrections are made for such errors, the investigator runs the risk of finding spurious college 'effects'. Such spurious effects tend to be highly believable, in that they ordinarily support the most plausible theory of how students are affected by their colleges. Since appropriate adjustments for such measurement error require a knowledge of the reliability of each input variable, researchers engaged in studies of college impact should consider collecting such reliability information routinely on each instrument that they use.

In spite of the many methodological and logical problems inherent in research on college impact, a number of checks and precautions are available to the investigator that will reduce his chances of committing inferential errors.

PART TWO

The Community Environment

In the first reading, by Marjoribanks, the community environment is defined by that social space which has been named elsewhere as the eth-class (see Gordon, 1964): that is, those social groupings that are formed in society by the intersections of horizontal social class stratifications with vertical ethnic group stratifications. In an analysis of the verbal, number, spatial and reasoning abilities of 11-year-old boys from five Canadian ethnic groups, each divided into two social class groups, it was found that significant ability differences existed among the children from the different social class and ethnic group backgrounds. Perhaps the most important finding was that when patterns of abilities were examined, it was found that the pattern of mental abilities for middle class children within each ethnic group was parallel to the pattern of abilities for lower class children. This result, which replicated some earlier research, suggests that ethnic groups are characterized by distinct patterns of mental ability scores and that social class influences do not alter the shapes of the patterns, but only affect the level of the patterns.

In an attempt to account for the social class and ethnic group influences on patterns of abilities, the social-psychological environments of the families from the different eth-classes were investigated. The results provided tentative support for the two propositions:

(1) that ethnic groups foster the development of different patterns of environmental forces and that these forces are related to the development of different patterns of mental abilities among ethnic groups; and
(2) social class groups foster the development of similar patterns of environmental forces and that these forces are related to the development of similar patterns of mental abilities between the social classes.

In the second reading, by Sewell and Armer, it is suggested that their study 'clearly casts doubt on the popular notion that the socioeconomic status of the neightbourhood in which the youth resides has a substantial influence on his educational aspirations'. Using a regression model of the following form:

$Y = a_1 X_1 + a_2 X_2 + a_3 X_3 + a_4 X_4 +$ constant, in which $T =$ college plans, $X_1 =$ sex, $X_2 =$ intelligence, $X_3 =$ socioeconomic status of family, and $X_4 =$ neighbourhood context, it was found that after accounting for the first three variables, neighbourhood context explained little additional variance in college plans.

The methodological and statistical framework of the study has been criticised (e.g. see Turner, 1967; Boyle, 1967; Michael, 1967). It has been suggested that there is no reason why the individual variables should take precedence over the contextual variables, and that the neighbourhood effect is minimal, in the study, because it is highly correlated with social class and intelligence. In essence, the criticisms of the study are related to the problems of environmental research which Astin discussed in the overview.

Another limitation of the Sewell and Armer study is the reliance on relatively global environmental measures. The first study in this section indicates that by using refined environmental measures, it is possible to increase our understanding of the complexity of environment-human behaviour interactions.

References

From: MARJORIBANKS, K. (1972)1 'Ethnicity and learning patterns: a replication and an explanation', *Sociology*, 6, 417–31.

From: SEWELL, W. H., and ARMER, J. M. (1966). 'Neighbourhood context and college plans', *American Sociological Review*, 31, 159–68.

3. Ethnicity and Learning Patterns: A Replication and an Explanation

KEVIN MARJORIBANKS

Introduction

IN AN examination of the learning patterns of children from different ethnic groups in the United States, Lesser *et al.* (1964), and Stodolsky and Lesser (1967) found that ethnic groups were characterized by distinct patterns of mental ability scores.[1] Contrary to the hypotheses of the studies, it was discovered that the patterns of abilities associated with ethnic group membership remained invariant across social class[2] divisions. Statistically, this meant that social class influences on the shapes of the patterns of mental ability test scores within each ethnic group were nonsignificant; that the pattern of abilities for middle class children within each ethnic group was parallel to the pattern of abilities for lower class children.

The pervasive influence of ethnicity as a determinant of patterns of mental ability test scores has tended to be accepted as almost axiomatic by subsequent reviewers and researchers. Considering the demonstrated power of social class influences upon numerous sociological, educational, and psychological variables, the findings of the Lesser studies and the unchallenged acceptance of them is surprising. Therefore, it was considered desirable that a replication study be undertaken in which the inter-relationships among the constructs of ethnicity, social class, and mental abilities be examined once again.

An investigation was thus made of the inter-relationships between Canadian ethnic group membership, social class background, and the levels and patterns of a set of mental ability test scores.

---

[1]In the first study four ethnic groups were examined: Negro, Puerto Rican, Chinese and Jewish. In the second study Chinese and Negro children were examined. Four mental abilities were investigated in each study: verbal, number, space and reasoning.

[2]'Social class' in this context (and as used in the present study) refers to social status groups and not the traditional concept of class.

Method

Mental Abilities

The levels and patterns of four mental abilities were examined: verbal, number, spatial, and reasoning. The abilities were operationalized by the scores on the sra Primary Mental Abilities subtests (1962 Revised Edition).

Sample

Members of five ethnic groups residing in Ontario, Canada, were included in the study: Canadian Indian (Iroquois), French Canadians (Franco-Ontarions), Jews, Southern Italians, and white Anglo-Saxon Protestants.

Approximately 100 11-year-old boys from each ethnic group were selected and tested, using first the California Test of Mental Maturity and then the sra Primary Mental Abilities test. The first test-taking situation was used: (a) to establish examiner-examinee rapport,[1] (b) to ensure that all the boys were able to understand the test instructions, and (c) to establish as far as possible uniform test-taking conditions. In the second test-taking situation, the sra test was administered. Only the scores from the latter test were used in the analysis.

Each boy in the sample was Canadian born and was attending a school in which English was the predominant language of instruction. In the Jewish schools a Hebrew studies programme was taken by each boy, and in the schools for the French Canadians, a French studies curriculum was also provided. The Canadian Indian students attended schools on an Indian reserve and the Southern Italian boys attended a Roman Catholic school system which served an urban Southern Italian neighbourhood. All of the schools, except those on the reservation, were in urban areas.

Social Class

The boys from each ethnic group were assigned to two social class categories, one designated as middle-class and the other as low-class. An equally weighted combination of the occupation of the head of the household and a rating of his (or her) education level was used as the basis of the classification. The social class data were initially obtained from student and school reports, but these were confirmed during a parent-interview session.

As part of the study, data were collected regarding the learning environment which was present in each boy's home. For this purpose the total sample of boys was divided into two parallel pools

---

[1]All testing was conducted by the author with the intention of creating uniformity in the test situation.

with the intention of obtaining 20 middle-class and 20 low-class families in each ethnic group. The reason for the substitute pools was to provide a set of alternate families which could be used in the study if families from the first pool did not agree to participate.

In the case of the Canadian Indians it was not possible to form completely parallel middle-class pools, and in the case of the Jewish families it was not possible to duplicate the low-class group. As a result, the final[1] sample within each ethnic group consisted of 18 families classified as middle-class and 19 as low-class. The analysis in the following sections is thus based upon data collected from 37 families, from each of five ethnic groups.

Results

The hypotheses which were examined were the same as those analysed in the Lesser studies:

(1) Significant differences exist among groups of children from different social class and ethnic group backgrounds in the level of each of the four mental abilities.
(2) Significant differences exist among groups of children from different social class and ethnic group backgrounds in the pattern of scores of the four mental abilities.
(3) Significant interactions exist between the variables of social class and ethnicity in determining the level of each mental ability and the nature of the patterns among them.

Levels of Abilities

A multiple regression model was used to examine the first hypothesis. The results of the analysis, which are presented in Table 5, provided support for the acceptance of the hypothesis and replicated the findings of the Lesser studies. On each of the abilities the middle-class boys had significantly higher scores than the lower-class boys, and in general the level of abilities of the Jewish and Protestant groups were significantly higher than the level of abilities of the other three groups.

Patterns of Abilities

The shapes of the patterns of the test scores for each social class group and each ethnic group have been presented in Figures 8 and 9. Scores on each of the mental abilities were converted to standard scores, calculated over the total sample, with a mean of 50 and a standard deviation of 10.

[1]In the Lesser study the sample was divided into two social class groups, 40 middle-class children (20 boys and 20 girls) and 40 lower-class children (20 boys and 20 girls) in each ethnic group.

TABLE 5: *Relationship between ethnicity, social class, and the mental ability test scores*

| Mental Ability | RELATION WITH SOCIAL CLASS | | RELATION WITH ETHNICITY[b] | |
	Multiple Correlation R_c^a	Percentage of Total Variance R_c^a	Multiple Correlation R_c	Percentage of Total Variance R_c^a
Verbal	·48**	23·2**	·66**	44·8**
Number	·35**	12·4**	·58**	33·5**
Spatial	·31**	9·7**	·21*	4·4*
Reasoning	·28**	8·2**	·29**	8·4**

a Corrected to allow for small sample size and cumulative errors in Multiple R·
b In the analysis the ethnic group data formed a set of mutually exclusive categories.
* p < ·05
** p < ·01

FIGURE 8: *Pattern of normalized mental-ability scores for each social class group*

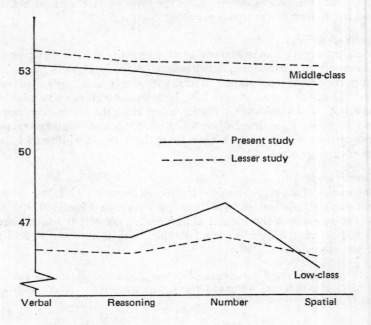

When an analysis of variance test for the existence of group psychometric patterns and configurations of test scores[1] was used to examine the shapes of the patterns, it was found that: (a) the two social class groups had patterns of similar shape, while (b) the shapes of the patterns for the ethnic groups were significantly different.

Again, the results of the present study replicated the findings of the previous research. In Figure 8, the patterns of abilities of each social class group in the original Lesser study have been presented. The two sets of patterns indicate the similarity of the results from the two studies. The shape of the pattern for the Jewish children is similar to the shape obtained in the Lesser studies, in which it was also found that Jewish children were characterized by high verbal and number ability scores and lower spatial and reasoning ability scores.

Interaction Effects

When levels of abilities were examined, the interaction effect of social class and ethnicity was significant only in relation to number ability. It was found that social class position produced more of a difference in the number ability scores of the French Canadian boys than in the number scores of the boys from the other four groups.

In the case of verbal, number, and spatial abilities, the influence of ethnicity was not significantly different across the social class levels.

All of the interaction effects in the Lesser studies were found to be significant. On each of the ability measures, social class position produced more of a difference in the scores of the Negro children than for the other groups.

When the relationships between the patterns of abilities and the interaction effect of ethnicity and social class was examined, it was found that only the Canadian Indian middle- and lower-class group patterns departed from parallelism. In Figures 10–14 the patterns of mental ability test scores for middle- and low-class boys from each ethnic group have been presented.

The overall findings of the study indicated, as did the Lesser studies, that (1) both social class and ethnicity influence the level of intellectual performance, and (2) while ethnicity fosters the development of different patterns of abilities, social class differences do not modify the basic shape of the patterns within ethnic groups.

An Explanation

In an attempt to account for the pervasive influence of ethnicity on the shapes of the patterns of abilities, a theoretical position developed by Ferguson (1954, 1956) was used as a framework for investigation.

[1] See Block *et al.* (1951); and Greenhouse and Geisser (1959).

FIGURE 9: *Patterns of mental ability test scores for each ethnic group*

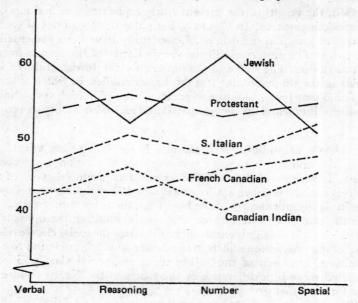

FIGURE 10: *Patterns of normalized mental ability scores for middle- and low-class Canadian Indian groups*

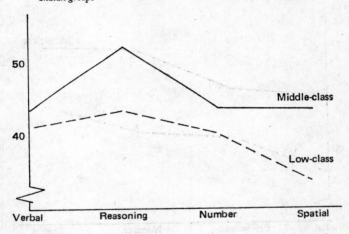

FIGURE 11: *Patterns of normalized mental ability scores for middle- and low-class French Canadian groups*

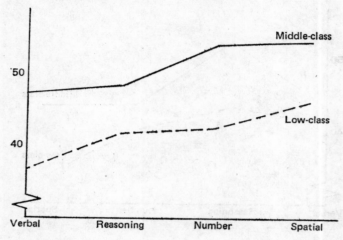

FIGURE 12: *Patterns of normalized mental ability scores for middle- and low-class Jewish groups*

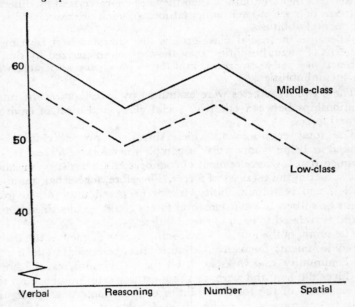

Essentially, Ferguson postulates that if different cultural groups are found to be characterized by different patterns of mental ability test scores, then they will also be characterized by different environments for learning. Therefore, the results of the present study suggested the following hypotheses:

(1) Because the ethnic groups are characterized by different patterns of mental abilities, then they are characterized by different patterns of a set of environmental forces which are associated with the mental abilities.

(2) Because the social class groups are characterized by similar patterns of mental abilities, then they are characterized by similar patterns of a set of environmental forces which are associated with the mental abilities.

These two hypotheses were examined by investigating the interrelationships between ethnicity social class, and a set of environmental forces.

The total environment which surrounds an individual was defined as being composed of a complex network of forces. It was assumed that the development of cognitive characteristics is related to a subset of the total set of forces. Therefore, for verbal, number, spatial, and reasoning ability, it was proposed that sub-environments or subsets of environmental forces could be identified which would be related to each of the abilities.

The union of the four sub-environments was defined as the learning environment. Such an environment may be present in the home, the community, and the school. Of these environments, the home produces the first and perhaps the most powerful influence on the development of the mental abilities of the child. As a result, the learning environment of the home was chosen as the focus of the study.

From a review of relevant theoretical and empirical literature a set of eight environmental forces was identified. (See later reading by Marjoribanks for a description of the environmental forces and for a description of the relation between the forces and the mental abilities.) The forces, which were labelled:

(1) press for achievement;
(2) press for activeness;
(3) press for intellectuality;
(4) press for independence;
(5) press for English;
(6) press for ethlanguage;
(7) mother dominance;
(8) father dominance;

accounted for about 50% of the variance in the verbal and number scores, 16% in the reasoning scores and 7% in the spatial scores.

Figure 13: *Patterns of normalized mental ability scores for middle- and low-class Southern Italian groups*

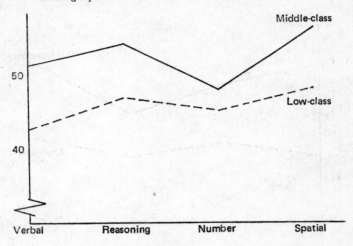

Figure 14: *Patterns of normalized mental ability scores for middle- and low-class white Anglo-Saxon Protestant groups*

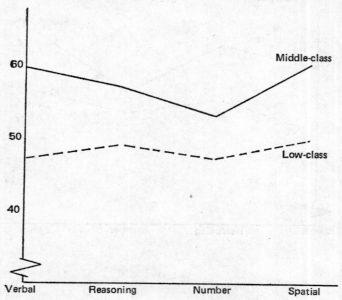

FIGURE 15: *Patterns of normalized environmental force scores for each ethnic group*

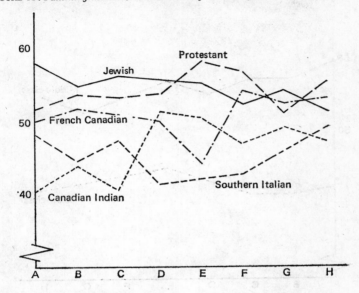

A-H correspond to forces 1-8 listed on page 80.

FIGURE 16: *Patterns of normalized environmental force scores for middle- and low-class groups*

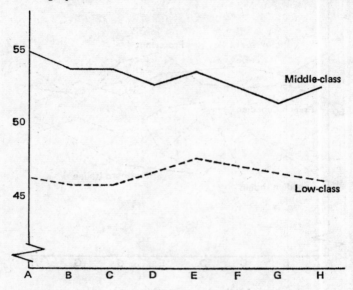

In Figures 15 and 16 the patterns of environmental force scores for each ethnic group and for the two social class groups have been presented. An analysis of the patterns indicated that: (a) the ethnic groups were characterized by significantly different patterns of environmental forces, and (b) the social class groups were characterized by patterns of environmental forces of similar shape.

The two sets of results provided support for the proposition that if cultural groups are characterized by distinctive patterns of mental abilities, then they are also characterized by distinctive patterns of a set of environmental forces which are related to the abilities.

Conclusion

By finding: (a) that ethnic groups and social class groups are markedly different in the absolute levels of a set of mental abilities, and (b) that while ethnicity affects the pattern of mental abilities, social class variations within an ethnic group do not alter the basic organization, the present study has replicated, and thus added some validity to the Lesser studies.

From the examination of the inter-relationships among the constructs of ethnicity, social class, environment, and mental abilities, it can be postulated:

(1) that ethnic groups foster the development of different patterns of environmental forces and that these forces are related to the development of different patterns of mental abilities among the ethnic groups, and
(2) social class groups foster the development of similar patterns of environmental forces and that these forces are related to the development of similar patterns of mental abilities between the social classes.

While the study is not a direct examination of the genetic hypothesis discussed by Jensen (1969) and Eysenck (1971), the results indicated that the smallest ethnic group and social class differences were in relation to spatial ability. Other studies have suggested that spatial ability scores may reflect innate intelligence better than other mental ability measures.

Because of the *ex post facto* nature of the study and its correlated design, inferences regarding the nature of the inter-relationships among the variables are, of course, restricted. But the study does provide, perhaps, a more detailed examination of the relationship between ethnicity, social class, environment, and mental abilities than has been presented so far. By developing a model of the learning environment, which is associated with ethnicity and social class, and which is predictive of a set of mental ability test scores, the study has moved beyond much of the previous research in this area of investigation which has used both gross classificatory environmental variables and global indicators of intellectual performance.

4. Neighbourhood Context and College Plans

WILLIAM H. SEWELL and J. MICHAEL ARMER

NUMEROUS STUDIES have appeared in recent years attempting to account for educational aspirations of high school seniors. To date, most research effort has been concentrated upon individual and family background attributes. Of all the factors studied, sex, intelligence, and socioeconomic status have been most frequently, consistently and clearly associated with educational aspirations. More recently the social environments or contexts in which individuals live have been examined for their bearing on educational aspirations. Such specific social context variables as rural-urban residence, peer group associations, the socioeconomic composition of the high schools, and the socioeconomic composition of the community or neighbourhood have been suggested by a number of investigators. The present paper reports an empirical examination of the influence of one of these social contexts, neighbourhood socioeconomic status, on the college plans of high school youth.

The most direct test of the thesis that community context influences the aspirations of youth comes from studies by Sewell (1965). This research, based on a large random sample of Wisconsin high school seniors, indicates that the community context, as measured by size of community, is clearly associated with the educational and occupational plans of youth. However, when sex, family socioeconomic status, and measured intelligence are controlled, the original relationship between community size and educational aspiration is greatly reduced. This permits the tentative conclusion that differences in aspirations may be due more to differences in the sex, socioeconomic, and ability composition of high schools than to normative differences in community contexts. Of course, tests employing more direct indices of community socioeconomic status and normative climates are necessary before more definitive conclusions can be drawn regarding the viability of the thesis as applied to communities.

Because of limitations of previous research, the question of the influence of residential segregation within large and complex communities on the educational aspiration of students, over and above the influence of the other known sources, remains largely unanswered.

The essential arguments and expectations of the thesis may be summarized as follows. Much evidence has accumulated to indicate that ecological processes in large cities result in socioeconomic segregation. It has also been shown that school segregation is in large part a consequence of residential segregation. Since high school enrolment areas represent functioning subcommunities for high school youth within larger urban complexes, it may be expected that informal mechanisms, such as normative climates or model levels of aspiration, would emerge and would have some pervasive influence on the aspirations of all youth residing in the neighbourhood, regardless of the socioeconomic status or ability levels of the youth. In other words, the prediction would be that the socioeconomic status of the high school district – since it presumably reflects the shared norms and aspirations of its members – would have an important effect on the educational aspirations of its youth over and above that of family socioeconomic status or individual ability. It is the purpose of this study to test this hypothesis using elaboration techniques and correlation analysis.

The Data

The principal source of the data on which this study is based is a survey of all high school seniors in public and private schools in Wisconsin in 1957. The total universe of public high school seniors in the Milwaukee metropolitan area (3,999 students) is included in this analysis. Information was gathered from these school students on a number of matters, including educational and vocational plans, socioeconomic status, and measured intelligence.

The County of Milwaukee was selected for study because it is the largest and most diverse metropolitan area in Wisconsin; its 1960 population was 1,036,041. It contains 20 public high schools: 13 in the central city and seven in independent suburbs. The high school enrolment districts were selected as the basic unit for analysis of neighbourhood context because they may be considered functional social areas within the larger community. This is true in the sense that a community of shared interests among students tends to form around the high school; students identify themselves with the school and its many curricular and non-curricular activities.

The index of socioeconomic status for each neighbourhood (school enrolment district) is the proportion of males 14 years and older living in the area who are employed in white-collar occupations. Since census figures are not reported for these areas, it was necessary to combine census tracts to fit as closely as possible the neighbourhood boundaries as defined in this study. The neighbourhood status for each student attending a given school is the percentage of white-collar workers in the area. The range in status was from 13–83 per cent for the 20 neighbourhoods. For the cross-tabular analysis, these neighbourhoods were divided into three neighbourhood context categories: high, 41–83 per cent white-collar; middle, 31–40 per cent white-collar; and low, 13–30 per cent white-collar. The high category consists of four high-status suburbs located on the northern and western borders of the city and two high-status neighbourhoods adjacent to them but within the city limits of Milwaukee. The low category includes five low-status neighbourhoods located in and surrounding the central business and lake-shore industrial district and two industrial suburbs. The seven middle-status neighbourhoods are scattered throughout the metropolitan area. Each of these three neighbourhood categories is distinct from the others not only in occupational distribution but also in such other relevant criteria as the percentage of adults with one or more years of college education, the average value of homes, and the percentage of non-whites. However, it should also be noted that the distinctions are not exaggerated in this study, as in much previous research, by purposely selecting only neighbourhoods which differ widely in socioeconomic status.

The college plans variable is based on the senior student's statement that he definitely plans to enrol in a degree-granting college or university (or one whose credits are acceptable for advanced standing at the University of Wisconsin) upon graduation from high school.

The control variables in the analysis are sex, intelligence, and socio-economic status. The intelligence variable is based on scores on the Henmon-Nelson Test of Mental ability which is administered annually in all high schools in Wisconsin. Students were divided into approximately equal thirds in measured intelligence: high (67th percentile and above), middle (38th percentile to 66th percentile), and low (37th percentile and below). The socio-economic status classification is based on a factor-weighted score of father's educational level, mother's educational level, an estimate of the funds the family could provide if the student were to attend college, the degree of sacrifice this would entail for the family, and the approximate wealth and income status of the student's family. The students were divided into three categories of approximately equal size, labelled high, middle, and low in socioeconomic status.

Results

The central hypothesis of this study is that the neighbourhood in

TABLE 6: *Percentage with college plans by neighbourhood status, for male and female Milwaukee public high school seniors*

NEIGHBOURHOOD STATUS	MALES		FEMALES		TOTAL
Low	30·5	(524)	20·3	(743)	24·6 (1267)
Middle	39·7	(658)	21·1	(833)	29·3 (1491)
High	62·2	(572)	53·2	(669)	57·4 (1241)
Total	44·3	(1754)	30·4	(2245)	36·5 (3999)

which the student resides has an important influence on high educational plans in addition to that of his sex, measured intelligence, and the socio-economic status of his family. To test this hypothesis the following questions should be considered: first, is neighbourhood status associated with college plans? Second, does the association persist when the effects of sex, socioeconomic status, and intelligence are separately controlled? Third, does the relationship persist when these variables are simultaneously controlled? Fourth, how much variance does neighbourhood status account for over and above that accounted for by sex, socioeconomic status, and intelligence?

The data bearing on the first question are given in summary form in Table 6. Less than a quarter of the students in low-status neighbourhoods plan on attending college, but more than half of those in high-status neighbourhoods have plans to attend college. Partialling out the effects of sex does not disturb the relationship except to reduce the difference between the low- and middle-status neighbourhoods for girls and to increase the difference for boys.

Table 7 shows the influence of intelligence and socioeconomic status on college plans. It is apparent that each of these variables is

TABLE 7: *Percentage with college plans by intelligence and socioeconomic status, for male and female Milwaukee public high school seniors*

	MALES		FEMALES		TOTAL
Intelligence					
Low	24·0	(516)	13·1	(863)	17·2 (1379)
Middle	42·1	(620)	34·6	(741)	38·0 (1361)
High	63·4	(618)	49·0	(641)	56·1 (1259)
Socioeconomic Status					
Low	24·6	(561)	14·1	(799)	18·5 (1360)
Middle	41·2	(610)	28·2	(791)	33·8 (1401)
High	66·6	(583)	53·0	(655)	59·4 (1238)
Total	44·3	(1754)	30·4	(2245)	36·5 (3999)

TABLE 8: *Percentage distribution of sex, intelligence, and socioeconomic status by neighbourhood status, for Milwaukee public high school seniors*

NEIGHBOURHOOD STATUS	A. SEX		
	Male	Female	Total
Low	41·4	58·6	100·0 (1267)
Middle	44·1	55·9	100·0 (1491)
High	46·1	53·9	100·0 (1241)
Total	43·9	56·1	100·0 (3999)

	B. INTELLIGENCE		
	Low Third	Middle Third	High Third
Low	41·3	36·5	22·2	100·0 (1267)
Middle	37·5	28·9	33·6	100·0 (1491)
High	23·9	37·6	38·5	100·0 (1241)
Total	34·5	34·0	31·5	100·0 (3999)

	C. SOCIOECONOMIC STATUS		
	Low Third	Middle Third	High Third
Low	43·8	35·3	20·9	100·0 (1267)
Middle	37·4	38·6	24·0	100·0 (1491)
High	20·0	30·5	29·5	100·0 (1241)
Total	34·0	35·0	31·0	100·0 (3999)

related to college plans. (In terms of the percentage differences, *either* variable is more closely related to college plans than is the neighbourhood context.) Those from high socioeconomic status families or of high intelligence are approximately three times as likely to plan on college as those of low socioeconomic status or of low intelligence. The same relationships hold for both boys and girls.

In Table 8, it will be noted that the lower status neighbourhoods have a disproportion of females, students from lower socioeconomic status families, and students of lower measured intelligence – each of these would tend to reduce the proportion of those planning on college. Because sex, intelligence, and socioeconomic status — all of which are related to college plans – are also all related to neighbourhood context, these variables must be controlled in assessing the influence of neighbourhood context on college plans.

TABLE 9: *Percentage with college plans by neighbourhood status and intelligence, for male and female Milwaukee public high school seniors*

NEIGHBOURHOOD STATUS	INTELLIGENCE			
	Low	Middle	High	Total
Males				
Low	15·9 (195)	31·4 (207)	52·5 (122)	30·5 (524)
Middle	24·5 (212)	35·6 (191)	55·3 (255)	39·7 (658)
High	37·6 (109)	57·7 (222)	77·6 (241)	62·2 (572)
Total	24·0 (516)	42·1 (620)	63·4 (618)	44·3 (1754)
Females				
Low	8·8 (328)	26·6 (256)	34·0 (159)	20·3 (743)
Middle	8·1 (347)	21·7 (240)	39·0 (246)	21·1 (833)
High	29·8 (188)	55·5 (245)	69·5 (236)	53·2 (669)
Total	13·1 (863)	34·6 (741)	49·0 (641)	30·4 (2245)

The effects of the control of sex and intelligence, on the relationship between neighbourhood context and college plans are given in Tables 9 and 10. Control of intelligence reduces the original relationship between neighbourhood context and college plans for boys – but not greatly – and in no case is there a single reversal in the ordering. For girls, the control of intelligence results in the virtual elimination of differences between the low and middle neighbourhood status groups, but there are still large differences between the college plans of girls in these two categories and those in the high-status neighbourhoods – for all three intelligence levels.

TABLE 10: *Percentage with college plans by neighbourhood status and socioeconomic status, for male and female Milwaukee public high school seniors*

NEIGHBOURHOOD STATUS	SOCIOECONOMIC STATUS			
	Low	Middle	High	Total
Males				
Low	22·6 (217)	29·3 (188)	47·1 (119)	30·5 (524)
Middle	21·1 (232)	40·9 (259)	63·5 (167)	39·7 (658)
High	35·7 (112)	55·2 (163)	76·1 (297)	62·2 (572)
Total	24·6 (561)	41·2 (610)	66·6 (583)	44·3 (1754)
Females				
Low	11·8 (338)	22·8 (259)	35·6 (146)	20·3 (743)
Middle	11·7 (325)	20·8 (317)	37·7 (191)	21·1 (833)
High	25·7 (136)	45·6 (215)	70·1 (318)	53·2 (669)
Total	14·1 (799)	28·2 (791)	53·0 (655)	30·4 (2245)

Thus controlling for intelligence does not explain the original differences either for boys or for girls.

Control for socioeconomic status (Table 10) greatly reduces the neighbourhood differences in college plans for boys from low socioeconomic status families, but large neighbourhood differences persist for middle and high socio-economic status groups. For girls, the partialling tends to eliminate the differences between the low- and middle-status neighbourhoods, but the differences between these two neighbourhood categories and the high-status neighbourhoods are marked – especially for girls from high socioeconomic status families. Thus, controlling for socioeconomic status does not explain the neighbourhood differences in college plans either for boys or for girls.

Since the results of the partialling thus far leaves large unexplained differences in college plans of students from neighbourhoods of varying status, the next step is to determine the effects of controlling sex, socioeconomic status, and intelligence simultaneously. The results of this operation produce, in effect, 18 tables showing the percentage of students with college plans according to neighbourhood context in all of the possible combinations of sex, socioeconomic status, and intelligence categories. These results are summarized in Table 11. For the boys, all but one of the sub-populations show marked reduction in the association of neighbourhood status with college plans, and in several sub-populations there are reversals in the low and middle categories. The only remaining comparatively large difference between the high and low neighbourhood contexts is for boys in the middle intelligence, high socioeconomic status category. In this instance, living in a higher status neighbourhood is clearly related to college plans.

For the girls, the influence of neighbourhood context is also reduced in all sub-populations except for those from high socioeconomic status families where the effects are about the same regardless of intelligence. In other words, girls living in higher status neighbourhoods tend to have high educational aspirations, regardless of their measured ability, if they come from high socioeconomic status families. There continues to be some relationship between neighbourhood context for girls from middle socioeconomic status families in the middle and high intelligence groups, and for highly intelligent girls from low-status families, but the association is not as large as in the preceding instances.

The results of this analysis suggest that neighbourhood context is associated more with the educational aspirations of girls than boys, and is strongest for girls from high socioeconomic status families. Why this should be true is not readily apparent from the analysis,

TABLE 11: *Percentage with college plans, by neighbourhood status, socioeconomic status, and intelligence, for male and female Milwaukee public high school seniors*

NEIGHBOURHOOD STATUS	A. LOW SOCIOECONOMIC STATUS		
	Low Intelligence	*Middle Intelligence*	*High Intelligence*
Males			
Low	13·0 (92)	23·8 (84)	41·5 (41)
Middle	11·9 (84)	18·3 (71)	33·8 (77)
High	27·3 (33)	25·0 (44)	57·1 (35)
Total	14·8 (209)	22·1 (199)	41·2 (153)
Females			
Low	4·8 (167)	17·1 (105)	21·2 (66)
Middle	4·8 (168)	17·4 (86)	21·1 (71)
High	13·8 (58)	30·0 (40)	39·5 (38)
Total	6·1 (393)	19·5 (231)	25·1 (175)

	B. MIDDLE SOCIOECONOMIC STATUS		
	Low Intelligence	*Middle Intelligence*	*High Intelligence*
Males			
Low	13·3 (75)	36·5 (74)	46·2 (39)
Middle	25·9 (85)	40·3 (72)	53·9 (102)
High	31·6 (38)	54·8 (62)	69·8 (63)
Total	22·2 (198)	43·3 (208)	57·4 (204)
Females			
Low	9·5 (116)	30·0 (90)	39·6 (53)
Middle	6·5 (123)	17·5 (97)	42·3 (97)
High	25·4 (71)	47·7 (86)	67·2 (58)
Total	11·9 (310)	31·1 (273)	48·6 (208)

	C. HIGH SOCIOECONOMIC STATUS		
	Low Intelligence	*Middle Intelligence*	*High Intelligence*
Males			
Low	32·1 (28)	36·7 (49)	69·1 (42)
Middle	46·5 (43)	54·2 (48)	79·0 (76)
High	52·6 (38)	71·6 (116)	86·0 (143)
Total	45·0 (109)	59·6 (213)	81·2 (261)
Females			
Low	22·2 (45)	37·7 (61)	47·5 (40)
Middle	21·4 (56)	35·1 (57)	51·3 (78)
High	50·9 (59)	69·8 (119)	78·6 (140)
Total	32·5 (160)	53·2 (237)	65·5 (258)

TABLE 11 (*cont.*)

NEIGHBOURHOOD STATUS	D. TOTALS OF LOW, MIDDLE AND HIGH SOCIOECONOMIC STATUS *Total Low, Middle, High Intelligence*
Males	
Low	30·5 (524)
Middle	39·7 (658)
High	62·2 (572)
Total	44·3 (1754)
Females	
Low	20·3 (743)
Middle	21·1 (833)
High	53·2 (669)
Total	30·4 (2245)

but deserves some speculation. One possible explanation is that those high socioeconomic status parents who place a high value on college education for their daughters are likely to insist on living in high-status neighbourhoods where their daughters can attend superior high schools, while those high-status parents who do not emphasize college education for their daughters are more likely to remain in lower status neighbourhoods. This explanation, of course, shifts the causal emphasis from the neighbourhood back to the family, and is essentially a straight ecological argument which cannot be tested directly with the data of this study because no information is available on residential mobility. A second and somewhat more social-psychological speculation would be that, since high educational aspirations are generally less common for girls than for boys and are less salient in terms of future occupational careers, girls are more susceptible to the influences of the social milieu than boys. This might help to account for the apparently greater influence of neighbourhood context on girls than on boys, but would not explain why high socioeconomic status girls are particularly responsive to neighbourhood context. Possibly the explanation is that the high-status girls in the lower status neighbourhood, who find themselves among associates with low aspirations, tend to reduce their own aspirations to the normative level of the group in order to be popular and possibly to improve their potential marriage opportunities with the boys in their neighbourhood. The high-status boys are less likely to be influenced by the desire for popularity and marriage prospects within the neighbourhood group because of the salience of college education to their later career plans and because in any event they probably intend to defer marriage until they finish college. For girls from low- and middle-status families, college aspirations are not high, in any case, because of lack of encouragement and support from parents; consequently, even a favourable neighbourhood context is not likely to have much effect on their educational aspirations. It should be emphasized again that this is only speculation – data are not available from our study to test this line of reasoning.

The results of partialling out the influence of sex, socioeconomic status, and intelligence indicate that neighbourhood context – although it apparently has special significance for some sub-populations – probably does not make a large contribution to the explanation of differences in the educational plans of this group of high school seniors. Actually the magnitude of its contribution has not been assessed either in the above tables or in other relevant studies. To provide a more accurate estimate of its contribution, the data have been analysed using correlation techniques (see Table 12). The results of this analysis are as follows: the zero-order correlation (r) of neighbourhood status with college plans is $+0.299$. The multiple correlation (R) of sex, socio-economic status, and intelligence with college plans is $+0.479$, and the coefficient of determination (R^2) is 0.229, which means that these three background factors account for 22.9 per cent of the variance in college plans. The addition of neighbourhood status as a predictor variable increases the multiple correlation (R) to $+0.497$ and the coefficient of determination (R^2) to 0.247. Thus, neighbourhood status results in an absolute increase of 1.8 per cent in the explained variance of college plans beyond the effects of sex, socioeconomic status, and intelligence $(0.247 - 0.229 = 0.018$ or 1.8 per cent). Consequently, it may be concluded that although neighbourhood

TABLE 12: *Correlates of college plans*

DEPENDENT VARIABLE: COLLEGE PLANS

INDEPENDENT VARIABLES	R	*Per cent of Variance Explained*	*Per cent Increase in Explained Variance Due to :*
Sex, intelligence, socioeconomic status and neighbourhood status	0.497	24.70	—
Sex, intelligence, and socioeconomic status	0.479	22.94	Neighbourhood status: 1.76
Sex, neighbourhood status, and intelligence	0.438	19.18	Socioeconomic status: 5.52
Sex, neighbourhood status, and socioeconomic status	0.430	18.49	Intelligence: 6.21

context makes some contribution to the explained variance in college plans over and above that made by the traditional variables, its added contribution is indeed small.

These results should not be interpreted to mean that neighbourhood context can be dismissed as a factor in educational aspirations of youth. Even the small amount of variance accounted for by neighbourhood status over and above that accounted for by sex, socioeconomic status, and intelligence makes some contribution to the understanding of educational aspirations. This contribution is important when the traditional variables leave a large proportion of the variance unexplained. Moreover, as the cross-tabular analysis indicates, the effect of neighbourhood context is considerably more important in some sub-populations than in others — a fact that is not revealed by the multiple correlation analysis. Nevertheless, the results of the analysis reported in this paper indicate that past claims for the importance of neighbourhood context in the development of educational aspirations may have been considerably overstated. Whether more direct measures of normative climates than the socioeconomic level of the neighbourhood or school, or other measures of neighbourhood or school climates, would reveal a closer relationship with educational aspirations must await new evidence based on actual assessments of these climates. Such evidence was not available in this study, nor has it been presented in any of the past studies. Whatever the prospects for future research, the present study clearly casts doubt on the popular notion that the socioeconomic status of the neighbourhood in which the youth resides has a substantial influence on his educational aspirations that cannot be explained in terms of his sex, ability, and socioeconomic status.

PART THREE

The Home Environment

SOME OF the earliest research related to the identification and measurement of subenvironments of social-psychological forces, involved the analysis of home environments. Using a sample of children and their parents in the United States, Dave (1963) examined the relationship between the home environment and academic achievement scores. Six environmental process variables were identified which were labelled: achievement press, language models, academic guidance, activeness of the family, intellectuality in the home, and work habits of the family. Each of the variables was defined in terms of a set of environmental process characteristics which provided a framework for the construction of a home interview schedule. It was found that the environment accounted for a moderate to large percentage of the variance in the achievement scores. For example, the percentage of variance accounted for by the environment in word knowledge was 62·2; reading, 53·1; arithmetic problem solving, 50·3; language, 46·8; and in spelling, 37·2.

Using the same sample as in the Dave study, Wolf (1964) analysed the relation between the home environment and intelligence test scores. The subenvironment for intelligence was defined as consisting of press for achievement motivation, press for language development, and provision for general learning. The measure of the environment accounted for approximately 50 per cent of the variance in the intelligence test scores. In the first reading, which provides an overview for the remainder of the section, Jensen lists the environmental process variables and the related environmental characteristics that were used in the Wolf study. In his review of studies Jensen indicates that the trend in environmental research related to the home as 'been away from rather crude socio-economic variables towards more subtle intrafamily and inter-personal psychological variables'. The four readings that follow are presented in order to reflect the trend as suggested by Jensen and as indicated in Figure 17.

The first reading by Marjoribanks draws together the results of a set of studies by Marjoribanks and Walberg (1974a, 1974b, 1974c)

FIGURE 17

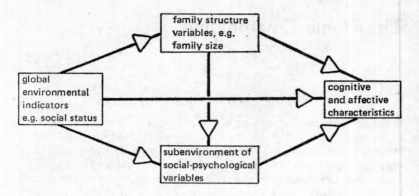

in which multiple regression models were used to gain a richer understanding of the relations between social class, family size and cognitive performance. The next three studies follow in the Bloom-Dave-Wolf tradition of defining and then measuring subenvironments. Weiss adopts the approach for an analysis of achievement motivation and self esteem while it is used by Marjoribanks to examine the environmental correlates of a set of mental abilities. In general, the results indicate that assessments of the learning subenvironment of the home are more powerful predictors of cognitive and affective behaviours than are global social status variables and family structure characteristics.

References

JENSEN, A. R. (1967). 'The culturally disadvantaged: psychological and educational aspects', *Educational Research*, 10, 4–20.

MARJORIBANKS, K. 'Academic achievement: family size and social class correlates'.

MARJORIBANKS, K. (1972). 'Environment, social class and mental abilities', *Journal of Educational Psychology*, 63, 103–9.

MARJORIBANKS, K. 'Environmental correlates of ability: a canonical analysis'.

WEISS, J. 'The identification and measurement of home environmental factors related to achievement motivation and self-esteem'.

5. The Culturally Disadvantaged: Psychological and Educational Aspects

ARTHUR R. JENSEN

THE LITERATURE on children called culturally disadvantaged that has recently proliferated is likely to give the impression to those who have not surveyed it in detail that much scientifically verified knowledge is now at hand as a sound basis for large-scale ameliorative action promising highly predictable and optimal results.

This is an incorrect impression. Although substantial knowledge about disadvantaged children, particularly of a demographic nature, is now available, the literature dealing with the psychological aspects of the problem is better viewed as a source of programmes for research and theoretical formulation. It is important to keep this in mind, not to discourage action programmes, which are obviously needed immediately, but to ensure that such action programmes are conceived of and conducted as research and not as the application of knowledge already established by research. This means that school programmes for the disadvantaged should be conducted, as far as possible, in the manner of scientific experimentation, which is to say with great attention to control and description of the 'input' variables (what we do with the children, their parents, their environments, etc.) and the 'output' variables (how the children respond). As in any investigation which attempts to evaluate the effects of an experimental variable, there should be appropriate control groups. Finally, there should be careful description of the population's social, economic, racial, family, and individual psychological characteristics.

The aim of this report is to indicate some of the main trends of thought and research on the psychology of disadvantaged children, to comment particularly on the research findings and hypotheses which seem to have the most direct implications for ameliorative action, and to point out a few of the most crucial-gaps in our current knowledge and the controversies issuing from them.

Description and Assessment of the Culturally Retarded

Descriptions of the disadvantaged have usually consisted of both environmental and personal characteristics. There is seldom any attempt to separate the causal, or background, factors from the supposedly resultant behavioural characteristics, of which the most important to the educator is the low educability of the disadvantaged child. In fact, low or mediocre intelligence (as assessed by standard intelligence tests) and particularly poor school achievement, are often included in the definition and identification of the 'culturally deprived', along with such criteria as low socioeconomic status and culturally impoverished home environment. The relatively rare slum child with a high IQ and superior school achievement is often not regarded as being culturally disadvantaged, while low IQ, low-achieving pupils from what may appear to be very similar home backgrounds are characterized as disadvantaged and their poor school performance is attributed largely to this condition.

The question raised by this type of definition is not without important practical implications. If we assume that the low IQ children actually have the potential both for higher intelligence and for normal progress in school, but have merely been 'depressed' by an unfavourable environment, we must ask if average or above-average culturally disadvantaged children are similarly depressed. A slum child with an IQ of 115 might thus have the intellectual potential of the middle-class child with an IQ of 130 to 140, and he might be able to realize this potential more fully if he were provided with the right kind of cultural stimulation at some stage of his development. Thus, in looking for potential college material among low socioeconomic status children, we might pin our greatest hopes on those already of at least average ability, despite a poor environment, and simply regard most low 'socioeconomic status' children (whose IQs are in the 'dull' range of intelligence, that is, from 75 to 95), though capable of benefiting educationally from intervention programmes such as Head Start, as more or less destined for intellectual and occupational mediocrity. This widespread belief gives rise to various plans for watered-down, less intellectual, and less academic educational programmes tailored to the apparent limitations of a large proportion (at least a half to two-thirds) of low socioeconomic status children. This is a harmful and unjust set of beliefs, if acted upon, since some evidence now makes it reasonable (though surprising) to hypothesize that a greater absolute amount of educational potential may exist among the low socioeconomic status children who, under present circumstances, obtain IQs in the range of 70 to 90 than among those whose measured IQs are in the above-average range from about 100 to 120. To state this proposition even more paradoxically, we can hypothesize that there is a greater chance of finding a potential IQ of 130, or 140, or 150 among the groups whose measured IQs are 70 to 90 than among the group whose IQs are 100 to 120, providing we are dealing with a population regarded by the usual criteria as predominantly culturally disadvantaged. All the evidence, which is massive, indicates conclusively that such a prediction with respect to children from middle-class families would be utterly ridiculous. With respect to low socioeconomic status children (especially, in the USA, Negroes; and possibly, in Britain, children of immigrant groups), however, it is a hypothesis worth investigating. No evidence as yet contradicts the hypothesis, and some evidence makes it seem reasonable, and, in fact, suggested this seemingly paradoxical idea in the first place (Jensen, 1963). But before we can elaborate on this line of thought, some supporting background information must be provided.

Differential Diagnosis of Cultural Retardation

In principle, intellectual and educational retardation can and must be clearly distinguished from what we will here refer to as primary retardation. Primary and cultural retardation are not all mutually exclusive; one may exist without the other, or they may exist in independently varying degrees simultaneously. There is substantial evidence of some degree of correlation, albeit quite low, between primary and cultural retardation in the total population (Burt and Howard, 1956; Tyler, 1965).

Primary retardation can be subdivided into three main types, all having an essentially biological causation: (1) an inevitable consequence of what geneticists call the multifactorial or polygenic inheritance of intelligence; (2) a result of a single, major gene defect; and (3) a result of brain damage. Factors 1 and 3 and factors 2 and 3 are not mutually exclusive, but may occur singly or together. Factor 2, however, always overrides factor 1, so that when factor 2 is involved, factor 1 is of almost no importance.

Polygenic Inheritance

Intelligence is inherited in much the same fashion as height (Burt, 1955, 1958, 1966; Burt and Howard, 1956; Huntley, 1966; Pearson, 1903). It is the result of a large number of genes each having a small additive effect. Because of random assortment of these genes, the total additive effect will be normally distributed in the population. Thus, the hereditary mechanism (in effect a random lottery) that results in one person's being bright, results in another's being dull, and the person who is dull or mentally retarded for this reason is, biologically speaking, no more abnormal or pathological than the average or bright person or the short or tall person. He is simply a part of normal variation. Being at the very low end of the distribution may be a personal misfortune from an educational standpoint, but it is not an abnormality in a medical or psychological sense, and is presumably not biologically or environmentally remediable. (In this respect dullness and brightness are genetically quite analogous to shortness and tallness of stature.) Persons at the low end of the distribution of intelligence need educational treatment somewhat different from that afforded average and bright persons. The majority of dull children in our schools who do not show neurological signs of organic impairment are of this type, regardless of their race or social class. For these children, education must be modified in accordance with their intellectual limitations, which is not to say that an appropriate education is not just as important for them as for the bright child. It must simply be a different kind of education, with different goals. The great misfortune of culturally disadvantaged children is that many are treated educationally (and they often perform accordingly) as if they were at the lower end of the genetic distribution of intelligence, when, in fact, they may be in the middle or even at the upper end of the distribution. Failure to distinguish between hereditary retardation and cultural retardation, as well as being a social injustice, results in a waste of educational potential and talent. The consequences are especially damaging to the social progress of minority groups, and the costs are borne by our whole society. The discrimination between cultural and genetic retardation in the culturally disadvantaged is a difficult diagnostic problem which does not even arise in middle-class children, with exceedingly rare exceptions, since retardation in this group is almost always of the primary type. There are, of course, gradations of cultural retardation, just as there are gradations of primary retardation. But it is unlikely that the degree of cultural retardation is a simple linear function of the degree of environmental impoverishment. There is evidence that the environment may act as a threshold variable in such a way that a quite severe degree of environmental deprivation must exist in order to produce cultural retardation in a child of normal genetic potential. This idea is explicated more fully in a later section of this paper.

Major Gene Defect

Practically all severe forms of mental deficiency, where the IQ is below 50, are the results either of severe brain damage or of major gene defects (Ellis, 1963, p. 276). Examples of major gene defects are Mongolism, phenylketonuria, and amaurotic idiocy. Genetically these intellectual defects are analogous to dwarfism in the trait of stature. They are caused by Mendelian inheritance of a single gene or by a mutant gene, which for all practical purposes may be regarded as completely overriding the normal polygenic determinants of intelligence. The resulting severe degree of mental defect, which is generally easy to diagnose in the first days or weeks of life, is not of concern in the present discussion except to distinguish it from retardation which constitutes a part of normal variation.

Brain Damage

Brain damage, especially prenatal and perinatal, is a continuous variable; that is, its effects can range from the negligible to the disastrous, and the effects can be manifest at all levels of genetic potential. Thus, a child who would have grown up to have an adult IQ of, say, 150, may, as a result of the brain damage incurred by anoxia at birth, have an actual IQ of 140. The literature on the subject suggests that brain damage to a degree that makes a difference in measurable mental ability is sufficiently rare not to constitute an appreciable source of variance in intellectual ability in the total population. An upper-limit estimate would be about five per cent of the total variance of measured intelligence, which means that, on the average, brain damage in individual cases may be intellectually devastating. There is also evidence that brain damage has a higher incidence in low socioeconomic status groups in which the mother's nutrition, prenatal care, and obstetrical practices are substandard (Osler and Cooke, 1965). All possible efforts should, of course, be made to minimize these conditions in order to decrease the chances of brain damage, but these amelioration efforts should prove considerably easier than combating the causal agents of *cultural* retardation *per se*.

All three types of primary retardation have three major effects in common: they result in below-average measured intelligence (IQ), in below-average educability in school subjects, and in a slow rate of what we shall refer to as basic learning ability. Cultural retardation, on the other hand, is distinguishable from primary retardation, at least in principle, on this third factor-basic learning ability. While cultural deprivation results in lowered IQ and lowered school achievement, it does not, except in extreme rare cases, result in lowered basic learning ability. This is a theoretically and practically important distinction, because it means that in trying to improve the educability of the culturally disadvantaged, we are trying not to make over genetically poor material but to allow sound innate learning potential to manifest itself. But now, to present further our thesis, we must clarify the special meaning we have given the terms *intelligence*, *basic learning ability*, and *educability*.

Intelligence, Learning Ability and Educability

Standard intelligence tests, such as the Stanford-Binet and the Wechsler, are measures of specific knowledge and problem solving skills which have been acquired by the testee at some time prior to the test situation. Mental age is determined directly from the amount of such knowledge and skill. By taking into account the amount of time the individual has had to acquire this knowledge, that is, his chronological age, we obtain a measure of learning rate expressed as the IQ. The validity of the IQ as a measure of learning ability, therefore, depends to a large extent upon equal opportunity for exposure to knowledge and skills that the test calls upon. Since intelligence tests were originally devised to predict school performance, they call upon knowledge and cognitive skills similar to the kinds of learning required in school – skills which are more or less prerequisite for school learning and which have considerable transfer value in the classroom.

Now, if IQ is a measure of learning rate, we should expect that learning tasks of the type used by experimental psychologists to study learning should show substantial positive correlations with IQ. This, in fact, is exactly what our research has found (e.g. Jensen, 1965). But here is the interesting thing: the correlation between IQ and learning ability, as measured directly in a controlled laboratory learning task, is much higher among middle-class children than among lower-class children (Jensen, 1961, 1963; Rapier, 1966). Furthermore, in comparing level of performance (i.e. speed of learning) as a function of IQ level and of social class (lower *v.* middle), we have found in several studies that low IQ (60–85) lower-class children are, on the average, markedly superior in learning ability to low IQ middle-class children. In the IQ range above 100, on the other hand, there are not significant differences in learning ability between lower- and middle-class children matched for IQ. This suggests that once the IQ has exceeded a certain level (somewhere in the neighbourhood of 100 and 110), it gives a fairly accurate assessment of learning ability regardless of social-class level. In the lower IQ range (which, incidentally, contains the modal performance of lower-class children), the IQ test grossly underestimates learning ability among lower-class children. We are speaking here, of course, only of averages, for a certain proportion of lower-class low IQ children are slow learners on the laboratory tasks just as are middle-class low IQ children. The middle-class low IQ group seems to be made up almost completely of slow learners. But the lower-class low IQ group contains all levels of learning ability. The probability of finding a very fast learner (i.e. learning speed comparable to that of 'gifted' middle-class children) seems to be greater in the low IQ low socioeconomic-status than in the average IQ range of either social class group. This suggests that the IQ is almost totally unpredictive of learning ability in the low IQ range for low socioeconomic-status children. It should be noted that the majority of low socioeconomic-status children are in the below-average IQ range. This is especially true for Negroes in the USA. On a national average only about 12 per cent of Negroes exceed the median IQ of the white population (McGurk, 1956; Tyler, 1965; Shuey, 1966).

In view of what has been said above, it might seem puzzling that the IQ is substantially correlated (correlations between 0·50 and 0·70) with school achievement regardless of social class. Ability for school learning may be referred to as *educability*. Educability is much more complexly determined than intelligence or learning ability. For one thing, it depends not only upon learning ability of the type measured in the laboratory, in which transfer from prior learning is relatively unimportant, but also upon a fund of prior knowledge, skills, and acquired cognitive habits, much of which is tapped by intelligence tests. But educability also involves much more than these intellectual abilities, as indicated by the fact that intelligence tests do not account for more than about 50 per cent of the variance in school achievement. A host of other factors must be taken into account to 'explain' the remaining variance. These are usually described under labels, such as attitudes, motivation, work habits, regularity of school attendance, parental interest, and help in school work.

Another point of interest and educational implication lies in a comparison of the heritabilities of intelligence and of educability. Despite the popular denigration of the genetic study of intelligence in educational circles in recent years, it is entirely possible to estimate the relative contributions of heredity and environment to the total variation in intelligence in a given population. The numerous studies done in this field over the past 50 years show a great consistency (Erlenmeyer-Kimling and Jarvik, 1963). They indicate that in Caucasian populations above the poverty line (and this is an important qualification), some 80 to 90 per cent of the variability in measured intelligence can be attributable to genetic factors and about five to 10 per cent to social environmental factors (Burt, 1958). (The remaining variance is divided between biological environmental factors and error of measurement.) The genetic component in school achievement or educability, on the other hand, is much less than for intelligence, accounting for only 40 to 50 per cent of the total variance (Burt, 1958; Jensen, 1967). Family influences largely account for the remaining variance. One of the obvious tasks of educational psychology and sociology is the analysis and isolation of these environmental influences on educability, so that they may be provided by one means or another when they are lacking in the child's natural environment. But before these environmental factors are discussed, a few other points need to be made concerning the inheritance of intelligence and the distribution of intelligence in the total population.

Environment as a Threshold Variable

By virtue of a largely fortuitous set of conditions, the Stanford-Binet intelligence test, when used on a white American population, which for the most part excludes the lowest segment of the socio-economic-status continuum, yields a distribution of IQs which conforms almost exactly to the so-called normal or Gaussian distribution. This is the distribution one would expect on the basis of polygenic inheritance of intelligence (Burt, 1957, 1963). In this same population, estimates of the genetic component in the variance of intelligence range between 80 and 90 per cent (Burt, 1958). Even the seemingly rather large environmental variations within this bulk of the American population apparently contribute very little to the variance in intelligence, as measured by an excellently constructed test such as the Stanford-Binet.

However, if the Stanford-Binet is administered to a large and truly representative sample of the total population (or to the *entire* population of school children, as was done in Scotland in 1947), we find that the distribution of IQ's departs in a very systematic way from the normal Gaussian distribution. There is a bulge (i.e. excess frequency) in the lower half of the distribution, especially in the IQ range from about 65 to 90 (Burt, 1957, 1963). This suggests the presence of some non-genetic influence which hinders intellectual development. (Another possible explanation is the differential fertility of dull and bright persons, there being a negative correlation of about $-0 \cdot 2$ between intelligence and family size, which would result in there being a slight preponderance of low IQs. This theory is seriously undermined by the fact that by far the best explanation for the negative correlation between family size and IQ involves strictly environmental causation; there is no equally reasonable genetic interpretation of this correlation.) An American study shows that if low socioeconomic status subjects are removed from the distribution, and especially if Negroes are removed, the distribution again closely approximates the normal (Kennedy, Van de Riet, and White, 1963). There is always a slight bulge, however, at the very lowest end of the distribution, below an IQ of 50, due to major gene defects and brain damage (Zigler, 1967).

These facts taken together are consistent with the hypothesis that the environment influences the development of intelligence as a threshold variable. (Actually it is best thought of as a number of thresholds.) That is to say, once certain kinds of environmental influences are present to a probably rather minimal degree, the individual's genetic potential for the development of intelligence will be more or less fully realized, and variations in the extent of these influences beyond this minimal threshold level will make only a slight contribution to the variance in measured intelligence. The situation is analogous to diet and physical stature. Once the diet is up to a certain miminal standard of adequacy with respect to vitamins, minerals, and proteins, the addition of more of these elements to the diet will not make any appreciable difference in physique; if they are present in the required minimal amounts, it will make no difference whether the person lives on beans and hamburger or on Oysters Rockefeller and pheasant-under-glass – the genes will entirely determine variations in stature. The case for intelligence seems much the same.

Another line of evidence is quite consistent with this threshold hypothesis, namely the studies concerned with upward changes in the IQ as a result of rather drastic environmental changes, either from 'natural' causes or by means of experimental manipulation of the environment. Environmental changes or manipulations seem to affect to any marked degree only those children whose social environments are quite wretched and clearly below what is presumably the environmental threshold for the normal development of genetic intellectual potential. Thus, when children are removed as infants from very poor homes, in which the natural parents have subnormal IQs, and are placed in foster homes, in which the foster parents are of average or superior intelligence, the children will grow up to obtain IQs that may be from 10 to 30 points higher than would be predicted if they had been reared by their natural parents, and their educational attainments will be even higher (Skodak and Skeels, 1966). (Of course, due allowance is made here for statistical regression.) It is only when there is a great discrepancy between the early environmental background of the natural parents and the environment provided for their children by the superior foster parents that we find evidence of a substantial boost in the children's IQs. It is simply a case of innate intellectual potential receiving the nurturance needed for its full development. It is also instructive to note that even though the IQs of foster parents may span a fairly wide range, the IQs of foster children are not correlated in the least with those of their foster parents (Honzik, 1957). Again, once the threshold of adequate environment is attained (the adoption agencies see that this is nearly always the case in foster homes), practically all the variability in the children's IQs will be determined by genetic factors.

Social Class and Intelligence

It has been hypothesized that the bulge in the lower half of the distribution of IQs is due to the proportion of the population reared under conditions which are below the threshold of those environmental influences necessary for the full development of genetic intellectual potential. Thus, presumably, if these environmental lacks were eliminated, the bulge in the distribution of IQs would be smoothed out and the distribution would more nearly approximate to the Gaussian curve required by genetic theory. The portion of the population which contributed to the bulge would become redistributed at various higher points along the IQ scale; some would make only very slight gains, while others would make considerable gains in IQ. It would be difficult to estimate precisely the average expected gain, but it is likely to be somewhere between 10 and 20 IQ points.

Differences in mean IQ among various social classes and occupational levels are, of course, a well-established fact. But it is commonly believed that all of the socioeconomic-status differences are due to environmental factors and none to differences in genetic potential. Though the evidence on this point is quite complex, and therefore cannot be presented in this brief paper, it suggests the conclusion that social classes probably differ in innate potential (Burt, 1961; Burt and Howard, 1956). Perhaps as much as half of the between-classes variance in IQ is genetically determined. Several lines of evidence lead to this conclusion. One of the most striking is the phenomenon of regression to the population means, which can be most satisfactorily accounted for in terms of genetic mechanisms. Even though low socioeconomic-status parents provide a poor environment for their children, their children, on the average, have higher intelligence than the parents; and though high socioeconomic-status parents provide a good environment for their children – often better than the environment they themselves grew up in – their children, on the average, have lower IQs than the parents (Burt, 1961; Jensen, 1968). This would be almost paradoxical from an environmentalist point of view, while it is completely in accord with genetic expectations. Also, it should be pointed out that the greater the equality of opportunity in a society and the fewer the restraints on social mobility, the greater will become the genetic differences between social classes. The educational and occupational hierarchies act as an intellectual screening device. Genetic differences between social classes could be minimized only by means of imposing rigid and impermeable class and caste boundaries that would rule out social mobility for many generations. This obviously is the very antithesis of a democratic society which, strange as it may seem at first glance, actually tends to maximize genetic differences and minimize environmental differences as a basis of social and economic rewards.

Racial Differences in Intelligence

The above statements concerning socioeconomic-status differences in innate potential cannot be applied to differences between racial groups when there are greater barriers to social and occupational mobility in one racial group than in another, as is clearly the case for Negroes and Mexicans as compared with Caucasians of European origin in the USA. There are probably socioeconomic-status differences in innate intellectual potential *within* any particular racial group, but these innate differences would be diminished to the extent that intellectually irrelevant genetic factors, such as lightness of skin colour and other caucasoid features, are important as determinants of social and occupational mobility. Therefore, the fact that Negroes and Mexicans are disproportionately represented in the lower end of the socioeconomic-status scale cannot be interpreted as evidence of poor genetic potential. For we know that there have been, and are still, powerful racial barriers to social mobility. Innate potential should be much more highly correlated with socioeconomic-status among white than among Negroes or other easily distinguishable minorities, who are discriminated against on the basis of intellectually irrelevant characteristics.

The Negro population in the USA as a whole has an average IQ about 15 to 20 points below the average for the white population, and the variance of Negro intelligence is less than 60 per cent than in the white population (Kennedy, Van de Riet, and White, 1963; Tyler, 1965). The Negro population (11 per cent of the total US population) is thus largely bunched up in that lower part of the IQ distribution where we find the bulge or departure from the so-called normal distribution. Since we know that the Negro population for the most part has suffered socioeconomic and cultural disadvantages for generations past, it seems a reasonable hypothesis that their low-average IQ is due to environmental rather than to genetic factors. A much larger proportion of Negroes (and Mexicans) than of white probably grow up under conditions that may be *below* the environmental threshold required for the realization of genetic potential. It also appears that the economic condition of the Negro, which has markedly improved over the past two generations, does not bear a close relationship to the really crucial environmental threshold variables. It has been pointed out that the rise of the Negro IQ since World War I has not been nearly commensurate with the improvement of the Negroes' economic condition (McGurk, 1956). But the important environmental threshold variables, mainly interpersonal and psychological in nature, seem to be only incidentally correlated with economic status. Except in the most extreme cases, economic factors in themselves seem to have little causal potency as determinants of IQ and educability.

Environmental Influences on Intelligence and Educability

It remains now to identify those environmental factors presently thought to be the most potent influences in the development of intellectual and educational potential. In recent years there has been a shifting of emphasis by psychologists working in this area. The trend has been away from rather crude socioeconomic variables towards more subtle intrafamily and interpersonal psychological variables. This shift in emphasis is given cogency by the fact that crude socioeconomic variables, such as income, occupation, and neighbourhood, do not correlate as highly with intelligence and educability as do ratings of more psychological variables, such as whether the parents read to the children during the pre-school years, whether the family eats together, whether children are brought into the conversation at the dinner table, and other features of parent-child interaction, especially involving verbal behaviour. The usual socioeconomic variables found to correlate with IQ and educability have shown correlations in the range from 0·30 to 0·50. At most, only about 30 per cent of the variance in intelligence can be predicted from a composite of various indices of socioeconomic status. Most variables that index socioeconomic status, however, are better thought of as incidental correlates of IQ rather than as causal factors. The quality of the parent-child relationship, on the other hand, may be thought of as causal correlation, even though one cannot overlook the high probability that the quality of the parent-child interaction is influenced to a not inconsiderable degree by the genetic potential of both the parents and their children.

What are some of the environmental variables most highly associated with the development of intelligence? Wolf (cited in Bloom, 1964, pp. 78–9) found that ratings on 13 process variables, describing the interactions between parents and children, would yield a multiple correlation with intelligence of +0·76. These variables may be classified as follows:

(a) Press for Achievement Motivation—
    1. nature of intellectual expectations of child;

    2. nature of intellectual aspirations for child;
    3. amount of information about child's intellectual development;
    4. nature of rewards for intellectual development.
(b) Press for Language Development—
    5. emphasis on use of language in a variety of situations;
    6. opportunities provided for enlarging vocabulary;
    7. emphasis on correctness of usage;
    8. quality of language models available.
(c) Provision for General Learning—
    9. opportunities provided for learning in the home;
   10. opportunities provided for learning outside the home (excluding school);
   11. availability of learning supplies;
   12. availability of books (including reference works), periodicals and library facilities;
   13. nature and amount of assistance provided to facilitate learning in a variety of situations.

Specific Experiential Deficiencies of the Culturally Disadvantaged Language Deficiencies

By far the greatest and most handicapping deficiencies of the culturally disadvantaged child are found in the realm of language. But the term language is here used in a much broader and psychologically more profound sense than is generally appreciated by teachers of English, speech therapists, and the like. The immediately obvious aspects of the language of the culturally disadvantaged – the lack of genteel English, incorrect grammar, poor pronunciation, use of slang, etc. – are psychologically the most superficial and the least important from the standpoint of intellectual development. This is not to minimize the social, economic, and occupational advantages of good oral and written English. It is simply important to realize that the language deficiencies of lower-class children have a much more detrimental psychological effect than the obvious social disadvantages of their language habits. Because the eschewal of certain lower-class language habits by the middle-class is perceived by some persons as undemocratic snobbery, there has grown up another utterly erroneous notion that lower-class language is just as good as any other kind of language, in the same sense that English, French and German, though obviously different from one another, are all equally good languages, so far as one can tell. Thus, social class differences in language habits are viewed as desirable or undesirable only according to one's acquired tastes, values and standards, and – to paraphrase the argument – who is to say that middle-class values are any better than lower-class values? This line of thinking can be quite discredited in terms of our growing understanding of the functions of language. Language not only serves a social function as a means of interpersonal communication but is also of crucial importance as a tool of thought. It is in this latter function that lower-class language deficiencies are most crippling psychologically.

General Language Characteristics

In general, it has been found that throughout the entire sequence of language development, from the earliest stages of speech in the first two years of life, there is retardation among culturally disadvantaged children (Bereiter and Engelmann, 1966; Jensen, in press; McCarthy, 1946, pp. 557–9). Furthermore, this retardation should not be thought of entirely as the disadvantaged child's merely lagging behind the middle-class child, with the same level of development merely being attained somewhat later. The characteristics of the language habits that are being acquired and the kinds of functions the language serves in the child's experience, actually shape his intellectual development, especially the development of the ability for abstraction and conceptual learning. Poor development of this ability places a low ceiling on educational attainment.

The most detailed analysis of social class differences in language characteristics, important to the development of cognitive abilities, has been made by Basil Bernstein (Bernstein, 1961). Except for minor details, his findings and conclusions seem to be applicable to social-class differences in the American culture as well as in the British, since social class differences in language behaviour of the type that concerns him are probably even more pronounced in America than in England. It is especially important that Bernstein's type of socio-linguistic analysis be applied to some of the various American low socioeconomic status sub-cultural groups.

In characterizing social class differences in language behaviour, Bernstein distinguishes two main forms of language, which he refers to as *public* and *formal*. In formal language, the variations of form and syntax are much less predictable for any one individual, and the formal possibilities for sentence organizations are used to clarify meaning and make it explicit. In *public* language, on the other hand, the speaker operates in a mode which individual selection and permutation are grossly restricted. In formal language the speaker can make highly individual selection and permutation. Formal language, therefore, can fit the speaker's purposes with much greater subtlety and precision and does not depend to any marked degree upon inflection, gestures, facial expressions, and a presupposed prior mutual understanding of the main gist of the communication, as expressed in the highly frequent use of the phrase 'you know what I mean' in lower-class speech. While middle-class persons can understand and use public as well as formal language, lower-class persons are more or less restricted to public language. Public language is almost completely limited to the single function of social intercourse within a community of tacit common understandings and values. It is not designed for expository functions, for detailed representation of past events or future plans, or for manipulating aspects of one's experience abstractly and symbolically. In public language, the quantity of speech is not reduced, but the variety of functions which speech can serve is limited. This becomes especially important in the realm of private or internal speech, where the person must use language to recall, review, structure, or otherwise mentally manipulate his past or his anticipated experience, aims, plans, problems, and so on.

Robert Hess, of the University of Chicago, has found considerable evidence of these two modes of language behaviour in the parent-child interactions of lower-class and middle-class Americans observed in situations in which the mother is required to instruct her child in learning a simple task (Hess and Shipman, 1965). The language of the lower-class mother does not provide the child with cues and aids to learning to the same extent as the language of the middle-class mother. Since children tend largely to internalize the language of their home environment, mainly that of the parents, the low socioeconomic status child acquires an inferior set of verbal techniques to apply on his own in learning and problem-solving situations.

Compensatory Education for the Disadvantaged

The most radical, yet probably most successful, of the pre-school programmes for the culturally disadvantaged is being conducted at the University of Illinois by Carl Bereiter and Siegfried Engelmann (Bereiter, 1965; Bereiter and Engelmann, 1966). It focuses intensively on training disadvantaged children to use the language in ways that facilitate learning and thinking.

The Bereiter programme is based on the premise that it would be practically impossible to make up every environmental disadvantage that slum children have experienced, and that we must therefore concentrate all our efforts only on those which are most crucial to the development of educability in a normal school setting. These crucial skills, Bereiter maintains, are concerned with the use of language as a tool of thought. His programme consists of drilling the kinds of language habits we have described into children by methods that produce high motivation, unanimous participation, and maximal concentration and effort on the child's part, with a minimal waste of time. The specific techniques have been described in greater detail elsewhere, and Bereiter and Engelmann have a book on their methods for use by pre-school teachers of the disadvantaged (Bereiter and Engelmann, 1966).

Bereiter correctly maintains that disadvantaged children must learn at not a normal but a superior rate in order to compete successfully with middle-class children. Otherwise they will never catch up to grade-level.

Other Intervention Programmes

Other systematically developed intervention programmes for culturally disadvantaged pre-schoolers are more or less typified by those of Martin Deutsch in New York City, and Susan Gray in Nashville, Tennessee (George Peabody College). These programmes cover a broader spectrum of activities and experiences than the Bereiter programme, though the emphasis is still on stimulating cognitive development. It is generally agreed that the traditional middle-class nursery curriculum, with its emphasis on personal-social adjustment, is inappropriate and inadequate as a means of pulling lower-class children up to the developmental level of high middle-class age-mates. The Deutsch and Gray programmes are described in articles by these investigators (Deutsch, 1962; Gray and Klaus, 1965).

Unfortunately, as of this date, the evidence regarding the efficacy of any of these programmes is still meagre. It is insufficient merely to report gains in IQ, especially when this is based on retest with the same instrument or an equivalent form of the test, and when there is a high probability that much of the gain in test scores is the result of highly specific transfer from materials and training in the nursery programme that closely resemble those used in the test. For example, the writer has noticed that in one pre-school programme, some of the nursery materials consisted of some of the identical equipment used in the Stanford-Binet IQ test, and IQ gains resulting from children's spending several weeks in the programme were based on pre- and post-training with the Stanford-Binet. Such unwitting self-deception must be guarded against in evaluating the effects of pre-school programmes.

The most important evidence for the efficacy of such programmes, of course, will be based on the child's performance in the elementary grades, especially his progress in reading. Probably the most significant predictor of satisfactory progress in the educational programme, as it now exists in the public sector schools, is reading ability. If a child can surmount the reading hurdle successfully, the prognosis for satisfactory educational progress is generally good. It is also at this early point in the educative process – the introduction of reading – that so many culturally disadvantaged children meet a stumbling block, and head down the demoralizing path of educational retardation. Pre-school programmes for the disadvantaged should concentrate, as does Bereiter's, on the development of cognitive skills basic to reading. In many cases this will probably require a greater attention to the development of perceptual-discriminative skills than is found in the Bereiter programme.

The motivational aspects of reading and reading-readiness are much less clear, but most teachers who are experienced with the disadvantaged believe there are social-class differences among children's attitudes towards reading that affect their desire to learn to read. The best guess is that this motivational component of reading has its origin in early parent-child interaction in reading situations. Social-class differences in this respect apparently are enormous. Can anything be done about it?

This brings us to the question of parent involvement in intervention programmes. Unfortunately, it has been the common experience that low socioeconomic status parents are difficult to change with respect to child-rearing practices. If these parents are not reached long before their children are four or five years of age, much valuable time is lost in terms of the development of the child's educational potential. The child will come to Head Start or to kindergarten without ever having looked at a book, without ever having been read to, and without ever having seen an older child or adult engaged in the act of reading. Some unknown, but possibly large proportion of the determinants of reading failure among low socioeconomic status children may be attributable directly to this set of conditions. Since it is unlikely that the majority of mothers of the most severely disadvantaged children can be reached by any feasible means that could create lasting changes in their mode of child-rearing, we should look elsewhere for practicable means of bringing appropriate influences to bear on culturally disadvantaged children early in their development.

One possible approach would be to require junior and senior high school girls to work with culturally disadvantaged children between six months and four years of age. It would be regarded as a practical course in the psychology of motherhood for all school girls, especially those from a low socioeconomic status background, extending from about the eight or ninth through to the 12th grade. Each girl would spend at least an hour a day with a child, either in a nursery or in the child's own home. Instruction and supervision would, of course, accompany the girls' activities in working with young children. Much of the activity would consist of type of play thought to promote cognitive development. Children would, for example, be read to regularly from about one year of age. There should be sufficient consistency of the relationship between the child and the student for emotional rapport to develop. In many cases, of course, low socioeconomic status high school girls will have to be taught and coached in detail about how to interact with infants and children in ways that promote cognitive development. They must be made to realize that these activities are probably the major hope for realizing the educational potential of low socioeconomic status children. An experiment essentially very much like this was carried out on a small scale by Skeels and Dye (1939) some 25 years ago, with extremely encouraging results, substantiated by follow-ups over a 25-year period (Skeels, 1966). Such a programme on a large scale would, of course, constitute a major educational undertaking, involving considerable expenditure of funds for additional personnel, facilities, and efforts to gain widespread public acceptance. It could first be tried experimentally on a modest scale to test its feasibility.

Finally, it must be emphasized that all educators who have worked with the disadvantaged are agreed that pre-school intervention without adequate follow-up in the first years of elementary school is inadequate, because the culturally disadvantaged child does not go home after school, as does the middle-class child, to what is essentially a tutorial situation. Middle-class parents take a greater interest in their children's school work and offer them more help than do low socioeconomic status parents. The educational system should make some provision for the lower-class child's opportunity for a tutorial relationship with an older child or an adult, at least throughout the elementary grades.

We are gradually having to face the fact that, in order to break the cycle of poverty and cultural deprivation, the public sector school will have to assume for culturally disadvantaged children more of the responsibilities of good child-rearing – responsibilities universally regarded among the middle-class as belonging wholly to the child's own parents. The brutal fact is that for culturally disadvantaged children, these responsibilities are not being met, for whatever reason. Whether or not the state school system should intervene where educationally important environmental lacks exist is, of course, strictly speaking, not a psychological or scientific question, but one of social policy.

6. Academic Achievement: Family Size and Social Class Correlates

KEVIN MARJORIBANKS

INVESTIGATIONS OF the relations between sibling constellation variables and measures of academic achievement have usually found that family size is negatively related to performance on the measures, especially verbal-type tests (e.g. Nisbet, 1953; Maxwell, 1969; Eysenck and Cookson, 1970; Oldman, Byoetheway and Horobin, 1971; Murray, 1971; Kellaghan and Macnamarra, 1972). Also, support has often been provided for Anastasi's (1956) proposition, that in the highest socioeconomic levels the negative relations may disappear (e.g. Cicirelli, 1967; Kennett and Cropley, 1970; Poole and Kuhn, 1973).

Some investigators have attempted to account for the relation between academic achievement and family size by controlling the effects of factors such as maternal age and social status (Record *et al.*, 1969; Lichtenwalner and Maxwell, 1969; Murray, 1971). But even when such influences are controlled, the findings remain equivocal as the studies rely on the use of restricted statistical techniques such as product-moment correlations, which reveal only bivariate relations, or on analysis of variance, which requires the grouping of variables into levels. As a result, the full range of possible relations between social status characteristics, family size and academic achievement has not been fully explored in research. In the present study, in order to overcome some of the statistical shortcomings of many previous studies, multiple regression models were used to analyse the interrelationships between social class, family size and academic achievement. Multiple regression provides a goodness-of-fit test for any functional form of the variables, and does not require grouping (Bottenberg and Ward, 1963; Cohen, 1968).

The study also departs from much of previous research in two ways. First, by analysing longitudinal data and second, by using a potentially more sensitive sibling constellation variable, the inverse of the size of the family. The variable was introduced as it was reasoned that since children share adult resources of intellectual stimulation in the home, the mathematical relationship between family size and parental stimulation is not linear but is of a hyperbolic form involving the term, one divided by the number of children in the family. That is, the amount of parental attention which each child receives decreases as the number of children in the family increases in such a way that with each additional child the successive decrements in shared attention become smaller. Therefore the expected percentages of parental attention given children in 1-, 2-, 3-, 4-, and 5-child families would be 100, 50, 33, 25 and 20 respectively. Thus a single child in a family may score higher on academic achievement tests because he receives all available parental stimulation, whereas a child with four siblings may have lower test scores because he receives more like one-fifth of the available parental stimulation.

Method

The data used in the study were collected in 1964 and 1968 as part of a national survey of English primary school children and their parents. The results of the first survey were published in the Plowden Report (1967).

In 1964 the sampling procedure had two stages. First, a random sample was taken from all types of maintained primary schools in England. Then a random selection was made of children within these schools. The total sample, which included 3,092 children from 173 primary schools was divided into three age-cohorts, each of approximately 1,000 children. The average age of the senior children in 1964 was approximately 11, of the middle group, eight, and of the youngest group, seven.

In 1968 when the three cohorts were surveyed again, the senior cohort was in the fourth year of secondary school, the middle cohort in the first year of secondary school, and the youngest group in the last year of the primary school. The number of children with complete records for both surveys is 2,350 with approximately 800, equally divided between boys and girls, in each of the cohorts.

During the surveys the children completed a series of cognitive tests. In 1968 the three groups were assessed using the Watts-Vernon English comprehension test, the Vernon graded arithmetic test and the Alice Heim non-verbal intelligence test (AH4). In 1964 the senior group was assessed using the Watts-Vernon reading test, and the other groups were assessed on reading tests developed by the National Foundation for Educational Research in England.

A structured home-interview schedule was used in the surveys to gain a measure of the social psychological environment of the family. During the interviews, data were also collected on father occupation, father education, number of children, eldest-only child, and income of the family. Social class was coded according to the Registrar-General's classification based on occupations (1960 edition) with unskilled occupations classified as category 1, manual semi-skilled occupations as category 2, non-manual semi-skilled as category 3, manual skilled as 4, non-manual skilled as 5, managerial supervisory as 6, and professional-managerial occupations as category 7.

Results and Discussion

A set of multiple regression models was used to examine the relations between the social status indicators, the sibling variables and the achievement scores. The 1968 measures of reading, arithmetic, and non-verbal ability formed the criteria while the predictors included the 1964 reading scores, the 1964 social status characteristics and the 1964 sibling variables. Also, the 1964 and 1968 measures of father occupation and sibsize were averaged to form two composite variables. It was assumed that the two new variables, father occupation and sibsize, would reflect the cumulative nature of the environment between the two time periods. (A more detailed analysis of the relationships among these variables is presented in the final reading of the text.)

In general, two-term equations containing the 1964 reading scores and the composite father occupation variable accounted for as much significant variance in the 1968 achievement scores as complex many-term equations containing all the measured variables, their quadratic forms (to test for non-linearity), and their products (to test for interactions). The inverse of sibsize explained no additional variance after taking into account prior reading scores and father occupation. As an example, the results for the 1968 reading scores are presented in Table 13.

Since the results indicated that the most potent predictor of the 1968 achievement scores was the 1964 reading scores, it was decided to examine the relation between the 1964 assessments of father occupation, inverse of sibsize, the product of the two variables and the 1964 reading scores. The results of the regression analyses, which are presented in Table 14, showed that social class accounted for a significant percentage of the variance in the reading scores for each group, while the inverse of sibsize explained significant additional variance in the two senior groups and for the middle boys. After accounting for father occupation and the inverse of sibsize, no additional variance was explained by the product of the two variables, in any of the groups.

A set of regression surfaces were constructed to show the re-

TABLE 13: *Multiple regression of 1968 reading scores on 1964 reading, father's occupation and inverse of sibsize*

1968 READING	1964 READING	FATHER OCCUPATION	SIBSIZE INVERSE	PRODUCT	MULTIPLE R
Senior boys	·987[a]	·558	2·315	− ·550	·852**
	·033[b]	·325	2·652	·639	
	·722**[c]	·003*	·000	·005	
Senior girls	1·058	·847	4·344	− ·936	·826**
	·040	·371	3·387	·786	
	·676**	·005**	·002	·012	
Middle boys	·643	1·218	5·513	− 1·087	·798**
	·030	·403	3·221	·813	
	·617**	·016**	·002	·002	
Middle girls	·631	·817	3·507	− ·446	·780**
	·031	·394	3·804	·862	
	·591**	·015**	·003	− ·000	
Junior boys	·414	·945	4·061	− ·241	·659**
	·028	·391	3·343	·836	
	·388**	·034**	·013**	·000	
Junior girls	·411	− ·160	−5·474	1·648	·617**
	·030	·416	3·831	·878	
	·357**	·015**	·003	·006	

[a] raw regression weights   * $p < 0.05$
[b] standard errors of weights   ** $p < 0.01$
[c] variance accounted for by variable

TABLE 14: *Multiple regression of 1964 reading scores on father's occupation and inverse of sibsize*

1964 READING	FATHER OCCUPATION	SIBSIZE INVERSE	MULTIPLE R
Senior boys	·510[a]	5·802	·363**
	·083[b]	1·313	
	·086**[c]	·045**	
Senior girls	·556	5·261	·400**
	·075	1·258	
	·121**	·038**	
Middle boys	·744	5·764	·360**
	·112	1·766	
	·104**	·025**	
Middle girls	·658	2·398	·313**
	·109	1·707	
	·092**	·005	
Junior boys	·558	− ·715	·247**
	·111	1·876	
	·061**	·000	
Junior girls	·511	3·075	·272**
	·100	1·685	
	·066**	·008	

[a] raw regression weights   * $p < ·05$
[b] standard errors of weights   ** $p < ·01$
[c] variance accounted for by variable

gression-fitted sibsize influence on the 1964 reading achievement scores at different socioeconomic levels.

The curvature of the surfaces in the figures for the junior groups and for the middle group girls indicated the overall lack of influence of sibsize on the reading scores, after accounting for the influence of social class. In the middle boys' group, there is a tendency (see Figure 18), in large families, for the inverse of sibsize to have an increasing influence on the reading scores as the socioeconomic level of the family decreases. For the two senior groups, 11-year-olds, the curvature of the surfaces reflects the potentially deleterious influence of large family size on reading achievement (see Figure 19, for the senior girls). Even at high socioeconomic levels, after the number of children increases beyond four, the reading scores start to decline rapidly.

The above relations between social class, sibsize, and academic achievement differ quite markedly from the results of a previous study (Marjoribanks and Walberg, 1974) in which the cognitive performance of Canadian 11-year-old boys was examined. In that study, it was found that three-term equations which included

FIGURE 18: *Fitted – 1964 reading scores in relation to sibsize and father occupation: middle group boys*

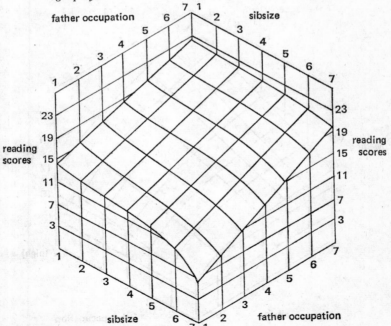

father's occupation, inverse of sibsize, and the interaction of the two variables parsimoniously accounted for as much significant variance in verbal and number scores as complex many-termed equations. Regression surfaces for the verbal and number scores indicated the increasing influence the inverse of sibsize has on the cognitive scores as the socioeconomic level of the family decreases. However, it was found that if children came from small families, their performances on the tests were quite similar regardless of their social class background. It was not until sibsize increased beyond two, in families of low social status, that family size appeared to have a deleterious influence on academic performance. In families of high social status, the effect of sibsize on the cognitive scores was attenuated and minimal. The curvature of the surface for the regression-fitted sibsize influence on verbal scores, at different socioeconomic levels, is shown in Figure 20.

The differences in the results from the two samples suggest that, in relation to Canadian families, working class English parents of even small families find it more difficult to provide a learning environment within the home for their children that is related to

FIGURE 19: *Fitted – 1964 reading scores in relation to sibsize and father occupation: senior group girls*

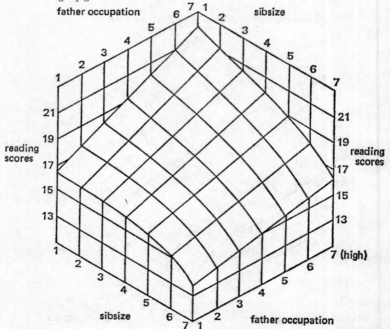

FIGURE 20: *Fitted – verbal scores in relation to sibsize and father occupation*

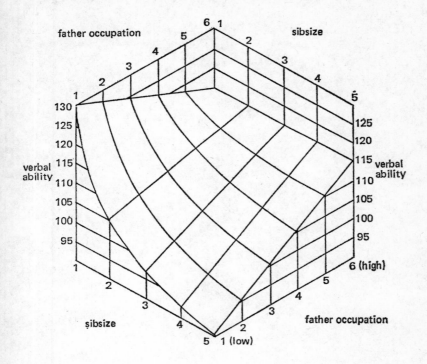

high academic achievement. However, studies such as the present one, that use global measures of the environment, provide only a general explanation of the environmental influences on cognitive performance. Social status characteristics and sibling variables are merely general unreliable indicators of more specific processes that operate within the family environment. In order to understand the complexities of the relations between the environment and cognitive development, research is required that investigates the relationships between sibling constellation variables, social status indicators, and detailed assessments of environmental variables that reflect parent-sibling interaction and which are related to measures of academic achievement.

7. Environment, Social Class, and Mental Abilities

KEVIN MARJORIBANKS

MUCH OF the research that has investigated the relationship between the environmental background of children and intellectual test performance has been limited by the inadequate measures of both the environment and student performance that have been used.

The environment has generally been defined in terms of social status characteristics such as the occupation and education of the parents or in terms of family structure variables such as family size and the crowding ratio of the home. For intellectual ability a global IQ score is often the only measure examined.

In an attempt to overcome the shortcomings of many of the existing environmental studies, it was decided to examine the relationship between a refined measure of the learning environment of the home and a set of mental ability test scores.

Method

Mental Abilities
Four mental abilities were examined: verbal, number, spatial and reasoning. These abilities were operationalized by the scores on the relevant SRA Primary Mental Abilities subtests (1962, revised edition). The test also provides a general measure of intelligence as well as the multifactored scores.

Environment
The total environment which surrounds an individual may be defined as being composed of a complex network of forces. It was assumed that a subset of the total network of forces is related to each human characteristic (Bloom, 1964). Thus for verbal, number, spatial, and reasoning ability, it was proposed that subenvironments or subsets of environmental forces could be identified which would be related to each of the abilities.

The union of the four subenvironments, which were postulated to be related to the four mental abilities, was defined as the learning environment. This learning environment may be present in the home, school, and community. Of these, the home produces the first and perhaps the most insistent and subtle influence on the mental ability development of the child. As a result, the home was chosen as the focus of the study.

From a review of relevant theoretical and empirical literature (Coleman, 1966; Dave, 1963; Plowden, 1967; Vernon, 1969; Weiss, 1969; Wolf, 1964) a set of eight environmental forces was identified. Subsets of these forces were postulated to be related to the mental abilities.

The forces were labelled:

(1) press for achievement;
(2) press for activeness;
(3) press for intellectuality;
(4) press for independence;
(5) press for English;
(6) press for ethlanguage;
    (refers to any language spoken in the home other than English)
(7) father dominance.
(8) mother dominance;

Each of the environmental forces was defined in terms of a set of environmental characteristics which were assumed to be the behavioural manifestations of the environmental forces.

A list of the environmental forces and their associated characteristics are presented in Table 15.

The environmental characteristics which are listed in Table 15 provided the framework for the construction of a new environmental measure. Initially, two instruments were developed which elicited responses from students regarding their home environments. In the first questionnaire, responses were of a true-false form, while in the second questionnaire a number of alternate responses were provided for each question. Although moderate relationships were found between the learning environment measures and a number of mental ability test scores, it was considered that such data included misperceptions and an absence of information regarding many of the environmental forces of the learning environment. It was also considered that these limitations would be greater if the questionnaires were administered to very young children.

Finally, it was decided to develop a semi-structured home interview schedule which could be used to elicit responses from both mothers and fathers. Because of the complexity and sublety of the environmental forces that were to be measured, it was considered desirable not to limit the interviewers and respondents to a completely fixed-alternative item schedule. It was also considered that a completely open-ended item schedule might reduce the reliability

TABLE 15: *Environmental forces and their related environmental characteristics used in the interview schedule*

ENVIRONMENTAL FORCES	ENVIRONMENTAL CHARACTERISTICS
1. Press for achievement	1a. Parental expectations for the education of the child.
	1b. Social press.
	1c. Parent's own aspirations.
	1d. Preparation and planning for child's education.
	1e. Knowledge of child's educational progress.
	1f. Valuing educational accomplishments.
	1g. Parental interest in school.
2. Press for activeness	2a. Extent and content of indoor activities.
	2b. Extent and content of outdoor activities.
	2c. Extent and the purpose of the use of TV and other media.
3. Press for intellectuality	3a. Number of thought-provoking activities engaged in by children.
	3b. Opportunities made available for thought-provoking discussions and thinking.
	3c. Use of books, periodicals, and other literature.
4. Press for independence	4a. Freedom and encouragement to explore the environment.
	4b. Stress on early independence.
5. Press for English	5a. Language (English) use and reinforcement.
	5b. Opportunities available for language (English) usage.
6. Press for ethlanguage	6a. Ethlanguage usage and reinforcement.
	6b. Opportunities available for ethlanguage usage.
7. Father dominance	7a. Father's involvement in child's activities.
	7b. Father's role in family decision-making.
8. Mother dominance	8a. Mother's involvement in child's activities.
	8b. Mother's role in family decision-making.

of the instrument. In the final instrument, a set of alternate responses was supplied for each item. In addition, an 'other answer' space was provided so that the interviewer could record a response that was not covered by those supplied.

A six-point rating scale was developed in order to score each item in the schedule. The score for each of the environmental characteristics was obtained by summing the scores on the relevant environmental items, and the score for each of the environmental forces was obtained by summing the scores on the relevant environmental characteristics.

As well as measuring the intensity of the present learning environment, the schedule attempted to gain a measure of the cumulative

E

nature of the learning environment over time. For example, as well as asking, how much schooling do you expect him to receive?, the schedule also asked, how long have you had these ideas about the amount of schooling you expect him to receive? For each such question, six possible answers were provided on the schedule for the guidance of the interviewer.

Three preliminary tests of the schedule were made before the final questionnaire was adopted.

Sample

Approximately 500 11-year-old boys were tested, using first the California Test of Mental Maturity, and then the SRA Primary Mental Abilities Test (1962, revised edition). The first test-taking situation was used to (a) establish examiner-examinee rapport, (b) ensure that all the children were able to understand the test instructions, and (c) establish as far as possible uniform test-taking situations. The boys were assigned to two categories, one classified as middle class and the other as low class. The social-class classification was based on an equally weighted combination of the occupation of the head of the household and a rating of his (or her) education. As far as possible, two parallel pools of boys were formed. The purpose of the substitute pool was to provide a set of alternate families which could be used in the study if families from the first pool did not agree to participate.

The final sample consisted of 90 boys and their parents, classified as middle class, and 95 classified as low class. Both parents from each family participated in the interviewing sessions. Each interview lasted for approximately two hours.

Hypotheses

In the development of the study it was postulated that subsets of environmental forces could be identified which would be related to each of the mental abilities.

Therefore the following hypothesis was investigated.

Hypothesis 1: The verbal, number, spatial, reasoning, and total ability test scores are significantly related to scores of environmental forces.

It was also proposed that the use of environmental forces was a means of moving beyond the use of gross classificatory variables such as social status factors (occupation of father, education of father, education of mother) and family structure characteristics (size of family, ordinal position in family, crowding ratio of home) as measures of the environment. The advantage of using the subenvironmental approach was investigated by examining the following hypothesis.

Hypothesis 2: Scores on the environmental forces are more highly related to measures of verbal, number, spatial, and reasoning ability than are other environmental measures such as social-status indicators and family structure characteristics.

Results

Before examining the hypotheses, the reliability coefficient of each of the environmental scales was estimated by evaluating coefficient alpha (Nunnally, 1967). The reliability coefficients are reported in Table 16.

It was considered that the reliability coefficients obtained in Table 16 were of an acceptable level.

The first analysis of *Hypothesis* 1 involved an examination of the zero-order correlations between the scores of the mental ability tests and the environmental force scores. These correlations, which are presented in Table 17, indicated that most of the relationships were statistically significant. For spatial ability the lack of a relationship with press for independence and father dominance scores is related to the inconsistent results found by Vernon (1969), who, from his analysis of cultural groups, indicated that 'there was only limited support for the hypothesis that masculine dominance in the home and encouragement of initiative are associated with perceptual-spatial abilities'.

A further examination of the relationship between the learning environment of the home and each mental ability was made by computing the multiple correlation between the eight environmental forces and each mental ability. In this analysis, the environmental forces formed a predictor set and the mental abilities formed the criterion vectors. The results of this analysis, which are presented in Table 18, indicated that when the environmental forces were

TABLE 16: *Reliability coefficients of the environmental scales*

SCALE	RELIABILITY COEFFICIENT	NUMBER OF ITEMS	SD OF SCORES
Press for achievement	·94	50	35·18
Press for intellectuality	·88	18	17·05
Press for activeness	·80	25	11·29
Press for independence	·71	16	8·72
Press for English	·93	20	17·83
Press for ethlanguage	·90	15	14·40
Father dominance	·67	22	9·22
Mother dominance	·66	22	10·33

TABLE 17: *Interrelationships between the mental ability test scores and scores of the environmental forces*

ENVIRONMENTAL FACTOR	ABILITY				
	Verbal	*Number*	*Spatial*	*Reasoning*	*Total*
Press for achievement	·66**	·66**	·28**	·39**	·69**
Press for activeness	·52**	·41**	·22**	·26**	·47**
Press for intellectuality	·61**	·53**	·26**	·31**	·59**
Press for independence	·42**	·34**	·10	·23**	·38**
Press for English	·50**	·27**	·18**	·28**	·40**
Press for ethlanguage	·35**	·24**	·09	·19**	·28**
Father dominance	·16*	·10	·09	·11	·15
Mother dominance	·21**	·16*	·04	·10**	·16*

$* p < ·05$
$** p < ·01$

combined into a set of predictors they accounted for a large percentage of the variance in verbal and number ability test scores, and a moderate percentage of the variance in the reasoning ability test scores. For spatial ability, the corrected multiple correlation coefficient did not reach statistical significance. These results are supportive of Cattell's theory (Cattell, 1963; Cattell and Butcher, 1968) which proposes that verbal, number, and reasoning abilities (crystallized abilities) depend more on environmental factors than does spatial ability (fluid ability).

The investigations of the zero-order and multiple correlations between the environment and mental abilities indicated that, in general, the environmental scales had (a) moderate to high concurrent validity in relation to verbal and number abilities, (b) low

TABLE 18: *Multiple correlations of each of the mental ability scores with the eight environment forces*

ABILITY	MULTIPLE CORRELATION	CORRECTED[a] MULTIPLE CORRELATION R_c	PERCENTAGE OF TOTAL VARIANCE R^2_c
Verbal	·72**	·71**	50·4**
Number	·72**	·71**	50·4**
Spatial	·32*	·26	6·7
Reasoning	·43**	·40**	16·0**
Total	·74**	·72**	51·8**

[a] R_c refers to the multiple correlation corrected to allow for cumulative errors in multiple R, and for small sample size.
$* p < ·01$
$** p < ·001$

to moderate concurrent validity for reasoning ability, and (c) low to negligible concurrent validity for spatial ability.

The relationship that was found between the environmental force scores and the total ability score replicates, in part, the studies conducted by Dave (1963), Wolf (1964), and Dyer (1967). Working with the same sample of white fifth-grade American children, both Dave and Wolf found that their measure of the environment accounted for approximately 50 per cent of the variance in global intelligence test scores. Dyer, who examined fifth-grade West Indian children, found that the environment scores accounted for 46 per cent of the variance in global intelligence test scores. In this present study it was found that 52 per cent of the variance in a global intelligence test score could be attributed to the measured environmental forces.

The relationship between the environment and the global ability test scores obscures, however, important relations between the environment and intellectual performance. In the present study the relationship between the environment and the verbal-educational abilities was found to be similar to the relationship between the environment and the global intelligence test scores. The relationship between the reasoning and spatial ability scores with the environment, however, was of a much lower order. These results indicate some of the limitations of using only global measures of intellectual ability in environmental studies. In relation to *Hypothesis* 2, which states that scores on the environmental forces are more highly related to measures of verbal, number, spatial, and reasoning ability than are other environmental measures such as social status indicators and family structure variables, a set of correlation analyses was conducted.

In Table 19 the zero-order interrelationships between the gross classificatory measures of the environment and each of the mental abilities are presented.

TABLE 19: *Interrelationships between gross indicators of the environment and mental ability test scores*

GROSS INDICATORS	ABILITIES				
	Verbal	*Number*	*Spatial*	*Reasoning*	*Total*
Education of father	·29**	·27**	·26**	·22**	·31**
Education of mother	·39**	·33**	·21**	·16*	·36**
Occupation of father	·43**	·30**	·31**	·29**	·43**
Number of children in family	− ·32**	− ·33**	− ·04	− ·03	− ·31**
Crowding ratio	− ·34**	− ·34**	− ·07	− ·09	− ·33**
Ordinal position in family	− ·26**	− ·25**	− ·04	− ·04	− ·24**

* p < ·05
** p < ·01

In general, the results that are reported in Table 19 support findings from previous research which have examined the relationship between global measures of the environment and intelligence test scores. It has been found that typical relationships between social-status characteristics and ability scores are represented by a correlation coefficient of 0·35 (Ausubel, 1968). In the present study the average correlation was 0·38. For family structure characteristics, moderate relationships have been found between family size and intelligence test performance. Fraser (1959) found a relation of −0·4, Whiteman and Deutsch (1968), a relation of −0·24, and Nisbet (1953) found relations of −0·19 on non-verbal tests and −0·33 on verbal tests. Similarly for the crowding ratio of the home and the ordinal position in the family, studies have found moderate relationships with verbal-educational ability scores. The present study replicated these results and also indicated a lack of a relationship with the spatial and reasoning ability scores.

Overall, the results indicated that the social status characteristics had a moderate relationship with the mental ability scores, and that the family structure characteristics, while having a moderate relationship with the verbal-educational ability scores, had a negligible relationship with the spatial and reasoning ability scores.

A qualitative inspection of Tables 17 and 19 indicated that, in general, the environmental force scores were more highly related to the mental ability scores than were the gross indicators of the environment.

In order to compare quantitatively the effectiveness of the environmental force scores, and the gross indicators as predictors of mental ability test scores, a set of multiple correlation analyses were conducted. In these analyses the amount of variance that could be attributed to the environmental forces was computed after accounting for the variance that could be attributed to the gross indicators of the environment. The results of these analyses, which are presented in Table 20, indicated that the environmental forces accounted for 25 per cent of the variance in verbal ability test scores, 34 per cent of the variance in number ability scores, and 12 per cent of the variance in reasoning ability scores after the variance due to the combination of status characteristics (occupation of father, education of father, education of mother, number of children, ordinal position, and crowding ratio) had been allowed for. For the spatial ability test scores, the corrected multiple correlation for 'environment' did not reach statistical significance. Thus the results provided support for the general acceptance of *Hypothesis* 2.

Discussion

The results that were obtained from an examination of the relation-

TABLE 20: *Relationship between mental abilities, environmental forces and gross indicators of the environment*

CRITERION	PREDICTOR VARIABLES	COMPUTED MULTIPLE CORRELATION R	CORRECTED MULTIPLE CORRELATION R_c	PERCENTAGE OF TOTAL VARIANCE R_c^2
Verbal ability	A = status variables + 8 environmental forces	·74***	·71***	51·0***
	B = 6 status variables	·53***	·51***	26·0***
	C = A – B = environment			25·0***
Number ability	A = 6 status variables + 8 environmental forces	·72***	·71***	50·0***
	B = 6 status variables	·42***	·40***	16·0***
	C = A – B = environment			34·0***
Spatial ability	A = 6 status variables + 8 environmental forces	·38**	·36*	13·0
	B = 6 status variables	·31**	·28*	8·0*
	C = A – B = environment			5·0
Reasoning ability	A = 6 status variables + 8 environmental forces	·47***	·42**	18·0**
	B = 6 status variables	·29**	·25	6·0
	C = A – B = environment			12·0**
Total ability	A = 6 status variables + 8 environmental forces	·78***	·75***	56·0***
	B = 6 status variables	·56***	·53***	28·0***
	C = A – B = environment			28·0***

* $p < ·05$
** $p < ·01$
*** $p < ·001$

ships among the constructs of environmental forces, global environmental meaures, and mental abilities provided support for the use of the subenvironment approach in the study of intellectual performance.

The *ex post facto* design of the study restricted, of course, the inferences that could be made about causation among the variables. Also the examination of the relationship between the environment and the mental abilities did not extricate genetic influences from 'pure' environmental influences. The disentanglement of these two influences would have required the study of children in which genotypes and environments were uncorrelated. Thus, some of the variance in the mental ability test scores that was attributed to the environment may, in fact, have a genetic base. However, the instrument which was developed for the study could be used in research that might attempt to extricate genetic from pure environmental forces. The study suggests that only through more rigorous research in this area of investigation and more rigorous attention to alternative explanations can we begin to understand the complexity of environment-organism interactions.

8. Environmental Correlates of Ability: A Canonical Analysis

KEVIN MARJORIBANKS

THE DATA from the previous study were analysed further by Walberg and Marjoribanks (1973). Canonical correlations were computed between the eight environmental scores and the four mental ability measures. Although Hotelling (1939) formulated canonical analysis four decades ago, it has been used very little in educational research. Just as multiple correlation is a generalization of simple correlation in that it relates several predictors to a criterion, canonical correlation is a generalization of multiple correlation in that it relates several predictors to several criteria. Also, just as multiple correlation yields a set of linear weights for the predictors to form a composite variate that is maximally correlated with the criterion, one or more pairs of canonical variates for the predictors and criteria are calculated that maximize the simple correlation between the paired linear composite variates from each set. Well worked out inferential tests are available to test the significance of successive canonical correlations, and the varieties may be characterized by calculating the 'canonical loadings', that is, the correlations of each composite variate with its original set of variables (Bock and Haggard, 1968; Darlington, Weinberg, and Walberg, 1973).

The canonical analysis revealed that the first two canonical correlations, ·781 and ·462 were significant (probabilities less than ·001 and ·005 respectively). The canonical loadings (plotted in Figure 21) reveal that with respect to the first canonical variate, verbal and number abilities and, to a lesser extent, reasoning ability, are more highly associated with the environmental scores than is spatial ability (also see Table 21).

The high loadings on the first canonical variate also indicate that the environmental forces contribute more strongly to the prediction of abilities than do the social status indicators and family structure characteristics.

After removing the variance of the first canonical variate from predictors and criteria, the loadings on the second variate reveal that the social status indicators and the environmental forces are

FIGURE 21: *Canonical loadings of environmental press and mental abilities measures*

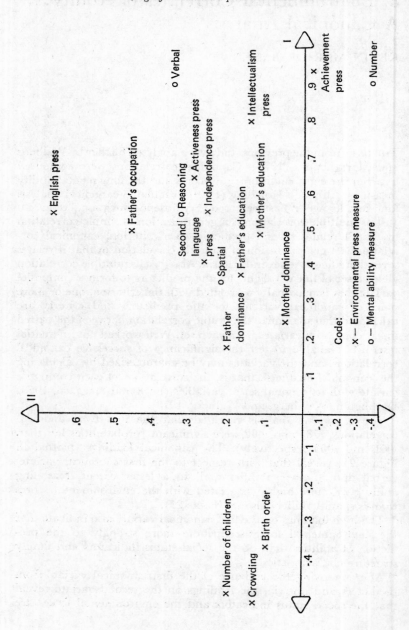

TABLE 21: *Correlations between two canonical predictor variates and four mental abilities*

ENVIRONMENTAL PREDICTOR VARIATE	MENTAL ABILITIES			
	Verbal	Numerical	Reasoning	Spatial
1	·716***	·702***	·401***	·280***
2	·153***	−·184***	·138***	·103
Multiple R	·733***	·726***	·425***	·298***

Note: Simple and multiple correlations significant at the ·05, ·01, and ·001 levels are indicated, respectively, by 1, 2 and 3 asterisks.

significantly related to differentially developed abilities. High ratings on press for English, father occupation, press for ethlanguage, and, to a lesser extent, press for activeness and father dominance, are associated on the second variate with high scores on verbal, reasoning and spatial abilities, but associated with lower number ability scores. The two language press scales reflect, in particular, a measure of parent-son interaction in activities such as reading, conversations after school at mealtimes and in the evenings, purposeful teaching of vocabulary, and the correction of syntactical errors in language use. The press-for-activeness scale measures parent-son involvement in both academic and non-academic situations while the father-dominance scale gauges the father's involvement in a son's activities.

Therefore, the second canonical variate suggests that the differential development of verbal, reasoning and spatial abilities, in relation to number ability, might be facilitated in homes characterized by high parent-son interation.

The findings have both substantive and methodological implications. By examining the canonical correlations between a set of environmental measures and cognitive abilities, the extra analysis of the data implies that differential environmental processes may operate selectively to develop certain potential abilities, and to leave others relatively underdeveloped. Feldman (1973) observed that, while the interest in the study of differential mental abilities has increased, the number of research studies has remained small. One reason for the paucity of studies has been the methodological difficulty of satisfactorily defining discrepant abilities without confounding the concepts of level and pattern of abilities. The use of canonical analysis as a technique for examining environmental correlates of differential mental abilities may overcome many of the previous difficulties.

9. The Identification and Measurement of Home Environmental Factors Related to Achievement Motivation and Self-Esteem

JOEL WEISS

THIS STUDY was concerned with developing and measuring models of the environment for selected individual personality characteristics. The present investigation explored a method for studying the relationship between individual personality characteristics and the environment which helps to shape them. A general model for describing the environment and its role in the prediction of two individual personality characteristics, self-esteem and achievement motivation, was tested. Any number of environmental settings could have been studied, but the home was chosen because of its assumed importance in early development.

Previous attempts to describe the environment have left much unexplained variance in individual personality characteristics. One approach borrows directly from Freudian psycho-analytic theory. This type of research tried to relate the development of selected personality characteristics to particular child rearing practices or experiences, during infancy or childhood. Using this approach has resulted in low and inconsistent relationships. Other researchers in the field have utilized a different approach by describing the environment in general terms. They investigated the relationships between global environmental indicators, such as social class, and personality characteristics of children. Only gross generalizations have emerged from this approach.

A more effective approach to the relations between the environment and personality characteristics was sought in light of these findings. One such strategy for research has been suggested by Bloom (1964). Somewhere between the total environment and the single experience is the concept of a subenvironment. Each subenvironment is seen as a set of forces which influence a particular human characteristic. The method utilized in this study departs from previous attempts in that it involved identifying and measuring a network of home environmental forces hypothesized to influence a particular selected personality variable.

The investigation limited itself to the study of two personality variables, achievement motivation and self esteem. The choice of these variables was dictated by an interest in the educational setting. Achievement motivation and self esteem were chosen because of their importance to the learning situation. Much research has been devoted to studying the influence of motivation upon school achievement. Curriculum specialists, teachers and school psychologists are all concerned with trying to increase the level of students' motivation. Similar reasons could be offered for the importance of self-esteem in the learning situation. For example, the work by Sears (1964) and others points to the negative effects that poor self image exerts upon educational progress.

Achievement motivation was operationally defined according to McClelland's (1958) dipolar criteria of need achievement theory. Specifically, a person with a high degree of achievement/motivation would exhibit the following: (1) competing with a maximal versus minimal standard of excellence; (2) long term versus short term involvement; (3) unique versus common accomplishments. Self-esteem was viewed as how a person evaluates himself with relation to his accomplishments and characteristics. Evaluation of self with regard to physical characteristics, intellectual abilities, social relations, temperament, and psychomotor competencies were considered.

A crucial problem was the identification of a set of environmental variables that constitute the subenvironments in the home for each of the personality variables. These environmental variables were identified from a review of the theoretical and empirical literature in the areas of child development, motivation and socialization. The subenvironment in the home for the development and maintenance of either of the personality variables consists of those forces and processes which are believed to affect the specific personality behaviour. The environmental process variables were defined as those social and psychological stimuli in the home which influence the development of either achievement motivation or self-esteem. In order to measure each environmental network the process variables were further delineated in terms of process characteristics.

A review of the relevant literature isolated three process variables for each of the two personality variables. The network for achievement motivation included:

I. *Generation of standards of excellence and expectations*
  1. Level of parental aspirations for themselves.
  2. Level of parental aspirations for the child.
  3. Emphasis on parents doing things well.
  4. Risk-taking behaviour of parents.

5. Parents' level of competitiveness.
6. Expectations of competitiveness held for child.
7. Work habits of parents.
8. Expectations of work habits for child.

II. *Independence training*
1. Freedom given to child for exploring environment.
2. Amount of aid given child.
3. Extent of dominance of parent of same or opposite sex.

III. *Parental approval*
1. Awareness of child's activities and behaviours.
2. Involvement in child's activities.
3. Extent of child's participation in decision making.
4. Quality and quantity of rewards and punishments.

The network for self-esteem included:

I. *Parental acceptance*
1. Awareness of child's activities.
2. Involvement in child's activities.
3. Quality and quantity of rewards and punishment.
4. Extent of parental self-acceptance.

II. *Evaluation of child*
1. Evaluation of child's physical characteristics.
2. Evaluation of child's intellectual qualities.
3. Evaluation of child's personality.
4. Evaluation of child's psychomotor competencies.
5. Evaluation of child's social skills.

III. *Opportunities for self-enhancement*
1. Extent of privacy for each person in family.
2. Encouragement given to child to explore new places and interests.
3. Child's participation in decision making.

A multi-method approach to the conceptualization of personality was adopted. Corresponding to the three categories that most definitions of personality can be placed (i.e. behavioural, social stimulus, and depth) are three different levels of viewing personality: self report, rating by other, and projective. Accordingly, three methods were used to measure each of the three different levels of personality. For both personality variables, ratings by the current teacher of the child were utilized in the rating by other instrument.

The major hypotheses of the study were concerned with the relationships between the measures of the environment and scores on tests of achievement motivation and self-esteem. The review of the theoretical and empirical literature in child development, personality, motivation and socialization with regard to particular forces in the home and their relations to the child's achievement motivation and self-esteem lead to the first major hypothesis, that:

The Indices of the Home Environment for Achievement Motivation and for Self-Esteem will be significantly related to measures of the child's achievement motivation and self-esteem, respectively.

Socioeconomic status and family structure variables such as ordinal position and size of family, have been utilized as predictors of achievement motivation and self-esteem. Results have been inconsistent for both personality variables. Since the Indices of Home Environment should contain more of the relevant features of the environment for each personality variable, they should be more highly related to measures of personality than the global indicators. Regardless of the level of predictability of status and family structure variables, it is difficult to assess the relevancy of such global indicators. In contrast, the Indices of Home Environment are an attempt to obtain information about the underlying relationships in the home situation for each of the personality variables. Accordingly, these Indices should better account for the dynamics of the relationships. Thus, the construct validity of the Indices of Home Environment was partially tested in the second hypothesis, that:

Scores on the Indices of Home Environment will be more highly related to the scores on measures of the child's self-esteem and achievement motivation than will (a) sociological variables such as socioeconomic status, (b) family structure variables, such as size of family and ordinal position.

Method

In order to test the hypotheses, data were collected on two randomly stratified samples of fifth-grade children, consisting of 27 boys and 29 girls. The samples were stratified on the basis of mother's education. Mother's education was chosen as the criterion because it has been shown to be related to variations in child rearing practices and also to social class. The subjects and their families lived in a heterogeneous community containing urban, rural and suburban components.

An interview schedule was developed in order to measure the hypothesized network of environmental forces. The interview was arranged into three categories of questions, those asked of the mother alone, the father alone, and the mother and father together. The questions for the Indices of Home Environment for Achievement Motivation were contained in six environmental process variables, three apiece for mother and father. While the number of environmental variables was originally the same for self-esteem and achievement motivation, the last variable for self-esteem, Father's Opportunity for Self Enhancement, was eliminated because of its extremely low reliability estimate.

Rating scales were developed for each question so that the verbal responses of the parents could be translated into scores. Many of the questions were precoded in order to facilitate the rating of responses. A score for an environmental characteristic was composed of the sum of scores on the rating scales for each question which was part of a characteristic.

Scores on the environmental process variables were determined by using principal component factor analysis to calculate principle component scores for each cluster of characteristics comprising each of the process variables.

An index of socioeconomic status was developed from four measures: father's occupation, amount of income, amount of father's education and amount of mother's education.

For achievement motivation, the self report, Student Choices, consisted of 46 forced choice items adapted from Farquhar's Generalized Situational Choice Inventory. The teacher rating or Teacher Achievement Motivation Rating, was adapted from Farquhar's (1963) Word Rating List and contained 20 adjectives to be rated on a four-point scale. A set of five pictures from the Thematic Apperception Test (TAT) was utilized as the projective device for achievement motivation.

Each of the three methods of measuring self-esteem was developed from a common set of 57 items derived mainly from Sears (1964) self report rating scale. For the self report, known as 'How Do I Rate Myself' Scale, the subject's task was to rate, using a six-point scale, what he thinks of himself in a particular area or activity. The teacher rating instrument, 'How Do I Rate My Student?' also called for a rating based on a six-point scale. The sentence completion technique was used as the projective method for measuring self-esteem. Each of the 57 rating items was converted into a sentence stem utilizing a third person name.

Since these instruments were used for both sexes, directions and items were changed accordingly. For the TAT, a set of pictures with female figures was developed for the female sample.

Results

A preliminary hypothesis concerned itself with the relationships among the different methods of measuring the personality variables. In general, the results confirmed the strategy of using three levels of personality. Analyses of the multi-trait, multi-method matrices indicated that for both achievement motivation and self-esteem, the different methods of measuring the same trait were generally independent of each other. For some measures methods factors seemed to be more pronounced than trait factors. In particular, there were indications that a teacher rating method factor may have emerged, indicative of the familiar 'halo effect' encountered when teachers are asked to make judgments of their students.

The major portion of the study concerned how well the models of the home environment predicted personality scores. The first major hypothesis stated that 'the Indices of Home Environment for Achievement Motivation and Self-Esteem would be significantly related to measures of achievement motivation and self-esteem, respectively'. Using multiple regression analysis, multiple correlations were determined between the combination of environmental process variables and the criterion measures. Table 22 presents the multiple correlations between the Indices of Home Environment and personality measures, as well as the results for the status and family structure variables (hypothesis 2). Results indicate a strong trend towards a relationship between the Indices of Home Environment and personality measures. More than half of the values, seven out of 12, were higher than ·50. The results for achievement motivation were especially pronounced, since five of the six values were ·50 or better.

TABLE 22 : *Summary table of relations between indices of Home Environment and socioeconomic status with personality measure*

PERSONALITY MEASURE		SOCIOECONOMIC STATUS$^{(r)}$	INDEX OF HOME ENVIRONMENT (R)	INDEX OF HOME ENVIRONMENT AND SOCIOECONOMIC STATUS (R)
Achievement Motivation				
Student Choices	Boys	− ·22	·57	·69*
	Girls	·15	·27	·39
Teacher Achievement	Boys	·53**	·66	·69*
Motivation Rating	Girls	·48**	·54	·65
TAT	Boys	·48	·56	·64
	Girls	·36	·51	·55
Self Esteem				
Student Self Rating	Boys	− ·01	·47	·47
	Girls	·26	·48	·48
Teacher Rating	Boys	·57**	·62*	·78**
	Girls	·16**	·53	·78**
Sentence Completion	Boys	·13	·43	·47
	Girls	− ·14	·43	·44

** p < ·05
** p < ·01

In terms of significance the values for boys' Teacher Self-Esteem Rating (R = ·62) and boys' Teacher Achievement Motivation Rating (R = ·66) were both significant at the ·05 level. When corrections for unreliability of instruments and shrinkage in small samples were made, a somewhat different pattern emerged with seven of the values being significant. For achievement motivation, Rs of ·81 (P < ·01) and ·70 (P < ·05) were obtained for boys' and girls' TAT, respectively. For self-esteem, significant values were obtained for the girls' self report (R = ·72, P < ·05), boys' and girls' teacher ratings (Rs of ·80 and ·79, P < ·01) and for boys' sentence completion (R = ·65, P < ·05). With the exception of the boys' self-esteem self report, the remaining relationships were difficult to interpret because of the low reliabilities of the corresponding Indices of Home Environment.

In general, these results support the thesis that a sub-set of the total environment can be identified and measured for individual personality characteristics. However, the results were dependent upon the criterion utilized. Unlike studies of cognitive characteristics it is more difficult to establish validity of criterion instruments for personality characteristics. It is likely that the situation was generalized to the relationships between environmental forces and certain criteria.

One way of determining the effectiveness of the overall strategy was to compare the Indices of Home Environment for Achievement Motivation and Self-Esteem with family status and structure variables as to their success in predicting personality scores. This was the second major hypothesis and served as a partial test of the construct validity of the Indices of Home Environment, since researchers have previously used status and family structure variables as predictors of personality behaviour. A comparison of the results presented in Table 22 shows that for both samples and all personality measures the Indices of Home Environment were better predictors than either ordinal position of child or size of family. In most cases the Index of Home Environment was at least as good as, or even better than, socioeconomic status as a predictor. The exceptions to this were the results for the teacher ratings where there was evidence of a strong halo effect.

Another way of looking at the relationships for the second hypothesis was to combine an Index of Home Environment and socioeconomic status into the same regression equation. This type of analysis enabled a test to be made of the contribution that socioeconomic status added beyond the predictive capacity of the Index of Home Environment. The multiple correlations obtained with the combination of these sets of predictors are presented in the last column of Table 22. For achievement motivation, with the exceptions of boys' self report and girls' teacher rating, there were no significant contributions made by socioeconomic status. The addition of socioeconomic status was only significant for the girls' teacher rating for self-esteem. To summarize, only one out of 12 regression analyses showed a significant contribution by socioeconomic status beyond that contributed by an Index of Home Environment.

In addition to a comparison between the different types of environmental indicators, these figures highlight the maximizing of personality prediction. In many cases, almost 50 per cent of the variance of a criterion score was explained, and, for girls' self-esteem teacher rating, the combination accounted for over 60 per cent of the variance. Thus, for predictive purposes, information about some of the underlying dimensions of the home as well as the socioeconomic status of the family helps to account for much of the variance in scores of personality behaviours of the fifth-grade children used in this study.

Discussion

The results of the study have important theoretical and methodological implications for future studies of environmental differences. Its theoretical importance lies in the concept of a model of environmental forces for each individual characteristic. Although other studies of the environment have utilized this strategy, it was applied to studying only a limited range of individual characteristics. This study, however, helps to extend the range from the cognitive area to variables illustrative of the social and/or emotional domains. While these models may not be definitive, results indicate that enough relevant forces have been isolated to warrant endorsing this concept of environment for further research. It is likely that work with a wider variety of personality variables, as well as interests and attitudes, will further illustrate the validity of this strategy.

From a methodological standpoint, this study has implications for further development of instruments for measuring environmental differences. While the instruments for this study are far from definitive, with improvement, they would represent useful additions to the sparse ranks of measures of environmental differences. Improvement of the instruments could be accomplished through further empirical revision of the parental interview. Also, it is possible that the lack of variation in the responses for some of the characteristics means that some information should be acquired by procedures other than the interview. Perhaps certain questions elicited socially desirable responses. One way of alleviating this problem would be to place parents in situations with and/or without the child, where some important behaviours could be demonstrated.

Another methodological implication of this study is derived from collecting information from each parent. In the main, previous studies of the home have tended to ignore the father as a source of information. A number of reasons may account for this situation: mothers can respond for both parents; fathers are rarely home when it is convenient for data collection. The results from this study point to the importance of the father beyond that contributed by the mother. Moreover, pilot testing highlighted problems that women have when asked to speak for their husbands. Therefore, it is of prime importance that fathers be included as respondents in instruments developed to measure evinronmental differences.

If the malleable aspects of the environment could be isolated, then possibilities exist for developing strategies for remediation and prevention of environmental deficiencies. Using environmental information in this fashion could provide one avenue for implementing more effective patterns of child rearing. It would be one direction in which Man's efforts to understand and control his environment could be furthered.

PART FOUR

The Classroom and College Environments

MUCH OF the research that has examined the relation between student performance and the learning environments of classrooms and schools has concentrated on the assessment of global environmental characteristics such as: per pupil expenditure, books in the library, class size, salaries of staff, age of buildings and qualifications of teachers (e.g. Mollenkopf and Melville, 1957; Goodman, 1959; Thomas, 1962; Coleman, 1966; Burkhead *et al.*, 1967; Plowden, 1967). Results from such studies have been inconsistent and they have accounted for a relatively small percentage of the variance in the performance of students (e.g. see Bowles and Levin, 1968; Dyer, 1968; Mosteller and Moynihan, 1972). Also, the global variables are too insensitive to allow any meaningful assessment of what is actually going on inside a classroom. The first three readings in this section present the results of research that has attempted to assess the social psychological environments of classrooms.

All of the difficulties that are associated with measuring environments, and which have already been discussed, apply probably with greater emphasis when the unit of analysis is a large institution of higher education. Universities, especially those which are not collegiate, are such diverse organizations that it is difficult to isolate well-defined subenvironments for learning. In the fourth reading in this section, Astin indicates and discusses three approaches that have been used to assess college environments. The most popular of these techniques have been those devised by Pace and Stern (1958), and Stern (1963).

However, rather than analysing the contributions by Stern, which are mentioned in a number of readings, a technique developed by McLeish is presented. Starting with the work of Pace and Stern, McLeish devised a questionnaire to measure environments in 10 Colleges of Education which are associated with the Cambridge Institute of Education, England. An Objective Evaluation Scale was also developed which measured factors such as: number of students, size of staff, rate of growth of college, library facilities, proportion of male staff, staff qualifications, and curriculum courses. It was found that a sufficiently large measure of agreement existed between the subjective and objective measurements of the college environments to allow the institutions to be arranged in an order of quality. A final 'quality of environment' measure was obtained by incorporating seven of the dimensions of the College Environment Index in the objective evaluation scale.

As in the readings related to the home environment, the present studies indicate that it is possible to move beyond the use of gross indicators of the learning environment and measure networks of more meaningful social psychological environmental forces.

References

ANDERSON, G. J., and WALBERG, H. J. 'Assessing Classroom Learning Environments'. Previously unpublished.

From: WALBERG, H. J., and THOMAS, S. C. (1972). 'Open Education: an Operational Definition and Validation in Great Britain and United States', *American Educational Research Journal*, 9, 197–208.

From: TRICKETT, E. M., and MOOS, R. H. (1973). 'Social Environment of Junior High and High School Classrooms', *Journal of Educational Psychology*, 65, 93–102.

From: ASTIN, A. W. (1970). 'The Methodology of Research on College Impact, Part Two', *Sociology of Education*, 43, 437–50.

From: MCLEISH, J. (1970). *Students' Attitudes and College Environments*. Cambridge: Institute of Education.

10. Assessing Classroom Learning Environments

GARY J. ANDERSON and HERBERT J. WALBERG

The Social Environment of Learning

SINCE 1966, a series of studies have demonstrated that student perceptions of the classroom learning environment can be measured reliably and that environmental measures are valid predictors of learning (Walberg, 1969a). Environmental variables themselves can be manipulated (Anderson, Walberg and Welch, 1969) and predicted from the class size, the biographical characteristics of its members, the mean intelligence, prior interest and achievement of pupils, and instructional variables (Walberg and Ahlgren, 1970). Moreover, powerful interactions have been identified between environment and both instructional variables (Walberg, 1969b) and individual differences in aptitudes and personality (Anderson, 1968; Bar-Yam, 1969).

The classroom environment may be conceptualized as one of four components of the learning process (Walberg, 1971) as shown in Table 23, and discussed in the first reading of the text. The working definitions in the Table indicate that the environment has the same relation to instruction as ability has to achievement: while environment has to do with the context of learning and ability with the student, both are more general, implicit, and enduring than their counterparts – instruction and achievement – that are more specific, intended and temporary. Thus, as factor analysts have sought those general abilities that underly surface academic achievements, we have sought the underlying environmental forces that are manifested in the context of learning through the content and method of instruction.

The research considered here involves three major research instruments which have been developed to assess aspects of the learning environment: the Learning Environment Inventory, the My Class Inventory, and the Class Activities Questionnaire. The 15 scales on the Learning Environment Inventory (LEI) are intended to be comprehensive and valid for predicting learning outcomes. The first version of the instrument was patterned by Walberg on

TABLE 23: *Definitions of, and relations between, four domains*

	RELATIVE CHARACTERISTICS	
Locus	*Specific, Intended, Temporary*	*General, Implicit, Enduring*
Student	Learning (or Achievement) – a change in (or state of) thought, feeling or behaviour	Aptitude (or Ability) – a characteristic of the individual that predicts learning
Context	Instruction – a stimulus intended to bring about learning	Environment – a stimulus, aside from instruction, that predicts learning

Hemphill's (1956) Group Dimensions Description Questionnaire, an instrument designed to tap 14 group characteristics that had been derived from one of the most extensive factor analytic studies of small adult groups ever conducted in terms of the numbers of groups and variables. While the LEI proved to be valid (Anderson and Walberg, 1968; Walberg and Anderson, 1968a), content, item, and factor analysis suggested a number of improvements that were carried out by Walberg and Anderson in the first revision that was again validated (Anderson, 1970; Walberg, 1971). On the basis of these results, Anderson (1971) prepared a final version by re-writing some items and adding a 15th scale.

A typical item on the 'Satisfaction' scale is the following: 'The students enjoy their class work'. The student responds by indicating his agreement or disagreement relative to the class he is attending in terms of the four responses: Strongly Agree, Agree, Disagree, or Strongly Disagree. Unlike teacher observation and counting schedules that require elaborate hand coding and processing, the LEI may be easily machine-scored by key punching the item responses and adding the appropriately keyed answers on a computer. There are seven items on each of the 15 scales listed in Table 24.

The LEI is convenient and easy to administer. It does not mention the teacher at all and, thus, does not pose the threat of other instruments that explicitly focus on teacher characteristics an behaviour. Moreover, in not singling out the teacher, the LEI reveals our assumption that the class members themselves, in addition to the teacher, constitute an important determinant of the learning environment. For research efficiency, the instrument has typically been administered to random halves of the class while other class members complete other instruments; however, all class members can complete the LEI if higher reliability is desired. Also, it is possible to omit some scales that are not of interest in a particular evaluation to cut down in testing time which would otherwise be about 35 minutes.

A few comments on why the LEI methodology has proven com-

TABLE 24: *Learning Environment Inventory scales*

Scales	Sample Items	Reliabilities		
		Individual		Class
		Alpha	Test/Re-test	Intraclass
Cohesiveness	Members of the class are personal friends	·69	·52	·85
Diversity	The class divides its efforts among several purposes	·53	·43	·31
Formality	Students are asked to follow a complicated set of rules	·76	·55	·92
Speed	The class has difficulty keeping up with its assigned work	·70	·51	·81
Environment	The books and equipment students need are easily available to them	·56	·64	·81
Friction	Certain students are considered unco-operative	·72	·73	·83
Goal Direction	The objectives of the class are specific	·85	·65	·75
Favouritism	Only the good students are given special projects	·78	·64	·76
Difficulty	Students are constantly challenged	·64	·46	·78
Apathy	Members of the class don't care what the class does	·82	·61	·61
Democratic	Class decisions tend to be made by all students	·67	·69	·67
Cliqueness	Certain students work only with their close friends	·65	·68	·71
Satisfaction	Students are well satisfied with the work of the class	·79	·71	·84
Disorganization	The class is disorganized	·82	·72	·92
Competitiveness	Students compete to see who can do the best work	·78	—	·56

paratively valid are in order here. First, the student is the intended recipient of instruction and other cues in the classroom, particularly social stimuli; and he may be the best judge of the learning context. Compared with a short-term observer, he weights in his judgement not only the class as it presently is, but how it has been since the beginning of the year. He is able to compare from the child-client point of view his class with those in past grades or perhaps with others he is presently taking or even of other small groups of which he is a member. He and his classmates form a group of 20 or 30 sensitive, well-informed judges of the class; an outside observer is a single judge who has far less data and, though highly trained and systematic, may be insensitive to what is important in a particular class.

On the other hand, the LEI scales are 'high-inference' measures in that they require subjective ratings of perceived behaviour unlike 'low-inference' measures which are objective counts of observed behaviour. Because they reflect psychology's current behaviouristic ethos, low-inference measures of teacher and class behaviour are far more prevalent. Low-inference scales would have the advantage that, if valid, they directly suggest changes in specific teacher behaviour, e.g. 'increase the number of questions you ask from two to four per minute'. However, low-inference measures are generally substantially less valid in predicting learning outcomes than high-inference measures. The reason for this is probably that counts of praise or questions measure quantity rather than quality, and may have limited relevance to student abilities, interests, and needs. For example, one profound and appropriate question may inspire learning more than 10 superficial ones; and one sincere 'Not bad' from an intellectually demanding teacher or student peer may be more potent than 'great, good, right' from one who often says it. Thirty students may be able to judge these things better than an evaluator or researcher who counts them.

Two additional instruments of interest in this review are the My Class Inventory (MCI; Anderson, 1971; Maguire, Goetz and Manos, 1972), and the Class Activities Questionnaire (CAQ). The MCI is a re-worked version of the LEI, containing five, nine-item scales incorporating a simple dichotomous agree-disagree format which is appropriate for younger children. The MCI with its scales Friction, Competitiveness, Difficulty, Satisfaction and Cohesiveness has proved useful in a variety of studies with six- to 12-year-olds.

The CAQ is similar to the LEI except that it was constructed to measure the six levels of Bloom's (1956) taxonomy. It would be interesting in subsequent research to investigate the relations of the LEI socio-psychological variables with CAQ cognitive dimensions. Moreover, both instruments might be used in evaluation research comprehensively to assess the affective-social and cognitive domains.

Determinants of the Learning Environment
What determines the learning environment? Nine studies are briefly described in this section under three subheadings: curriculum, class size, and other correlates.
Curriculum. Anderson, Walberg and Welch (1969) reported a study conducted with the LEI on a national sample of 150 high school

classes. A national random sample of physics teachers was randomly assigned to teach Harvard Project Physics (HPP), a new course undergoing evaluation, or the course they ordinarily taught; also, a group teaching HPP for a second year was included in the analysis. Multivariate and univariate statistical tests revealed that, as the course developers had hoped, HPP was seen as less difficult, more diverse and as providing a more stimulating environment than other courses; cliques and friction among class members were perceived to be less frequent among HPP students. Teachers using HPP for the first time had classes viewed as more democratic and cohesive than those of the other two groups of teachers.

The main comparative evaluation of the HPP course (Welch and Walberg, 1972) contrasted only the randomly assigned groups for a true experiment. While it confirmed that the HPP classes are perceived as less difficult and the activities more diverse, the two studies taken together suggest that the environmental differences between courses increase with teachers' increasing experience with a new course.

Anderson (1971), using discriminant function analysis, compared the learning environments of 62 science, mathematics, humanities and French classes in Montreal. Mathematics classes were seen as relatively high on Favouritism, Difficulty, Disorganization and Cliqueness and low on Formality and Goal Direction; thus, despite the elegant formality and organization of the subject, mathematics classes at the high school level apparently do not have these features. A second dimension of differences between the courses showed that science classes are more formal, difficult, and fast moving while humanities courses are relatively disorganized and easy. The last dimension showed that French classes are comparatively high on Goal Direction and low on Friction and Disorganization.

Walberg, Steele, and House (1972) followed upon this study and compared several subject areas on the CAQ ratings of cognitive emphasis in 121 classes. Three discriminant functions were found. The first, termed 'Convergence-Divergence', contrasts mathematics with other subjects; the second, 'Substance-Syntax', social studies and science with language arts and mathematics; and the third, 'Objectivity-Subjectivity', contrasts science with social studies. The pattern of cognitive press on the first two functions was very reminiscent of Anderson's first two functions despite the instrument differences.

These four studies involving subject matter differences in social environment and cognitive press suggest there are important heretofore un-analysed differences in the various parts of the curriculum. More research is needed to produce a typology of social and cognitive stimulation provided in different courses and subject areas.

Class Size. Many studies of class size have failed to produce significant and consistent correlates with cognitive and affective qualities. However, two studies of the LEI replicated two significant correlates. Walberg (1969c) using 149 physics classes and Anderson and Walberg (1972) using 61 Montreal classes in several subject areas both found smaller classes to be significantly higher on Cohesiveness and Difficulty. While small groups of many kinds are generally perceived as more cohesive (Cartwright and Zander, 1968), we speculate that smaller classes are perceived as more difficult because students are less able to use them to conceal low personal productivity. Smaller classes might be encouraged not only because teachers and students want them more, but because the two significant correlates have been associated with cognitive and affective outcomes in other studies (see the next section). The LEI may be tapping those aspects of environment that stimulate educational growth that are not well measured by conventional achievement tests.

Other Studies. Walberg, House and Steele (1973) investigated the relation of grade level with cognitive press and affective characteristics measured on the CAQ. A cross-sectional study made of 121 sixth-to-12th grades revealed that students in higher grades saw their classes as less stimulating and enjoyable than students in the lower grades. High school students also found their classes emphasizing factual memorization while elementary school students saw greatest emphasis on higher-level cognitive processes such as analysis, synthesis and evaluation. The most undesirable classes in the students' perception were at the sophomore and junior levels, the years of highest drop-out rates.

Walberg and Ahlgren (1970) investigated the predictability of the LEI scales from other educational variables in 144 physics classes. Initial class interest and ability in physics were associated with high levels of perceived Difficulty, Disorganization, and Speed and low levels of Formality, Goal Direction, and Democracy. With respect to biographical characteristics of class members, classes with sociable, less bookish members were rated higher on Cohesiveness; classes with more college-bound students, science prize winners, and those with high school marks were scored higher on Difficulty.

Walberg, Sorenson, and Fischbach (1972) adapted the LEI for use in the middle grades to measure the school environment and administered the scales to all fifth-grade students in 40 Wisconsin high schools. The analysis revealed that the higher the socioeconomic (SES) levels of the school, the less competitive the high-SES children perceive the school, but the more competitive low-SES children see it. Thus, the LEI is sensitive to the composition of the student body of the school, and it can be used as one set of indicators for the success of social interventions, such as bussing for integration, and also to measure the effectiveness of the school in providing a good learning environment for different types of children.

In addition to these nine studies, several others can be cited to illustrate the range of variables that have been related to perceptions of the learning environment. Walberg (1968) examined the relationship of measures of teacher personality to the environment of their classes; graded schools have been compared to continuous progress schools by Ranayya (1971); and, the effects of bussing for integration have been explored using the MCI (Walberg, 1970).

Environments and Learning

The past five years saw a variety of research on the correlates of classroom social climate and various measures of student learning. These LEI studies have included a variety of units of analysis, measures of learning outcomes, and have employed a great many statistical techniques. Researchers have examined the relationships between individual and class-mean measures of the learning environment on the one hand and individual and class mean learning outcomes on the other. Thus, there are four combinations of individual and group variables that can be compared. Note that the various combinations address themselves to different kinds of questions. To answer the question, 'how does an individual student's perception of his learning environment affect the amount of learning which he himself can demonstrate over the course of the year', one would compare individual classroom climate scores with measures of individual learning. The bulk of research done to date, however, suggests that measures of the learning environment are essentially group characteristics and the most meaningful way of analysing the effects of the learning environment on outcomes is to utilize climate measures as class variables by calculating the class mean score or the mean for some fraction of class members. We can, moreover, examine the effects of group climate both on the learning of the group as a whole and the learning of individual members within it. It must be stressed that measures of learning for the class mean are not readily transferable to individual students. In many cases, the effects are similar but this is not necessarily so.

The first major question which needs to be answered is as follows: 'Is the Learning Environment Inventory a useful predictor of student learning?'. To answer it adequately we should examine the effects of other well-known predictors of student learning and determine whether or not such instruments as the LEI predict substantially more variance in learning than do well-established predictors. Several of the research studies have attempted to do this by using the most successful predictor of learning yet devised, namely, measures of IQ. We can determine both whether the LEI predicts more variance in learning than does IQ and whether it predicts different variance from that predicted by IQ.

Table 25 lists a number of studies in which this question was considered. As shown from the studies in the Table, IQ generally accounts for no more than 16 per cent of the variance in learning, when the effect of pre-test scores has been removed. The combination of all the LEI scales accounts for between 13 per cent and 46 per cent and a substantial percentage of this variance in learning outcomes is predicted uniquely by the LEI. The various studies in Table 25 have considered cognitive, affective, and behavioural learning outcomes. While the methods of assessing the latter have not always been optimal, they have generally been predictable from LEI scales.

What are the effects of individual measures of classroom social climate on student learning? To consider this question, let us consider three studies. The three studies have been selected since they represent three different samples of subjects and they are rather comprehensive in scope. Their findings would seem to supplement the work in earlier studies using earlier forms of the Learning Environment Inventory.

TABLE 25: *General predictability of learning outcomes from LEI scales*

	PER CENT LEARNING VARIANCE PREDICTABLE[a]		
	IQ Alone	LEI Scales Alone	LEI Scales with IQ Partialled Out
Anderson and Walberg (1968)			
Cognitive$_1$	0	33	—
Cognitive$_2$	7	46	—
Cognitive$_3$	0	34	—
Walberg and Anderson (1972)			
Cognitive$_1$	7	43	38
Cognitive$_2$	12	46	36
Walberg (1971)			
Cognitive$_1$	16	30	—
Cognitive$_2$	12	21	—
Cognitive$_3$	13	18	—
Affective$_1$	3	19	—
Affective$_2$	1	17	—
Behavioural	0	13	—

a Note: In these studies learning criteria have been adjusted for pre-tests, reducing considerably the amount of variance predictable from measures of IQ alone

Anderson (1970+) utilized class means on the LEI and related them to individual cognitive, affective and behavioural measures of student gains in learning. The sample of subjects included those participating in the evaluation of HPP and specific students were randomly selected who had fulfilled certain criteria; thus, the analysis incorporated the effects of students' IQ interactions between LEI class scores and individual student IQ, as well as non-linea LEI effects on the various measures of learning. In overall terms, individual scales on the LEI were significantly related to cognitive and affective measures of student learning, but there were fewer relationships with paper-and-pencil measures of behavioural outcomes. Positive effects on learning were reported for cohesiveness, and for the Difficulty scale. Friction bore negative relationships to learning but in one instance, with the female sample, friction was positively related to a measure of 'science understanding'. For the two cognitive measures, class mean IQ accounted for five per cent to 25 per cent of variance in learning, whereas the best LEI scales practically doubled these figures to a maximum of 36 per cent. This study illustrates that some environments are best for students at high IQ levels while other environments are more appropriate for other types of students.

Walberg (1971) examined the relationships of a large number of student and class characteristics to six learning criteria. His sample included over 150 classes in the Harvard Project Physics Evaluation and the analysis revealed positive correlations between class difficulty and cognitive learning and satisfaction with measures of interest. Negative correlations were reported between class friction and perceived apathy and the various measures of learning. For apathy and cliqueness, there were negative relationships to measures of behavioural learning which included science activities pursued by students.

The Walberg and Anderson (1972) study had the advantage of incorporating a sample which included 64 classes in eight different subject areas: mathematics, physics, chemistry, biology, English, history, geography and French. As reported in the other two studies, the scales Cohesiveness, Environment, and Satisfaction bore positive relationships to cognitive learning, while Friction, Cliqueness and Apathy were negatively related to learning measures. Speed, Favouritism and Disorganization were also negatively related to learning. This was the only one of the three studies incorporating the Competitiveness scale which bore both positive and negative relationships to learning in the various subject areas. For example, Competitiveness was positively correlated with learning in mathematics classes and bore an equally high negative correlation with achievement in physics classes. In this study, the learning criteria

F

included course achievement measures and similar measures with the effect of class IQ statistically removed. In the latter case, the correlations were reduced by about 10 per cent, again indicating the power of the LEI to predict learning outcomes.

In total, these studies imply that approximately half the LEI scales, namely, Cohesiveness, Environment, Friction, Cliqueness, Satisfaction, Disorganization, Difficulty and Apathy account for substantial variance in measures of student learning. While the directions of relationship are generally what one would expect, the studies have served to document these relationships.

The data reported so far have involved overall effects on samples. In many cases these studies have been subdivided and analyses have included different subject matter, different student sexes, levels of initial ability and other such important variables. It is beyond the scope of this chapter to include all the findings incorporating these combinations of variables. A few of them will be reported to indicate the types of effects which have been uncovered.

Anderson (1970) found that classroom climate scores were positively related to scores on the Science Process Inventory for females but the relationship was negative for male subjects. Scales such as Cohesiveness, Apathy and Environment have been differentially related to student learning in the various subject areas. Strong relationships were found between these scales and the learning of history, physics and mathematics, but the relationships were much less strong in subject areas such as chemistry, biology and English. Clearly these types of differential findings indicate a need for much more intensive, in-depth study of the relationships between classroom social climate and student learning.

Using Measures of Environment in Research

How can measures of the learning environment be best used in evaluative research? A major concern of researchers is the use of appropriate measures for comparing various educational methods, treatments, curricula, student groups and teaching strategies to name just a few of the hundreds of research questions of this type. The high inference measures described in this chapter have proven to be extremely sensitive in tapping differences among groups – to the extent that these measures of the learning environment have often been the only source of statistically significant comparisons. Researchers are learning increasingly that valid and useful differences among educational treatments are often reflected first and most strongly in changes in students' perceptions of their learning environment. Later, and in moderated form, these changes also show up in terms of student learning and other such indicators of outcome. Thus, dimensions of the MCI, LEI, and CAQ are useful additions to the types of instruments typically used in evaluative research.

The sensitivity of the LEI-type instruments in *post hoc* analysis should not be an excuse for weak experimental designs. Indeed, the instruments are probably most useful when administered both 'pre' and 'post' in experimental treatment. Though little work has been conducted to date on the changes in environmental perceptions as a result of intervention, such a line of inquiry should become a preoccupation in the future. The usefulness of documenting how children's feelings about their classes change as a result of curricular, organizational, or indeed, even behaviour modification methods, can hardly be denied by researchers or practitioners.

In conclusion, educators interested in affective areas of school evaluation must include in their studies measures of the learning environment itself. Cognitive, and even affective measures do not in themselves go far enough. Evaluation must take into account the group characteristics and social climate properties of groups of learners, however they may be organized in schools and beyond. Evaluators should explore the use of measures of the social climate of learning as a means of assessing the product of their educational efforts; in this case a desirable classroom climate would be a primary process goal of the school rather than a means to increase measurable learning outcomes.

11. Open Education: An Operational Definition and Validation in Great Britain and the United States

HERBERT J. WALBERG
and
SUSAN CHRISTIE THOMAS

'OPEN EDUCATION', 'the British Infant School', 'the Developmental Classroom', 'the Leicestershire Plan', 'the Integrated Day' – these phrases refer to an educational movement that began in Great Britain and is growing rapidly and generating a great deal of interest among administrators, teachers, and parents in the United States (Silberman, 1970). However, there has been very little research and evaluation on Open Education, aside from testimonials by exponents and reporters. Recently Educational Development Centre, a United States Office of Education-sponsored educational laboratory, commissioned TDR (Training-Development-Research-Associates, Inc.) to review available Open Education literature, analyse the concept into its component parts, verify the analysis with prominent Open Educators, and develop instruments for classroom measurement of its properties (Walberg and Thomas, 1971). The present paper presents a validation of the instruments in United States Open and Traditional classes and British Open classes.

Before turning to validation, a few words on the concept and a brief summary of our recent literature review are in order. It seems better to try to present a fair representation of the concept rather than advocating or attacking it. Open Education is difficult to characterize in the manner that behavioural scientists are accustomed to operationalizing concepts. For the approach is founded upon contingency and uniqueness; each student, teacher, and event is *sui generis*. The feelings and behaviour of the Open teacher cannot be easily categorized because her guiding principle is to repond as sensitively and reflectively as possible to the unique child at precise moments in the temporal stream and situational Gestalt of her interaction with him. Also implicit in the approach is a view of the child, especially in the primary grades, as a significant decision-maker in determining the direction, scope, means and pace of his education. Open Educators hold that the teacher and the child, in complementary roles, should together fashion the child's school experience. Thus, Open Education differs from teacher-centred, child-centred, and programmed, textbook, or other materials-centred approaches in that it combines all three, with both the teacher and the child determining learning goals, materials, and activities (Gardner and Cass, 1965; Plowden, 1967; Bussis and Chittenden, 1970; Walberg and Thomas, 1971).

The Open Education movement seems to grow out of many old truths, perhaps clichés, about children and the learning process (Walberg and Thomas, 1971). But Open Educators seem to take the ideals described above seriously and practically and to teach and relate to children accordingly, instead of rationalizing and convincing themselves *ex post facto* that existing practices are consistent with such ideals. Open Education has grown out of practical experience rather than philosophical or scientific foundations. It is not a theory or system of education, but a related set of ideas and methods. Content analysis reveals that the movement resonates strongly with the educational thoughts of Rousseau in France, Tolstoy in Russia, and in America the methods used in the one-room prairie school house in the 19th century and by some Progressives during the 1920s and '30s (Walberg and Thomas, 1971). Philosophically it would rest on phenomenology rather than positivism, and the position of Open Education is antipathetic to a line of mainstream educators from Plato to programmed instruction advocates who classify the curriculum into subjects, group learners by ability, and view knowledge as represented authoritatively by the teacher or in prescribed vicarious materials of instruction (Walberg, 1971). Their point of view is far more consonant with developmental, humanistic, and clinical psychology than with the branches that have been most influential in education, connectionism, behaviourism, and psychometrics.

The foregoing description of the assumptions and nature of Open Education does not immediately suggest operational definitions of its components. The analytic writings found most useful for this purpose are by Barth (1970), Bussis and Chittenden (1970), and Rathbone (1970). Bussis and Chittenden, from interviews with Open Education teachers, identified 10 distinctive themes of the movement. While these themes seemed most promising for scale construction, a review of Barth, Rathbone, and 16 other informed writers suggested that the Bussis-Chittenden themes had to be transformed somewhat and reduced to eight (Walberg and Thomas, 1971). It seemed that not only would the eight themes be distinguishable from one another but would also distinguish Open from Traditional Education. The next section describes the themes and how the scales were constructed.

Method

Instrument Development

The major works on Open Education were scanned for concrete examples of the eight themes listed in Table 26. Those found were recorded verbatim under each theme (Walberg and Thomas, 1971, Appendix A, pp. 1–76). Based on the quotations, 106 specific, explicit statements were drafted which were intended to define explicitly Open classroom characteristics (see Table 26 for examples). A total of 29 nationally prominent Open Educators responded to a request to agree or disagree with statements and to criticise and to suggest changes for any they found deficient. From their reactions, the original list was revised and 50 items were selected for inclusion on an Observation Rating Scale and parallel Teacher Questionnaire. The number of items for each theme reflects the attention given to the theme in the original writers and the extent of agreement by the panel of experts as well as meeting the criterion of possible observability; for example, half the items are related to Provisioning because it is so strongly emphasized by Open Educators and also because it can be more readily observed. To diminish response set in drafting the final set of scales, some items were stated negatively so that agreement would imply Traditional classroom characteristics.

Observers

The observations in the United States were done by 14 college-educated women ranging in age from early 20s to mid 30s. Eleven of them had applied for part-time work at Educational Development Centre or had responded to an advertisement posted at a job bulletin board frequented by wives of Harvard graduate students. The other three were already working on the project which led up to this data collection. One of the three, who had been responsible for the pilot testing of the instruments, trained the other 13 observers in the use of the Observation Rating Scale.

The training covered a total of two days. All observers were gathered for the first full day session; they were apprised of the kinds of situations they would be entering and instructed in what behaviour was expected of them. However, they were not informed of the differences between Open and Traditional education; neither were they told which sample classes were designated Open and Traditional; and an effort was made throughout the training

TABLE 26: *Eight Open Education themes and their item representation on the rating scale and questionnaire*

SAMPLE ITEMS	NUMBER OF ITEMS	CORRELATION BETWEEN QUESTIONNAIRE AND OBSERVATION
1. *Provisioning for Learning:* Manipulative materials are supplied in great diversity and range with little replication, i.e. not class sets. Children move freely about the room without asking permission. Talking among children is encouraged. The teacher does group children by ability according to tests or norms.* Children generally group and re-group themselves through their own choices.	25	·81***
2. *Humaneness, Respect, Openness and Warmth:* Children use 'books' written by their class-mates as part of their reading and reference materials. The environment includes materials developed or supplied by the children. Teacher takes care of dealing with conflicts and disruptive behaviour without involving the group.* Children's activities, products, and ideas are reflected abundantly about the classroom.	4	·46***
3. *Diagnosis of Learning Events:* Teacher uses test results to group children for reading and/or maths.* Children expect the teacher to correct all their work.* Teacher gives children tests to find out what they know. To obtain diagnostic information, the teacher closely observes the specific work or concern of a child and asks immediate, experience-based questions.	4	·48***
4. *Instruction, Guidance, and Extension of Learning:* Teacher bases her instruction on each individual child and his interaction with materials and equipment. The work children do is divided into subject matter areas.* The teacher's lessons and assignments are given to the class as a whole.* Teacher bases her instruction on curriculum guides or text books for the grade level she teaches.* Before suggesting any extension or redirection of activity, teacher gives diagnostic attention to the particular child and his particular activity.	5	·60***

TABLE 26 (*cont.*)

Sample Items	Number of Items	Correlation between Questionnaire and Observation
5. *Evaluation of Diagnostic Information:* Teacher keeps notes and writes individual histories of each child's intellectual, emotional, physical development. Teacher has children for a period of just one year.* Teacher uses tests to evaluate children and rate them in comparison to their peers.* Teacher keeps a collection of each child's work for use in evaluating his development. Teacher views evaluation as information to guide her instruction and provisioning for the classroom.	5	·48***
6. *Seeking Opportunities for Professional Growth:* Teacher uses the assistance of someone in a supportive, advisory capacity. Teacher has helpful colleagues with whom she discusses teaching.	2	·18
7. *Self-Perception of Teacher:* Teacher tries to keep all children within her sight so that she can make sure they are doing what they are supposed to do.	1	·42***
8. *Assumptions about Children and Learning Process:* The emotional climate is warm and accepting. The class operates within clear guidelines made explicit. Academic achievement is the teacher's top priority for the children.* Children are deeply involved in what they are doing.	4	·11
Total and Canonical Correlation	50	·86***

* Reverse coding; throughout this paper 1, 2, and 3 asterisks respectively indicate statistical significance levels of ·05, ·01, and ·001.

and actual observing to inculcate objective attention to explicit, specific, concrete indicators of classroom processes. In the morning session, the instrument was distributed and directions for filling it out were given. The trainees completed the Observation Rating Scale after viewing a mathematics project training film in which an exceptional teacher instructs an eager class using a Traditional lesson format. After all observers completed the Rating Scale, the same observer/leader provided feedback training through group examination of each item, checking for aberrant choices and mis-interpretations, entertaining questions, and bringing the group to general consensus on each item. In the afternoon session, the observers watched a 60-minute film of an Open classroom, and then marked the Observation Scales and participated in a similar feedback session. During the following two days, each trainee completed the instrument twice more. Each made a practice observation in a Traditional classroom and a Open classroom specially selected as training sites. Inspection of the training and site data revealed no tendency for the 'naive raters' to be less accurate than the three who knew the purpose of the study.

An additional two observers were trained in London during the last two weeks of the data collection. They corresponded to their US counterparts except that one of them was British. They spent an afternoon with one of the experienced observers who had worked on the project from its inception. Together they went through the instrument carefully and talked at length about the kinds of circumstances they might run into or have difficulty coding based on the experienced observer's four weeks of observing US sites. A check of these two observers was obtained by comparing their ratings with those of the two experienced American observers with whom they shared the task of making the British observations.

Sites and Procedure

The sites for observations were selected on basis of reputation and also on the personal knowledge of the investigators. The sample was by no means random, but represented urban and suburban public and private schools with administrators and teachers co-operative enough to permit intrusive observers. An effort was made to gain access to both Open and Traditional classes with teachers regarded as excellent by outside experts and their principals, and the sample was further restricted to classes of five- to seven-year-old children in their first three years of school.

About 20 classes each of the US Open, US Traditional, and British Open (see Table 27 for exact figures) were selected. In the US, classrooms were observed in three major cities (Boston, Chicago, and New York), one small city (Cambridge, Massachusetts); several suburban towns; and one university town. In Britain, classes were visited in two major cities (London and Bristol); one university town (Cambridge); and two villages in Leicestershire (where the movement originated).

The selection of sites was made to balance roughly the number of disadvantaged to lower-class schools with the number of middle- to upper-class schools within each of the three groups (see Table 27). As would be expected from demographic data, the disadvantaged schools were concentrated in US and British inner cities. This selection was guided by informants familiar with potential sites. The socio-economic levels were later verified during interviews with principals and teachers during the observation period.

At least two different observers visited each classroom three times in the US. For economy, only two observations were made in each British classroom. In both countries, a questionnaire which paralleled the observation scales, was left with teachers during the first visit and picked up during the second visit.

The questionnaires were scored by summing the coded item responses for each scale. Each observer rating was scored the same way, and then the means of the two (for Great Britain) or three (for US) ratings were computed for the analyses. The questionnaire format was a four-point (strongly disagree, disagree, agree, strongly agree) format; and the observation rating was also a four-point scale (no evidence; weak, infrequent evidence; moderate, occasional; and strong, frequent evidence).

Results and Discussion

Cross-Method Correlations

A canonical correlation was computed between the eight observation scales and the eight questionnaire scales. The canonical correlation is ·86 (p < ·001), and six of the eight simple correlations between corresponding scales were significant (p < ·05; see Table 26). With the exception of the substantial correlation, ·81, for the Provisioning scale, the significant correlations between measurement methods for corresponding scales are moderate (from ·42 to ·60). Moderate cross-method correlations probably resulted not from lower validities, but from lower reliabilities because all scales but Provisioning had few items per scale. As might be expected under this inference, these corresponding scale correlations, when corrected for unreliability (see Table 28 for internal consistencies), are substantial

TABLE 27: *Cell sizes for analysis*

| Socioeconomic Status | Group | | | |
	United States Traditional	United States Open	Great Britain Open	Total
Higher	12	11	11	34
Lower	9	10	9	28
Total	21	21	20	62

(above ·8). Thus on six of the eight themes, the observers' perceptions appear to agree quite well with the way the teacher views her own behaviour and that of her pupils. The two scales that are non-significantly correlated across methods, Seeking and Assumptions, are relatively unreliable (see Table 28); from the item content (see Table 26), one suspects that observers could not rate these themes very easily and that the questionnaire items for these two scales might be subject to acquiescent response bias.

Multivariate and SES Effects

Table 28 shows the multivariate and univariate F-ratios for the effects of socioeconomic status (SES), educational group, and the interaction. In a multivariate sense, SES is significant for the questionnaire variables, while educational group (US Open and Traditional and GB Open and its interaction with SES are significant on both the questionnaire and observation variables. Both the multivariate and univariate F-ratios indicate that educational group has far larger effects than SES and its interaction with group. Inspections of the means reveal that teachers in higher SES schools tended to agree more often with five Open Education themes on the questionnaire, and on four of these – Provisioning, Instruction, Self Perception, and Assumptions – the observers also rated these teachers higher than teachers in lower SES schools. Since SES did not interact strongly with educational group on these four variables, it may be inferred that classes in higher SES schools, whether British or American, Open or Traditional, tend to be more 'open' (as operationalized here) than counterpart classes in lower SES schools. Indeed, since the interactions are ordinal and comparatively small and were not hypothesized, they are not reported here.

Open versus Traditional Classes

Inspection of Table 28 reveals the very great differences between educational groups on the questionnaire and observation criteria. The group differences were significant for all eight themes on both methods with one exception, observation ratings on Seeking Opportunities for Professional Growth; this more than the other themes might be difficult to rate because it may not be manifest in obvious ways in the classroom.

Aside from this exception, the scales clearly distinguish Open from Traditional classes. Figure 22 is a plot of the standardized contrasts of US and GB Open with US Traditional classes; these are the estimates of the raw differences in means divided by the within-cells standard deviations of the corresponding critieria (see Bock, 1966); thus, they measure the differences between group

TABLE 28: *F-tests for two effects and their interaction on two sets of criteria*

CRITERION		SOCIOECONOMIC STATUS	GROUP	INTERACTION
Observation Multivariate		1·5	9·4***	1·8*
Provisioning	(·97)	5·7*	79·3***	1·2
Humaneness	(·68)	2·3	30·0***	1·1
Diagnosis	(·77)	1·9	50·0***	1·5
Instruction	(·88)	4·0*	51·5***	·0
Evaluation	(·57)	·7	29·7***	3·1*
Seeking	(·59)	·4	1·2	2·4
Self-Perception	(—)	3·3*	22·4***	3·3*
Assumptions	(·41)	10·0**	7·6***	1·0
Questionnaire Multivariate		4·0***	8·7***	2·0*
Provisioning	(·90)	16·1***	48·7***	1·5
Humaneness	(·33)	1·9	25·1***	6·6**
Diagnosis	(·34)	2·8	8·0***	·2
Instruction	(·71)	13·5***	20·9***	2·3
Evaluation	(·41)	·0	22·3***	·3
Seeking	(·44)	7·2**	5·4**	3·0
Self-Perception	(—)	14·3***	14·0***	·7
Assumptions	(·22)	9·8**	3·1*	1·0

Note: Alpha internal consistency reliabilities of criteria given in parentheses; since Self-Perception has only one item, internal consistencies could not be computed for this scale; 1, 2, and 3 asterisks indicate respectively the ·05, ·01, and ·001 significance levels.

means in units of standard deviation, and the contrasts are comparable across all criteria. It can be seen that Open classes differ sharply from Traditional on five of the eight criteria – Provisioning, Humaneness, Diagnosis, Instruction, and Evaluation. Moreover, British and US Open classes are highly similar, especially on the observation criteria. British Open teachers were close to US Traditional teachers on the questionnaire scales, Seeking and Assumptions, but both Open groups are similar to one another and well differentiated from Traditional groups on the corresponding observation scales.

Conclusion
An earlier report (Walberg and Thomas, 1971) demonstrated a consistency among major analytic and descriptive writings on Open Education with respect to eight themes. Here we have found strong empirical evidence that the themes distinguish Open from Traditional teachers whether a teacher questionnaire or an observer scale are used to measure the differences between groups. Moreover, the differences between Open ond Traditional teachers are far larger

FIGURE 22: *Standardized contrasts of US and GB Open with US Traditional classes*

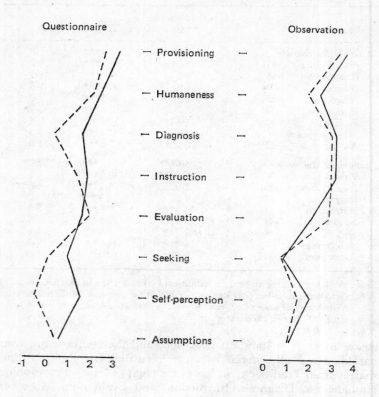

Note: US Open means are shown with a continuous line; GB Open means, with a broken line; US Traditional means are at zero point; the standard error of all contrasts is ·31; Seeking as observed is the only non-significant criterion.

than the differences found either between schools of different socio-economic strata or between schools in United States and Great Britain. Thus we have found consistencies between the conceptualization and anecdotal descriptions of Open Education on the one hand and its classroom practice as viewed by insiders and outsiders on the other.

There are many additional valid questions to ask about the concept of Open Education. Here perhaps we have identified some of the crucial elements of these questions. As pointed out at the outset, the concept has been the subject of very little evaluation and research, aside from testimonials by proponents. Before it is expanded from the limited number of extant experimental settings in this country, administrators, teachers, and parents quite properly should know if it leads to more learning, to higher levels of performance in reading, to greater self-esteem and self-determination, to the good life. We have developed some exploratory instruments that are indicative of presumably important aspects of Open classroom processes. Seeing if these processes are related to valued educational outcomes is an obvious next step for those who wish to evaluate Open Education.

12. Social Environment of Junior High and High School Classrooms

EDISON M. TRICKETT
and
RUDOLPH H. MOOS

THE PURPOSE of this paper is to describe the development of a technique to assess the psychosocial environment of the high school classroom. The classroom is a critical locus for student interpersonal and educational development, and the notion that classrooms have distinct atmospheres or climates which mediate this development has been in the working vocabulary of educators and researchers for years (e.g., Anderson, 1939; Withall, 1949, 1951).

Three dominant trends are reflected in much previous research on 'classroom climate'. First, the primary target for these assessments has been the elementary, not the high school, classroom. Second, much of the work has concentrated on constructing coding categories for *teacher verbal behaviour* as indicants of classroom atmosphere. The early work of Anderson (Anderson, 1939; Anderson and Brewer, 1945, 1946) and Withall (1949, 1951) typify this approach, and more recent work by Flanders (1960, 1965) demonstrates the increasing sophistication of this procedure. Third, the two most oft-used methodologies for gathering teacher verbal behaviour have been classroom observations (Barr, 1929; Mitzeland and Rabinowitz, 1953) and tape-recording or videotaping of classrooms (Bellak, 1964; Biddle, 1967).

The present research offers a somewhat different approach from the normative patterns suggested above. First, it focuses explicitly on the psychosocial environment of the high school classroom and conceptualizes that environment as a dynamic social system which includes not only teacher behaviour and teacher-student interaction, but student-student interaction as well. The relevance of student-student classroom interactions is suggested by the increasing importance of peer associations in adolescence. Thus the focus of conceptual concern is somewhat different from much prior work. Second, rather than using ratings of outside observers, the classroom environment in the present study is defined in terms of the shared perceptions of students in that environment. This procedure has the dual advantage of seeing the classroom through the eyes of the actual participants, and allowing one to solicit information about long-standing attributes of the classroom not as easily or parsimoniously derived by observational methods.

This general approach to assessing environments has been utilized in a wide variety of settings, including psychiatric wards (Moos and Houts, 1968) and colleges (Stern, 1970). In the area of classrooms, Walberg and Anderson (Walberg, 1968a, 1968b; Anderson and Walberg, 1968; Anderson, 1970), have utilized a somewhat similar approach. The present work differs from their work in some of the specific aspects of the classroom chosen for inclusion in the scale, and in the methodology used for item selection and test construction.

Method
The basic strategy of the project was to identify aspects of the psychosocial environment of the classroom which were salient for students and which could be conceptually grounded. In so doing, we drew on conceptual and empirical inquiry in both educational and organizational psychology (Gage, 1962; Argyris, 1964; Katz and Kahn, 1966). The social system perspective helped in delineating two primary sets of variables: (a) *interpersonal relationship variables*, including student-teacher and student-student relationships; (b) *organizational or system maintenance variables*. Explicit recognition was given to the fact that the role of teacher involved both friendship functions (interpersonal relationship variables) and authority functions (organizational maintenance variables) (see Bidwell, 1965).

Dimensions were selected as being consistent with the overriding conceptual framework and as being important to students and faculty. Once a conceptual dimension was selected and defined, test items were written which were presumable indicants of that particular dimension. For example, one such concept was that of student involvement. The question was then asked 'What might be characteristic of a classroom in which students are very involved?' Items were chosen to represent a variety of degrees of abstraction. Thus, with respect to the dimension of student involvement, the more behavioural items included 'very few students take part in the class discussions or activities' (a negatively keyed item), while the more inferential ones included 'students really enjoy this class'. After the original pool of items was constructed, they were reassigned to dimensions on the basis of independent agreement by two naive raters that they belonged in a particular dimension. If the raters did not agree on a particular item, that item was discarded.

The initial version of the Classroom Environment Scale consisted of 242 items representing 13 conceptual dimensions. On each dimension approximately half the items were keyed true and half keyed false. To each statement in the scale the respondent answers true if he believes it to be a general characteristic of this particular classroom and false if it is not a general characteristic. This version (Form A) was given to 504 students in 26 classrooms in six public high schools and one private high school. Grades 9–12 were represented as were such diverse subject matter as physics, art, and social studies. All students also took a 20-item version of the Marlowe-Crowne Social Desirability Scale (Crowne and Marlowe, 1964) so that CES items which were particularly sensitive to social desirability could be eliminated.

Analysis of the data indicated very low correlations between the individual CES items and the Social Desirability Scale (·20 or lower). For some of the dimensions, too few items were left to merit their retention in the scale. On other dimensions, some items were dropped because of redundant content and extremely high or low inter-correlation with other items on the particular dimension. As these were eliminated, a 10 dimension, 120 item scale emerged (Form B).

Because some of the subscale intercorrelations of Form B were excessive (e.g., 6 or greater) and because some important concepts were not 'captured' in the shortened Form B, additional observations and interviews with teachers and students were initiated. On the basis of this additional information, new items were written and added to Form B. This resulted in a 208 item Form C representing 13 dimensions of the classroom environment.

Form C of the CES was then administered to students in 38 high school classrooms. As before, the classrooms were selected to represent a variety of grade levels (9–12), subject matter (art, science, psychology), and kind of school (public, private, vocational). To reduce the amount of data, 22 classrooms containing 443 students were randomly selected for data analysis.

Results

The first analysis of the data included one way analyses of variance with each of the 208 test items across the 22 classrooms to determine whether each individual item discriminated between classrooms. Of the 208 items, 185 (89 per cent) discriminated significantly between classrooms at the ·05 level. In addition, 169 of the 208 (81 per cent) discriminated at the ·01 level.

Next, items were evaluated for the 13 rationally derived subscales on the following criteria: (a) each item should discriminate signifi-cantly between classrooms; (b) the overall item split (percentage in the total sample who answer it true or false) should be as close to 50–50 as possible (this should help avoid items which significantly discriminate between classrooms but which are characteristic of extreme classrooms only); (c) there should be approximately the same number of items scored true as false within each subscale so as to control for acquiescence response set; (d) each item should correlate highly with its subscale score.

The use of these criteria resulted in 13 subscales of 10–12 items per subscale. When these subscales were intercorrelated, however, several showed unacceptably high scale intercorrelations. Through dropping some dimensions and combining those with high scale intercorrelations, the current form of the CES, a nine dimension scale with 10 items per dimension, was achieved. The nine subscales of the CES, their definitions, and examples of items are given in Table 29.

Consistent with the conceptualization, the dimensions fall into interpersonal relationship variables, system maintenance and system change variables, and goal-orientation variables. Thus, order and organization, rule clarity, and teacher control are conceptualized as differentiated 'maintenance' or 'authority' functions, while innovation is seen as a system change dimension. Teacher support, involvement, and affiliation relate to 'friendship', or personal, affective teacher-student and student-student relationships. This dual role of responsibility of maintaining conditions in which a group of students can learn and providing affective support for such learning is at the heart of the role of teacher (Bidwell, 1965). Goal-orientation variables are assessed by the task orientation and competition subscales.

Table 30 summarizes the internal consistencies for the nine subscales following Stern (1970) and using Cronbach's alpha and average within-classroom item variance. Results indicate that all of the subscales show acceptable internal consistency.

Next, the nine subscale scores were obtained for each student in the 22 classrooms. Means and standard deviations of the subscale scores were then calculated for each classroom. The question was whether or not the subscales, in addition to the individual items, significantly differentiated the classrooms. The results of the one-way analyses of variance indicated that all nine subscales differentiated the 22 classrooms at better than the ·001 level. The F ratios ranged from 6·93 (affiliation) to 21·56 (innovation).

Estimated omega-squared (Hays, 1963) was used to calculate the amount of each subscale's 'total variance' accounted for by differences among the 38 classrooms. Percentages vary from 21 per cent (affiliation) to a high of 48 per cent (innovation),

TABLE 29: *Classroom Environment Scale (CES), Form D*

SUBSCALE	DESCRIPTION OF SUBSCALE AND EXAMPLES OF ITEM
1. Involvement	Measures the extent to which students pay attention to and show interest in the activities of the class. Students put a lot of energy into what they do here. (T) Students daydream a lot in this class. (F)
2. Affiliation	Measures the extent to which students work with and come to know each other within the classroom. Students in this class get to know each other really well. (T) There are groups of students who don't get along in this class. (F)
3. Support	Measures the extent to which the teacher expresses a personal interest in the students. The teacher goes out of his way to help students. (T) Sometimes the teacher embarrasses the students for not knowing the right answer. (F)
4. Task Orientation	Measures the extent to which the activities of the class are centred around the accomplishment of specified academic objectives. Almost all class time is spent on the lesson for the day. (T) This teacher often takes time out from the lesson plan to talk about other things. (F)
5. Competition	Measures the amount of emphasis on academic competition within the class. Students try hard to get the best grade. (T) Students usually pass even if they don't do much. (F)
6. Order and Organization	Measures the emphasis within the classroom on maintenance of order and the degree to which the activities of the class are well organized. Activities in this class are clearly and carefully planned. (T) The teacher often has to tell students to calm down. (F)
7. Rule Clarity	Measures the degree to which the rules for conduct in the classroom are explicitly stated and clearly understood. The teacher explains what will happen if a student breaks a rule. (T) Rules in this class seem to change a lot. (F)
8. Innovation	Measures the extent to which different modes of teaching and classroom interaction take place in the class. What students do in class is very different on different days. (T) Students do the same kind of homework almost every day. (F)

TABLE 30: *Internal consistencies for CES from D subscales across 22 classes*

SUBSCALE	ALPHA
Involvement	·85
Affiliation	·74
Support	·84
Task Orientation	·84
Competition	·67
Order and Organization	·85
Rule Clarity	·74
Teacher Control	·86
Innovation	·80

Note: Abbreviation: CES = Classroom Environment Scale

suggesting that percentages of variances accounted for by classroom differences are variable but generally substantial. Table 31 shows the percentages of variance accounted for by classroom differences.

TABLE 31: *Percentages of total variance attributable to between-classroom differences*

SUBSCALE	PERCENTAGE
Involvement	32
Affiliation	21
Support	33
Task Orientation	47
Competition	26
Order and Organization	43
Rule Clarity	28
Teacher Control	38
Innovation	48

Thus, the purpose of creating a measure of the perceived environment of the high school classroom which clearly differentiates the environments of different classrooms was achieved.

An additional analysis of the data involved intercorrelating the nine subscales to discover if any further collapsing or deletion of scales may be mandated. Table 32 shows these intercorrelations. The highest intercorrelation is ·51 which accounts for less than 26 per cent of the variance. The average intercorrelation of each subscale with the other subscales ranges from ·01 to ·31, and the average intercorrelation among all nine subscales is ·26. There are some clusters of moderately intercorrelated scales, following closely the conceptual underpinnings. Thus, the system maintenance variables intercorrelate moderately with each other, as do those scales related to teacher-student affective relationships. Since these groups of subscales are indeed differentiated aspects of the same general conceptual concern, this moderate degree of intercorrelation

TABLE 32: *CES Form D subscale intercorrelations across individuals*

Subscale	2	3	4	5	6	7	8	9
1. Involvement	·49	·45	·15	·15	·49	·19	− ·15	·44
2. Affiliation		·34	·14	·17	·30	·12	− ·09	·38
3. Support			− ·25	·05	·19	·00	− ·48	·51
4. Task Orientation				·41	·42	·41	·49	− ·21
5. Competition					·19	·26	·32	− ·02
6. Order and Organization						·37	·09	·19
7. Rule Clarity							·44	− ·09
8. Teacher Control								− ·33
9. Innovation								

Note: Abbreviation: CES = Classroom Environment Scale.

is to be expected. Thus, the nine subscales of the CES appear to measure distinct, albeit correlated, dimensions of the psychosocial environment of the high school classroom.

A final analysis of the profile stability of the CES was made over a two-week period. Two classrooms took a two-week test-retest administration of the scale, and the stability of the classroom profile on the nine subscales was computed by doing a rank-order correlation of the subscales on each class from Time 1 to Time 2. The correlations of ·91 and ·98 indicate a high degree of profile stability over a two-week period.

Sample Profiles and their Interpretation

Since a major purpose was to develop an assessment instrument for describing the psychosocial environment of the high school classroom, sample profiles of the two contrasting classrooms may be useful in concretizing the nature of the data derived from the scale. The two classroom profiles are superimposed on the same figure for purposes of comparison (see Figure 23). Each profile compares the average student subscale score to the current standardization sample of the 38 classrooms in the study.

Classroom 8 is a distributive education class of high school juniors in a rural high school. Classroom 14 is a ninth-grade mathematics class in a suburban junior high school. The profiles of these different classes provide some similarities as well as differences. Both classes, for example, report an equivalent emphasis on competition and order and organization, and an average emphasis compared to the standardization sample. Within the peer relationship variables, however, the students of Classroom 8 report more positive affiliative relationships than those in Classroom 14. Classroom 8 students are more likely to endorse such test items as 'students in this class get to know each other really well' and are

FIGURE 23. *Comparison of sample profiles of students in two classes*

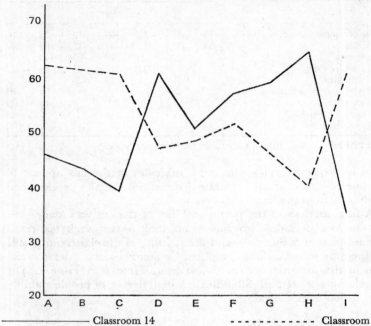

———————— Classroom 14   - - - - - - - - - - - - Classroom 8

A. Involvement	B. Affiliation	C. Support
D. Task Orientation	E. Competition	F. Order and Organization
G. Rule Clarity	H. Teacher Control	I. Innovation

more likely to rate as false such items as 'there are groups of students who don't get along in this class'. In addition, students in Classroom 8 report more involvement and innovation in the class. They look forward to coming to the class and 'dig in' when they arrive. The class offerings are perceived as more diverse, and 'new ideas are always being tried out here'. In addition, the differences in the innovation subscale indicate that in Classroom 8 'students are allowed to make up their own projects' and are not expected to follow a prescribed procedure in doing their work. Finally, students perceive a more personal and supportive relationship with the teacher of Classroom 8 than do students in Classroom 14. They are more likely to see the teacher as 'taking a personal interest in students' and less likely to perceive the teacher as 'talking down to students'.

In terms of the remaining system maintenance variables, the students in Classroom 14 report a classroom where the class sticks to classwork and seldom gets sidetracked (high task orientation), where the rules for behaviour are clear and the consequences for breaking them generally unambiguous and consistent (high rule clarity), and where the teacher maintains control in the class and 'runs a tight ship' (high teacher control). In contrast, the teacher in Classroom 8 is perceived by students as less demanding in terms of work for the class and more prone to discussing outside topics (low tack orientation). He is also more ambiguous about the rules governing classroom behaviour (low rule clarity), and is much more 'laissez faire' about classroom management than the teacher of Classroom 14 (low teacher control).

In sum, the two profiles offer similarities in some areas of the perceived environment and contrasts in others. The profiles present a differentiated picture of teacher-student relationships and in the area of student-student rapport, a large perceived difference. One can make some rather general statements about differences in teacher style, with the teacher of Classroom 14 adopting a tighter classroom management policy and being less personal with students. But such statements need qualification. For example, both class-rooms have an equivalent emphasis on order and organization. In addition, while two classrooms may differ from each other, the comparison with the standardization sample allows one to put these differences in the context of a broader perspective. The data from the sample profiles of the CES, then, demonstrate comparisons with two different frames of reference: (a) comparisons between classes themselves and (b) comparisons of each class with a wider range of classes on which the norms are derived.

Discussion

The CES which assesses nine psychosocial dimensions of the high school classroom has been developed, and the underlying conceptual and methodological rationale discussed. The moderate inter-correlations of the subscales generally fall into patterns consistent with the conceptual rationale, and the psychometric properties of the items and subscales are satisfactory. The CES does indeed discriminate among classrooms on the nine dimensions or subscales, and in so doing gives a differentiated picture of the environment of diverse classrooms. Thus, while an obvious need exists for studies on the validity of the instrument and its relation to observational technique and other questionnaires (e.g. Anderson and Walberg, 1968), the CES appears to be a promising instrument.

As one example of an approach to the assessment of social environments, the CES has important implications for the assessment and prediction of behaviour. If one can assess empirically the environment of the classroom, one can study the effects on students of being in a particular classroom for a period of time. Are there, for example, select classroom environments that increase a student's self-esteem or the amount of academic material he has learned? In short, such assessment techniques can aid in understanding the socialization effects of differing classrooms and differing teaching styles. In addition, it becomes possible to test varied assumptions about 'where' classroom environment comes from and who sets the tone. Great emphasis, for example, is often placed on the role of the teacher in creating and maintaining the atmosphere of the classroom. Much of this work involves elementary schools, however, and usually does not include the numbers or heterogeneity of students which public high school teachers see daily. Do the classroom environments of the same teacher across heterogeneous samples of students differ greatly and, if so, can this be better explained in terms of student rather than teacher characteristics? The CES can facilitate research on these kinds of questions as well.

In addition to studying the 'main effects' of diverse classrooms on students, the CES may be useful in testing interactional or transactional hypotheses about student and teacher behaviour. Trickett and Moos (1970) found, for example, that in high school classrooms a significant amount of variance in student reaction was accounted for by the interaction of student and classroom. The CES can aid in testing more specific dimensions of this interaction variance. Are students high in exploratory coping style (Edwards, 1971) more likely to be dissatisfied in classrooms high in teacher control than in low-control classrooms? Are students who differ in their need for structure likely to be differentially productive in contrasting classroom environments? These interactive questions relating to more general issues of person-environment fit (Pervin, 1968) can be profitably attacked when the environment of the classroom is systematically assessed.

On a descriptive level, the CES can provide systematic data about classroom environments differing on a number of dimensions and, by implication, generate information about the demand characteristics of different kinds of classrooms. Does subject matter, for example, necessitate differences in teaching style that may be reflected in classroom environment? What are the differential implications of class size for the psychosocial experience of students? Larger and more systematic sampling can shed light on these kinds of issues.

The development of the CES may be seen as having pragmatic implications as well. Measures of the environment of the classroom over time can provide teachers and students with the opportunity for self-analysis or analysis of how the class is doing compared with how it wants to be. Data from the CES can thus be used to formulate planned change within the classroom and to evaluate that change in terms of student perceptions of whether or not it has actually occurred. For example, Pierce, Trickett, and Moos (1972) have successfully used a similar instrument, which assesses the environment of psychiatric wards to generate discussion and produce programmatic changes in an inpatient psychiatric ward, and Moos (in press) has reported a similar project in an adolescent residential centre. Both these studies used an ideal form of the appropriate environment scale, on which respondents were asked to describe their ideal psychiatric ward or residential centre. The discrepancies between the real and ideal environments were then used as bases for deciding what aspects of the environment should be changed. A similar strategy can be applied to the CES.

Thus the CES can have theoretical, descriptive, and pragmatic implications for understanding behaviour and for changing an environment of importance to the development of adolescents. Beneath much of this discussion, however, is an additional concern – that of relating dogma to data. Several of the dimensions of the CES have consensus value labels associated with them. Teacher support, for example, seems to be a clear instance of consensus about what constitutes a 'good' teacher-student relationship. The educational correlates of such support are often more presumed than demonstrated, however, and in all probability interact with other aspects of the teacher-student relationship. The perspective here is one of encouraging investigation of the multiple and differential impacts of varied classrooms on students. The promise of the CES lies in its utility in articulating these complicated relationships.

13. The Methodology of Research on College Impact, Part Two

ALEXANDER W. ASTIN

Environment Measurement

Between-College Measures

SEVERAL INSTRUMENTS have been devised for measuring characteristics of college environments. In many ways, these instruments
resemble personality inventories designed for assessing the traits of
individuals; they include the *College Characteristics Index* (CCI) (Pace
and Stern, 1958; Stern, 1963); the *College and University Environmental Scales* (CUES) (Pace, 1960, 1963); the *Environmental Assessment
Technique* (EAT) (Astin and Holland, 1961); and the *Inventory of
College Activities* (ICA) (Astin, 1968a). Reviews and discussions of
these instruments have appeared elsewhere (Astin, 1968a; Menne,
1967). Each presents certain problems in inferring causation that
merit some discussion.

These various instruments embody three conceptually different
approaches to the assessment of environmental characteristics: The
'image' approach of the CCI and the CUES, the 'student characteristics'
approach of the EAT, and the 'stimulus' approach of the ICA.

In the image approach, observers (usually students) are asked to
report their impressions of what the college is like. The answers of
all respondents at a particular institution are aggregated or averaged
for each item, and the items are grouped into scales to form the
environmental measures. Although the CCI and CUES use between
15 and 30 items per scale, data from the ICA (Astin, 1968a) indicate
that highly reliable estimates of college 'image' factors can be
obtained with only two or three items. Apparently, when scale
scores are averaged or aggregated across relatively large numbers
of individuals, the advantages to be gained from basing each scale
on a large number of items diminish.

The student characteristics approach is based essentially on an
interpersonal theory of environmental influence. The objective is to
assess the average or modal characteristics of the students at each

institution. Although the EAT is based on only eight measures of the student body (size, ability, and six measures of personality), the possible number of relevant student characteristics actually is much larger.

The stimulus approach to measuring college environments was developed primarily because of certain interpretative difficulties connected with the image and student characteristic approaches. In the stimulus approach, the environment is seen as consisting of all the stimuli that are capable of changing the student's sensory input. A 'stimulus' is defined as 'any behaviour, event, or other observable characteristic of the institution capable of changing the student's sensory input, the existence or occurrence of which can be confirmed by independent observation' (Astin, 1968a: 5). This definition suggests that neither the college image nor the personal characteristics of the students satisfies the criterion of a potential stimulus. Thus, although the student's perception of his environment may influence his behaviour toward his fellow students, his perception alone cannot function as a stimulus for others. Similarly, the student's intelligence, attitudes, values, and other personal characteristics do not constitute stimuli by this definition, even though such traits may be manifested in certain behaviours which in turn can serve as stimuli for fellow students. The stimulus approach was developed in the belief that environmental measures based on such information would provide a better conceptual basis for interpreting causal relationships than either the image or the student characteristic approaches.

A major difficulty presented by the image approach to measuring environmental characteristics is that the student's perception of his college can be influenced not only by what the college really is like but also by how it has influenced him. Thus, if a particular image factor is found to 'affect' some student outcome, we can not be sure that we have explained the observed effect adequately simply because the student's perceptions may have been influenced by the effect itself.

A fourth category of between-institution environmental information – one which has not as yet been used in developing an inventory to measure college characteristics – is the structural and organizational characteristics of the institution. There are many such measures that might be used, both qualitative and quantitative. Among the more common qualitative measures are: type of control, religious affiliation, type of curriculum, highest degree conferred, geographic region, sex, and race of the institution. Among the many possible quantitative measures are: size of the institution, faculty-student ratio, tuition charges, endowment, operating budget, research funds, percentage of PhDs on the faculty, and library size. Such character-istics present certain interpretative difficulties because they are remote from the student and his development. From a practical standpoint, however, they are of particular importance, being more amenable to direct manipulation than are most of the measures that characterize the various environmental inventories. This fact sug-gests that we need to do research on the manner in which these structural administrative characteristics affect the college environ-ment, and in turn, the development of the student.

In one recent multi-institution longitudinal study, Astin and Panos (1969) compared image, personal characteristics, and stimulus mea-sures in terms of their effectiveness in accounting for differential institutional impact on the undergraduate student's educational and career plans. In general, the stimulus measures accounted for larger proportions of the differential institutional effects than did either the personal characteristics or the image measures. Nevertheless, some outputs were most highly dependent on personal characteristic measures; others appeared to be most highly dependent on college image measures.

This same study also compared the relative efficiency of continuous measures of environmental 'traits' (ICA factors, for example) and discrete or 'type' measures of college attributes (Protestant colleges, for example). Virtually all of the outputs were much more highly predictable from college trait measures, although, in a few cases, certain college type characteristics appeared to carry substantial weight. In particular, technological institutions and men's colleges appeared to have certain effects on student's career plans which could not be accounted for by the several trait measures used.

In short, the empirical evidence so far indicates that differential college impact, whatever the output being investigated, cannot be attributed to any single college environmental characteristic. Furthermore, while certain types of measures appear to be more effective in accounting for differential impact than others, no single class of measures derived so far seems to assess all the important institutional attributes. The lesson to be drawn from this is that investigators should use multiple measures of college characteristics rather than limit their measures to a single class of institutional attributes. At the same time, further intensive research is needed to develop improved taxonomic procedures for measuring college environments.

Within-College Measures

Some educators object to the use of between-college measures, such as those discussed in the preceding section, on the grounds that a measure of the environment of the total institution may be a poor reflection of the environment actually encountered by individual students. Since unquestionably there are many distinct subenvironments within given institutions, especially within the complex universities, measures of the 'total' institutional environment will confound these distinctions. One practical problem in using between-institution measures to describe subenvironments within institutions is to define the appropriate environmental sub-units. This task may be relatively simple in many universities, where colleges or schools are well defined, although the mere existence of such colleges or schools does not necessarily mean that they are functionally independent. In some universities, for example, the students attending the technical college have little or no contact with students or professors in any of the other colleges. On the other hand, in other universities, such students may live in dormitories and attend classes with students from a variety of other colleges. Nevertheless, if functionally independent sub-units within institutions can be identified, there seems to be no reason why these units cannot be treated as separate 'institutions' in the analysis of between-college environmental effects.

There are a great many within-college environmental experiences that cut across organizational sub-units like the colleges of schools. The methodological challenge to the researcher is to identify such experiences, devise an appropriate means for measuring them, and determine whether or not each of his subjects encountered these experiences during college. Below is just a partial list of the many types of within-college environmental experiences which can affect the student's development:

(1) The characteristics of individual professors and individual courses.
(2) His course of study.
(3) The amount of time he spends at various activities (studying, outside reading, recreation, sleeping, etc.).
(4) The type and amount of counselling or advisement he receives.
(5) His participation in special educational programmes (honours programme, year abroad, Washington semester, undergraduate research participation, etc.).
(6) His living arrangements (dormitory, fraternity house, commuting from home, private apartment).
(7) Number and types of his room-mates.
(8) His use of drugs (tranquillizers, barbiturates, hallucinogens, narcotics, etc.).
(9) The type and amount of financial aid he receives.
(10) The hours he works and the type of work he does.
(11) His marital status and number of children.

(12) The availability to him of a private automobile.

Information about most of these within-environment experiences can be obtained directly from the student by means of a follow-up questionnaire. However, self-reports present certain potential dangers, depending upon the nature of the experience. Those experiences that require relatively little interpretation, such as whether the student had a scholarship, seem to present few problems; however, reports of how many hours the student spent in outside reading, or ratings of his professors or room-mates, may be biased systematically, thereby producing interpretive ambiguities similar to those described earlier for measures of the college 'image'. In theory, of course, no student's report of his own environmental experiences can be regarded as experimentally independent of data on his input and output characteristics. In practice, however, the bias resulting from this lack of independence probably is minimal, as long as the environmental experience being reported is relatively objective and not open to misinterpretation by the student.

A related problem concerns the 'randomness' of the experience itself. The basic problem here is to determine the extent to which the student himself was directly responsible for his being exposed to the particular experience, or, in cases where exposure was determined by others, the extent to which their decision was based on a knowledge of the student's input characteristics. In some colleges, for example, the assignment of students to dormitories, classes, professors, and other experiences is virtually random or at least haphazard. In others, the student has almost complete control over where he lives, who his room-mates are, and what courses he takes. The most difficult interpretative problems arise in the case of experiences over which the student has very direct control (drug use, for example).

This discussion of environmental measurement indicates that a stepwise analysis of college impact would control successively the effects of various independent variables on the output variable in the following logical sequence:

1. Main effects of student input variables.
2. Interaction effects among student input variables.
3. Main effects of *within*-college environmental variables.
4. Interaction effects among *within*-college variables.
5. Interaction effects between student input and *within*-college environmental variables.
6. Main effects of *between*-college environmental variables.
7. Interaction effects among *between*-college environmental variables.
8. Interaction effects between student input and *between*-college environmental variables.

G

9. Interaction effects between *within*-college and *between*-college environmental variables.

Of course, the higher-order interaction effects among student input, within-college and between-college variables also can be studied, although the possible number is so large that the investigator ordinarily would limit his research to those higher-order effects that test specific hypotheses.

Methods of Data Collection

One methodological question which has received very little attention is the technique used for collecting empirical data in studies of college effects. Unfortunately, logistical considerations often limit the techniques available to an investigator. One difficulty in multi-institution studies, for example, is that the conditions for collecting data may vary systematically from institution to institution, particularly if the tests or questionnaires are administered to groups of students. Important institutional biases may be introduced by variations in the instructions given, in the manner in which students' questions are answered, in the time allotted for completing the task, and in the physical surroundings where the task is carried out. The major problem with such biases, of course, is that they affect most of the students at a given institution and thereby introduce systematic error into the inter-institutional comparisons.

Serious systematic errors of this kind probably are more likely to occur with group follow-ups or post-testing than with initial group pre-testing, since the general environmental conditions associated with freshman orientation and registration (assuming that this is the period during which the pre-test is administered) probably are much the same at most institutions.

The most serious problem with group follow-up testing at the institution is that it excludes dropouts and early graduates. As a consequence, generalizations concerning environmental influences are limited to what may be the least affected group of students. A more subtle problem is that the effects of college on the student's tendency to drop out may be confounded with college 'effects' on other outcomes. If dropout-proneness is correlated with changes in other student outcomes, then those institutions that encourage potential dropouts to stay in college also will appear to 'affect' these other outcomes. One protection for the researcher here would be to see if these other 'effects' hold up once he has controlled for the institution's dropout rate as a kind of input or control variable.

Perhaps the most realistic alternative to group follow-up testing at the institution is the mailed questionnaire sent to the student's home. This technique permits the investigator to follow-up all or a random sample of all entering students, including those who have dropped out or transferred. In one sense, the self-administered questionnaire represents the most *un*standardized of all data collection techniques. The real methodological advantage here, of course, is that these extreme variations in the conditions of administration are confounded in the inter-institutional comparisons. The reduction in precision that results from this confounding is a small price to pay in order to eliminate the systematic biases that almost inevitably result from follow-ups carried out at the institution.

Summary
The principal function of environmental measurement in research on college impact is to provide an interpretive frame of reference for any significant effects that might be observed. The generalizability and usefulness of information about college impact depends very highly on the number and kinds of the environmental measurements used. Although the most popular approaches to environmental measurement have been based on student perceptions of the environment, such measures present interpretive difficulties in view of the possibility that the effect itself may have influenced the student's perception of his institution. One possible solution to this problem is to develop environmental measures based on directly observable events rather than on perception.

Data collection in connection with multi-institutional longitudinal studies of college impact are subject to certain systematic errors which may bias the inter-institutional comparisons. Follow up data collected by means of group-administered questionnaires are especially vulnerable to such errors. Although data obtained from questionnaires mailed to the students' homes are less likely to contain systematic institutional biases, such data introduce other possible errors because of nonrespondents. Several techniques are available, however, for adjusting for nonrespondent bias in mailed follow-up surveys.

14. Students' Attitudes and College Environments

JOHN McLEISH

MEASURING THE COLLEGE ENVIRONMENT

A. The Subjective Evaluation Scale – Construction of the Index

THE WORK done in America seemed a useful starting point, especially the *College Characteristics Index* devised by Pace and Stern (1958). The main weaknesses of the Pace and Stern Index were found to be: (1) it is over long, consisting of 300 statements; (2) it refers to American college environments so that many statements are irrelevant, ambiguous and inappropriate when speaking of a College of Education in England; (3) many statements seem to be totally irrelevant to any college environment, or so it appeared to the writer; (4) the particular dimensions alleged to be evaluated by the Pace and Stern Index seemed ill-established and perhaps heterogeneous.

This Index was therefore thought of as a source of statements for a questionnaire specifically designed for the Cambridge Institute Colleges of Education, and especially with the three-year course students in mind. Ten dimensions were settled upon at this stage: (1) Student energy, (2) Concern for individuality, (3) Social commitment, (4) Staff-student relations, (5) Scholarship, (6) Curriculum courses, (7) Loyalty to college, (8) Humane regulations, (9) Group participation, (10) Lack of anxiety. One hundred statements were written down as descriptive of college climate and directed towards particular dimensions of interest in this project. In the case of each dimension, 10 statements were made, the respondent being invited to say T (true) or F (false) depending on whether the statement referred to the particular college attended. The total score on the environment index was intended to yield a valid and reliable measure of the student's view of the total college environment: the average of the student group score should measure the attitude of the given group to the particular college under consideration. Thus, it should become possible to compare each college with every other in terms of the subjective judgments given from the students' perspective. By using the average scores of the 10 dimensions, it should also be possible to give a detailed picture of each college from the same point of view.

Having carefully analysed the students' responses from each of the colleges in terms of these dimensions and having discussed the Index in relation to their own college with members of the college staff, it was decided that the names of some dimensions should be changed. It was considered that the new names were better descriptions of what was actually being measured. The revised dimensions are given below, with representative statements under each heading to convey something of the 'flavour' of the Index.

1. *Student Energy*

The 10 statements taken together refer to the enthusiasm with which students pursue their group and leisure activities, whether these be quasi-academic in character, or physical and recreative. Examples of statements (students writing T or F respectively if they thought the statement true or false about their college) are:

11. Students get so absorbed in various activities that they often lose all sense of time or personal comfort.
31. Discussions get quite heated here, with a lot of display of feeling.
91. A controversial speaker always stirs up a lot of student discussion.

2. *Concern for Individuality*

The statements belonging to this dimension assess the degree to which the given college values the expression of individual viewpoints and independent judgment – however much these may differ from the majority view or that of the staff. It is a measure of the extent to which the college is interested in students' working towards their own value systems and commitments. Colleges which, in the students' view, are more interested in conformism and established tradition will score low on this dimension. Illustrative statements are:

12. In college discussions, essays and exams, the main emphasis is on breadth of understanding, perspective and individual judgement.
32. The expression of strong personal belief or conviction is quite acceptable here.
42. The students' right to personal privacy is respected here and adequate provision is made for it.

3. *Social Commitment*

The statements here refer mainly to activities of a very specific nature, such as, work with the handicapped or field trips to slum areas, as well as some more general questions about the stress laid by the college staff on such things as responsibility for leadership, the expression of ideals in action and responsibility for social and political life. Representative statements are:

3. The emphasis on the responsibility of educated people to give leadership is very strong in this college.
23. Tutors encourage students to think about taking up unusual aspects of teaching, e.g. handicapped children, socially disadvantaged children, etc.
93. National elections generate a lot of strong feeling in this college.

4. *Staff Image*

This dimension (previously called 'staff-student relations') is concerned with three aspects of the student's picture of their teachers. A favourable image is taken to include such matters as staff concern for students as persons, staff objectivity as this is experienced by the individual student, and staff breadth of outlook. The flavour of this dimension is conveyed by such statements as:

14. The teaching staff and administration are seldom joked about maliciously or criticised in student conversations.
34. The staff of this college have a very objective and well-based view of each student's achievement and understanding.
74. Individual tutorials and pastoral care by tutors are a feature of this college.

5. *Intellectual Climate*

This was originally called 'scholarship' but, on reconsideration, 'intellectual climate' seems to be a better description. The dimension appears to be concerned primarily with two different aspects of intellectual climate: (a) the tendency for students to interest themselves in intellectual matters outside their prescribed academic programme; and (b) the variety of the intellectual stimulus actually provided by the college in such forms as general lectures of a high intellectual calibre and the availability of advanced courses of a specialized nature.

25. Long, serious intellectual discussions are common amongst the students here.
55. The college offers opportunities for hearing about recent significant advances in scientific knowledge.
85. To most students here music and art are to be studied as well as experienced.

6. *Clarity and System*

This dimension was originally referred to as 'curriculum courses', the idea being that it would provide a measure of the effective preparation of the students for teaching by an assessment of the systematic and purposeful nature of the college courses which deal with methods of teaching key subjects in schools. On consideration, and in the light of the comments made by lecturers and students, it seems as though we are dealing here with statements which refer to the ability of the teaching staff to present all their college courses in an effective way. Teaching 'effectiveness' is assumed to be based on very careful preparation of materials, clarity about objectives, enthusiasm for the subject, and the degree to which staff are able to involve students in independent and systematic study. Typical statements are:

6. Most of the lecturers are very thorough teachers who really probe into the fundamentals of their subjects.

36. Most courses are very well organized and progress systematically from week to week.

66. Assignments are usually clear and specific, making it easy for students to plan their studies effectively.

7. *Loyalty to College*
This dimension refers to the feeling of group loyalty which the college tends to produce, or not to produce, as the case may be. This does not necessarily imply that colleges which score low on this dimension have a large group of disaffected students: it may be that a low score indicates merely that the students tend to be individualists. Amongst items which count on this dimension are:

47. I would recommend this college above others to a friend or close relation without reservation.

37. Students exert considerable pressure on one another to live up to the expected codes of conduct.

87. The main college events call out a lot of enthusiasm and support from students and staff.

8. *Humane Regulations*
The naming of this dimension has presented some difficulty. It refers to the existence, or absence, of an 'adult' atmosphere in which status differences, especially as between staff and students, are minimized, and the relationships between the various college groups are easy and personal. In a college which scores high, one would expect an atmosphere of tolerance, where deviations from the strict letter of college regulations would be regarded with a certain 'tender-mindedness'. Representative statements are:

18. No one is expected to suffer in silence if some regulation happens to create a personal hardship.

48. Students are encouraged to criticise the standards and methods of teaching by college staff.
88. In most classes there is a good deal of joking and laughing.

9. *Group Participation*

This dimension measures the cohesion of the student peer group, as indicated by the fact that a great number of activities involve substantial sections of the student body. It is clearly distinguishable from dimension seven ('loyalty to college') which is concerned with loyalty to the institution. Representative statements from dimension nine are:

9. Students frequently study or prepare for examinations together.
49. It's easy to get a group together for card games, singing, going to the cinema, etc.
89. Students spend a lot of time together in common rooms, snack bars and in one another's rooms.

10. *Lack of Tension*

It will have been observed that all the statements given so far in illustration are *positive* in character. In constructing the *College Environment Index* the deliberate decision was made to use only statements *favourable* to the college. This decision was based mainly on two considerations: (i) if statements were undirectional, and the response given was either 'T' or 'F', a simple count of the 'T' responses could be taken as the measure of the 'goodness' of the environment; (ii) it was discovered that members of College showed a certain sensitivity to the idea of asking a *negative* question of students. It was believed by some lecturers that asking students to agree with an unfavourable statement might 'put ideas into their heads which weren't there already', the most probable outcome of which would be student unrest.

In spite of the fact that presenting only favourable statements would almost certainly produce a 'response set' favourable to the colleges, it was decided that, since our main purpose was to use the same instrument to *compare* the 10 college environments, no serious interference with the objectivity of the comparisons would be produced. It was believed that the effect of the 'response set' on the average score for each college would either be the same in each case, and hence could be disregarded, or would have the effect of spreading the average scores over a larger range without at all affecting rank order of the colleges. However, to test the possibility that students might simply accept the statements given, without really considering their truth or falsehood, it was decided to include a kind of 'lie scale'. The nine dimensions illustrated above are based on favourable statements only. In the case of the 10th dimension, however, only statements which were *unfavourable* to the college image were used. In this dimension the scoring scheme works in reverse: 'F' statements are counted as though they were 'T', and vice-versa; the resulting score is called 'lack of tension'. Selected statements are given below:

40. Most students get extremely tense here, especially during exam periods.
70. Many students here worry about their future prospects.
90. A substantial number of the students here take sedatives or tranquillizing pills round about exam times.

The Index was completed by 1,247 students who had completed their courses after three years of full-time study. It would appear that they had nothing to lose by answering frankly. They had been assured of the complete confidentiality of their replies. They had been told that the main object of the investigation was to delineate the reality: this should suggest by implication – and in some cases by explicit statement – how the quality of college life and college courses might be improved. They understood that their answers would be taken directly from their colleges and scored by research workers who were not concerned with them in any capacity as individuals and who had no particular association with any specific college.

B. Analysis of the Index
If we intercorrelate the scores on the 10th dimensions of the *College Environment Index* for the three-year course students (n=1,247), we find that all the correlations are positive, with the exception of the 10th dimension ('lack of anxiety'). Here correlations with the other nine dimensions are almost uniformly negative: this is true of every college and of the colleges as a whole. Reversing the signs (and direction) of the 10th dimension, we find that the correlations can be accounted for in terms of two factors. The first factor arranges the 10 dimensions in the order shown in Table 33.

This factor is clearly a general factor of approval and takes up about 60 per cent of the variance (the standardized differences between individual respondents). The saturation coefficients indicate the weights which the student body as a whole assigns to the various dimensions in defining implicitly by the pattern of their responses the qualities of a 'good' college environment. This factor can therefore be interpreted as 'general excellence' of the college environment as seen from the student viewpoint. Of the greatest significance in their view is the quality of student energy, but this is

TABLE 33: *Factor analysis of College Environment Index: first factor*

FACTOR SATURATION	DIMENSION OF INDEX
·900	Student energy
·850	Human regulations
	Social commitment
	Staff image
·800	Concern for individuality
	Clarity and system
	Loyalty to college
·750	Intellectual climate
·640	Group participation
·200	Anxiety

closely followed by humane regulations, social commitment and quality of the staff. Concern for individuality, clarity and system in the college courses and loyalty to the college as an institution tie for next place in student esteem. The intellectual climate is next in importance, followed by group participation. Lastly, and of little significance in the students' judgement is the anxiety level generated by the various demands made on students and the sanctions operating in case of failure.

When the influence of this factor is removed from the matrix by the appropriate mathematical technique, the residual correlations yield a second (bipolar) factor. This second factor arranges the dimensions as shown in Table 34.

This factor accounts for only five per cent of the total variance. It can be interpreted as a dimension which contrasts on the one hand the social satisfactions of group relationships provided by one kind of college with the concern for intellectual and professional matters shown by another kind of college. These may be regarded as the opposite poles of a dimension which classifies our sample of respondents (and of colleges) according to whether they regard a 'good' college environment as manifesting, on the one hand, high intellectual quality and an excellent training programme, but

TABLE 34: *Factor analysis of College Environment Index: second factor*

POSITIVE SATURATIONS	NAME OF DIMENSION	NEGATIVE SATURATIONS	NAME OF DIMENSION
·400	Intellectual climate	— ·300	Loyalty to college
·300	Clarity and system	— ·230	Group participation
·150	Social commitment	— ·200	Humane regulations
·130	Anxiety	— ·050	Concern for individuality
·000	Student energy		

looking outside itself for the achievement of worthwhile purposes, or on the other hand as a happy institution where the group is dedicated to worthy and humane purposes which find their main focus in the institutional group itself.

It is possible now to combine the information obtained up to this point about the college environment in a single diagram (see Figure 24).

FIGURE 24: *Classification of colleges on two criteria*

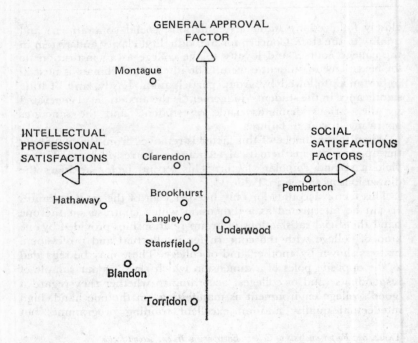

PART FIVE

Multiple Environmental Influences on Student Behaviour

THE FINAL section includes readings that have attempted to assess the impact of multiple environmental influences on behaviour. Large representative samples of Negro and Mexican-American children from kindergarten to eighth grade are compared with white children, by Jensen, in the first reading. A comprehensive battery of tests of mental abilities and scholastic achievement are used, in addition to personality variables and indices of socioeconomic and cultural disadvantage. The McDill Meyers and Rigsby contribution analyses the relative influence on academic achievement of (1) the socio-economic context of the school and (2) a number of normative dimensions of school environment, while controlling personal variables such as ability level and father's education. Classroom, peer-group and home environments are analysed in Keeves' study of a sample of Australian children in what is one of the most sophisticated pieces of environmental research yet undertaken.

Building on (a) the conceptual frameworks that have been proposed by Bloom, Walberg and Moos, (b) the statistical techniques suggested by Astin and (c) the research results reported in the

FIGURE 25

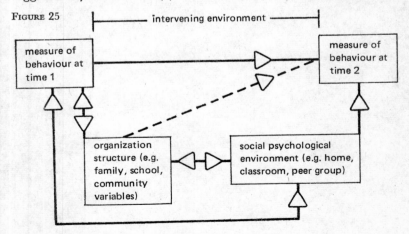

readings, Walberg and Marjoribanks, in the final contribution, have developed a basic paradigm for future environmental research. It is suggested that as a minimum, the paradigm needs to include the variables in the path diagram (Figure 25), where the single-headed arrows portray possible causal effects while double-headed arrows indicate possible correlated causal variables. The broken lines show distal measures hypothesized to be mediated through more proximal variables.

From an analysis of the path diagram, using longitudinal data involving the environmental correlates of reading development, Walberg and Marjoribanks present a mathematical model which, it is proposed, might provide the framework for the development of the study of environmental social psychology.

References
From: JENSEN, A. R. (1971). 'Do Schools Cheat Minority Children?', *Educational Research*, **14**, 1, 3–28.

From: McDILL, E. L., MYERS, E. D., and RIGSBY, L. C. (1967). 'Institutional Effects on the Academic Behaviour of High School Students', *Sociology of Education*, **40**, 181–99.

From: KEEVES, J. P. (1972). *Educational Environment and Student Achievement*. Stockholm: Almquist and Wiksell.

WALBERG, H. J., and MARJORIBANKS, K. Social Environment and Cognitive Development: Toward a Generalized Causal Model. Previously unpublished.

15. Do Schools Cheat Minority Children?

ARTHUR R. JENSEN

A KEYSTONE of public education is the promise that no child should be denied the opportunity to fulfil his educational potential, regardless of his national, ethnic, or socioeconomic background. When substantial inequalities in educational achievement are evident between large segments of the population nominally sharing the same educational system, serious questions are raised, and rightly so.

The causes of educational inequalities, in terms both of input and output, cannot be discussed very fruitfully in general terms. There are considerable regional and local differences in educational expenditures and facilities and in their distribution within local districts. In assessing the existence and degree of educational inequities, we must get down to specific cases. That is what is intended in this article. We shall take a rather close look at some of the questions and answers involved in assessing inequalities within a single Californian school system which serves three sub-populations: a majority group, which we shall refer to as Anglos, and two sizeable minorities, Negroes and Mexican-Americans. Before going into the details of this study, however, a few more general points should be reviewed.

School Comparisons of Academic Achievement

The now famous Coleman Report (Coleman *et al.*, 1966), which surveyed 645,000 pupils in more than 3,000 schools in all regions of the United States, found relatively minor differences in the measured characteristics of schools attended by different racial and ethnic groups, but very great differences in their achievement levels. The Report also argued that when the social background and attitudes of students are held constant, per pupil expenditures, pupil-teacher ratios, school facilities and curricula show very little relation to achievement. The Report concluded '. . . that schools bring little influence to bear on a child's achievement that is independent of his background and general social context' (p. 325). A critical examination of this study by Bowles and Leven (1968) led them to the conclusion that Coleman's methodology could have resulted in an underestimation to some unknown degree of the extent of the relationship between school differences and pupil achievement. They also criticise the conclusion of the Coleman Report that 'There is a small positive effect of school integration on the reading and mathematics achievement of Negro pupils after differences in the socioeconomic background of the students are accounted for' (pp. 29–30). Bowles and Levin claim that '. . . the small residual correlation between proportion white in the schools and Negro achievement is likely to be due, at least in part, to the fact that the proportion white in a school is a measure of otherwise inadequately controlled social background of the Negro student. Thus, we find that the conclusion that Negro achievement is positively associated with the proportion of fellow students who are white, once other influences are taken into account, is not supported by the evidence presented in the Report.' Here then is one critique of the Coleman Report which suggests just the opposite of the most popularly held conceptions of what was proved by the Report. Bowles and Levin argue that school effects are probably larger than suggested by the study, and racial composition of the school *per se* is a probably more negligible factor than suggested in the Report's conclusions. A smaller-scale but statistically more thoroughly controlled study by Wilson (1967) found that after controlling for other factors, the racial composition of the school had no significant direct association with Negro achievement, thus supporting the conclusion of Bowles and Levin, at least in the one California school district studied by Wilson.

But probably the most compelling argument for requiring racial balance in schools is not the direct effect of a school's racial composition *per se*, but the fact that it could lead to a greater equalization. of school facilities for majority and minority groups so that disadvantaged minorities would not be largely confined to schools with inferior resources. This may be a valid argument in some parts of the country, but one may justifiably question whether it is a cogent factor in California schools.

Consider the following evidence. A rather coarse-grained analysis of the relationship between the proportion of minority enrolment and certain school characteristics in California is made possible by the State Department of Education's recent publication of statistics on several scholastic variables for all school districts in the State. The present analysis, carried out by the writer, is based on only the total of 191 school districts in the 10 counties of the greater Bay Area.

The variables on which all school districts were ranked were: Grade 6 Reading Achievement (age 11), Grade 10 Reading (age 15), Grade 6 Median IQ, Grade 10 Median IQ, Proportion of Minority Enrolment, Per Pupil Expenditure, Teacher Salary,

Teacher-Pupil Ratio (grades four to eight), Number of Administrators per 100 Pupils, and General Purpose Tax Rate in the school district. The rank order correlations among these variables for the 191 school districts show that minority enrolment has quite negligible correlations with all the school facility variables except number of administrators per 100 pupils, and this correlation is positive. On the other hand, there is a strong negative correlation between minority enrolment and the sixth and tenth grade reading and IQ scores. The correlation matrix can be elucidated by factor analysing it, thereby reducing it to three independent components which account for most of the variance (78 per cent). This was accomplished by a varimax rotation of the first three principal components. The rotated factors are shown in Table 35. Factor I is scholastic aptitude (IQ), reading achievement and minority enrolment. Factor II represents the financial resources of the schools, with the highest loading on teacher salary. Factor III is teacher/pupil ratio and that part of per pupil expenditure not associated with Factor II. What this analysis shows most clearly is the absence of any appreciable correlation between the aptitude-achievement variables and the school district's financial outlay. If there were a substantial relationship between the financial resources and the reading achievement of the various school districts, the factors shown in Table 35 could not be so clearly separated. Note also that while minority enrolment has a negative correlation ($-\cdot82$) with Factor I (IQ-reading), it has a small positive correlation ($+\cdot19$) with Factor II (expenditures). The negative correlation ($-\cdot09$) between minority enrolment and Factor III indicates a slight disadvantage to districts with a high proportion of minorities in terms of average class size. Overall, these data suggest that there is

TABLE 35: *Rotated factor loadings for ten educational variables in 191 California school districts*

VARIABLES	FACTORS		
	I	II	III
1. Grade 6 Reading (age 11)	·95	·12	·15
2. Grade 10 Reading (age 15)	·92	·00	$-\cdot08$
3. Grade 6 IQ	·92	·13	·17
4. Grade 10 IQ	·95	·06	$-\cdot17$
5. Minority Enrolment	$-\cdot82$	·19	$-\cdot09$
6. Per Pupil Expenditure	·10	·67	·55
7. Tax Rate	·11	·75	$-\cdot15$
8. Teacher Salary	·06	·83	·17
9. Teacher/Pupil Ratio	·03	·01	·96
10. No. of Administrators	$-\cdot13$	·71	·01
Percent of Variance	42·0	22·8	13·6

no appreciable relationship between these particular school resources and minority enrolment, and if anything the correlation is in just the opposite direction to the popular belief that educational facilities are relatively inadequate in districts with a higher percentage of minority students.

Since this analysis is based on data in which the smallest unit for analysis is the school district, it permits no inference concerning the allocation of educational resources to the various schools, which probably differ in minority enrolments, within the districts. A similar analysis could be performed within a district, using the individual schools as the unit of analysis, but different indices of a school's resources would have to be used, since there would be relatively little variance on such variables as teacher salary and per pupil expenditure *within* any given school district. More fine-grained indices of the school's specific educational facilities should be included. In any case, the first and most obvious step in assessing the equality of educational facilities is to make a direct examination of the facilities, per pupil expenditures, etc. The recreational, hygienic, safety, and aesthetic aspects of the school plant should be considered no less than those facilities deemed to have more direct educational consequences, such as pupil/teacher ratio and special services.

The Misuse of National and State Norms

School boards, the public, and the press commonly misuse the published and state norms on standardized achievement tests. Schools and districts are compared against 'norms' which are intended to represent national or state averages, as if achieving a close approximation to the norms, if not exceeding them, should be the primary goal of every school system. Deviation from the norm, above or below, is commonly regarded as a credit or a discredit to the particular school system. The fallacy in this, of course, is the fact that the average level of scholastic achievement in a community is highly predictable from a number of the community's characteristics over which the local schools have no control whatsoever. A school's or district's deviation from the mean achievement predicted from a multiple regression equation based on a host of community characteristics would make much more sense than a mere comparison of the school's average with national or state norms.

Majority/Minority Comparisons within a School District

Even when a school district has equalized the educational facilities in all of its schools in terms of physical plant, amenities, teacher salaries and qualifications, per pupil expenditures, teacher/pupil ratios, special services, curriculum, and the like, the question may still be asked whether majority-minority differences in scholastic achievement are a product of more subtle and less tangible factors operating in the school situation. We have in mind, for example, such factors as racial and socioeconomic composition of the school, and different teacher attitudes and expectancies in relation to majority and minority pupils. Is there any way we can assess the degree to which schools afford unequal educational advantages to majority and minority pupils over and above what can easily be reckoned in terms of pupil expenditures and the like?

I have tried to answer this question as best as I believe it can be answered with the psychometric and statistical methodology now available and with the rather modest resources within the financial means of most school systems. Although it would be impossible to present all the technical details and results of this study within the limits of this paper, it is possible to indicate some of the methods and the most relevant results they have yielded.

The study was conducted in 1970 in a fairly large (35 schools) elementary school district of California. This school district was ideal for this kind of study for four main reasons: (1) the district's school population has substantial proportions of Negro (13 per cent) and Mexican-American (20 per cent) students; (2) the majority (Anglo) population is very close to state and national norms for Anglos in IQ, for both mean and standard deviation, and the same is true for the two minority groups in relation to norms for their respective populations in the US; (3) the schools are largely *de facto* segregated due to rather widely spaced residential clustering of the three ethnic groups, and (4) the district had made a thorough effort to provide equal educational facilities in all of its schools, if anything favouring those schools with the largest minority enrolments to whom additional federal and state funds were allocated for special compensatory programmes.

Large representative samples totalling 28 per cent of the school population from kindergarten to the eighth grade (age 13) were selected for study. A total of 6,619 children were tested; more or less equal numbers were tested at each grade. The three main ethnic classications were Anglo (N=2,453), Mexican-American (N=2,263), and Negro (N=1,853). Approximately half the sample (selected randomly with the classroom as the unit of selection) were tested by a small staff of specially trained testers, and half were tested by their regular classroom teachers. Because of the large sample sizes the tester and teacher results often differ significantly but do not differ appreciably or systematically, except that the results of teacher-administered tests consistently have somewhat greater variance and lower reliability which would tend to attenuate intercorrelations among measures and lessen the statistical significance of group differences. Parallel analyses for testers and teachers were run on all the data, which were combined when there were no significant or systematic differences between the two forms of testing. For the sake of simplicity in the present summary, only the tester results are reported here when the two sets of data were not combined.

Rationale of the Study

In terms of this study one can think of the educational process as being analogous to an industrial production process in which raw materials ('input') are converted to a specified product ('output'). The output will be a function both of the input and of the effectiveness of the process by means of which the input is converted into output. In the case of schooling, the input is what the child brings with him to school by way of his abilities, attitudes, prior learning, cultural background, and personality characteristics relevant to learning in the classroom. The school itself has relatively little, if any, control over these input variables. The school, however, can have considerable influence on one variable – prior learning – for children who are already somewhere along the educational path, and if the school's instructional programme is deficient for some children, the deficiences in prior learning in earlier grades should show up increasingly in later grades as a cumulating deficit in scholastic achievement.

Whatever else one may say about it, schooling is essentially a process whereby children are helped to acquire certain skills, which are the output of the system. The effectiveness of the process can be judged, among other ways, in terms of the relationship between input and output. Meaningful comparisons cannot be made between the output (scholastic achievement) of different pupils, classes, schools, or school districts without reference to the input variables. The main purpose of the present study is the comparison of the ouputs, i.e. educational achievements, of three categories of pupils – Anglo, Negro, and Mexican-American – when these groups are statistically equated on the input variables. In this way we can make some judgement concerning the relative efficiency of the educational process for each of the three groups. The adequacy of the statistical equating of the groups in terms of input depends upon a judicious selection of instruments for measuring the input variables. The chief aims in selecting the input control variables are (1) to represent the domain of educationally relevant abilities, personality, and home background factors as broadly as feasible, and (2) to include only those ability and background variables which are not explicitly taught by the school or are not under direct control of schools. That is to say, they should represent the raw materials that the schools have to work with. The output, on the other hand, should represent objective measures of those skills which it is the school's specific purpose to teach. These are best measured by standardized tests of scholastic achievement.

The input variables can be classified into three categories: (1) ability or general aptitude tests, (2) motivation, personality, and school-related attitudes, and (3) environmental background variables reflecting socioeconomic status, parental education, and general cultural advantages.

Input Variables

Ability Tests

Lorge-Thorndike Intelligence Test. This is a nationally standardized group-administered test of general intelligence. In the normative sample, which was intended to be representative of the nation's school population, the test has a mean IQ of 100 and a standard deviation of 16. It is generally acknowledged to be one of the best paper-and-pencil tests of general intelligence.

Figure Copying Test. The Figure Copying Test was given in grades K-6. Beyond grade six (age 11) too large a proportion of children obtain the maximum possible score (30) for the test to be useful in making group comparisons. In fact, by grades five and six group differences are very probably underestimated by this test, since a larger proportion of the higher-scoring group will obtain the maximum score and this 'ceiling' effect will prevent the group's full range of ability from being represented. The ceiling effect consequently spuriously depresses the group's mean and reduces the variance (or standard deviation). Nevertheless, this test is extremely valuable for group comparisons because it is one of the least culture-loaded tests available and successful performance on the test is known to be significantly related to readiness for the scholastic tasks of the primary grades, especially reading readiness.

Raven's Progressive Matrices. This non-verbal reasoning test, devised in England, is intended to be a pure measure of g, the general factor common to all intelligence tests. It is a highly reliable measure of reasoning ability, quite free of the influence of special abilities, such as verbal or numerical facility. It is probably the most culture-free test of general intelligence yet devised by psychologists. The test mainly gets at the ability to grasp relationships; it does not depend upon specific acquired information as do tests of vocabulary, general information, etc. The test, which is group-administered, begins with problems that are so easy that all children by third grade can catch on and solve the problems even without instructions.

Two forms of the test were used. The Coloured Progressive Matrices, which is the children's form, was used in grades three to six. The Standard Progressive Matrices were used in grades seven and eight. These begin as easily as the coloured matrices but advance in difficulty more rapidly and go up to a level appropriate for average adults. There are 60 matrix problems in all, and the subjects are encouraged to attempt all of them, without penalty for guessing.

Listening-Attention Test. In the Listening-Attention Test the child is presented with an answer sheet containing 100 pairs of digits in sets of 10. The child listens to a tape recording which speaks one digit every two seconds. The child is required to put an X over the one digit in each pair which has been heard on the tape recorder. The purpose of this test is to determine the extent to which the child is able to pay attention to numbers spoken on a tape recorder, to keep his place in the test, and to make the appropriate responses to what he hears from moment to moment. Low scores on this test indicate that the subject is not yet ready to take the Memory for Numbers test which immediately follows it. High scores on the Listening-Attention Test indicate that the subject has the prerequisite skills for taking the digit span (Memory for Numbers) test. The Listening-Attention Test thus is intended as a means for detecting students who, for whatever reason, are unable to hear and to respond to numbers read over a tape recorder. The test itself makes no demands on the child's memory, but on his ability for listening, paying attention, and responding appropriately – all prerequisites for the digit memory test that follows.

Memory for Numbers Test. The Memory for Numbers test is a measure of digit span, or more generally, short-term memory. It consists of three parts. Each part consists of six series of digits going from four digits in a series up to nine digits in a series. The first sub-test is labelled Immediate Recall (1). Here the subject is instructed to recall the series *immediately* after the last digit has been spoken on the tape recorder. The second sub-test consists of Delayed Recall (D). Here the subject is instructed not to write down his response until after ten seconds have elapsed after the last digit has been spoken. The ten-second interval is marked by audible clicks of a metronome and is terminated by the sound of a 'bong', which signals the child to write his response. The Delayed Recall condition invariably results in some retention loss. The third sub-test is the repeated series test, in which the digit series is repeated three times prior to recall; the subject then recalls the series immediately after the last digit in the series has been presented. Again, recall is signalled by a 'bong'. Each repetition of the series is separated by a tone with a duration of one second. The repeated series almost invariably results in greater recall than a single series. This test is very culture-fair for children in second grade and beyond and who know their numerals and are capable of listening and paying attention, as indicated by the Listening-Attention Test. The maximum score on any one of the sub-tests is 39, that is the sum of the digit series from four through nine.

Motivational and Personality Tests

Speed and Persistence Test (Making X's). The Making X's Test is intended as an assessment of test-making motivation. It gives an indication of the subject's willingness to comply with instructions in a group testing situation and to mobilize effort in following those instructions for a brief period of time. The wide range of individual differences among children at any one grade level would seem to reflect mainly general motivation and test-making attitudes in a group situation. The test also serves partly as an index of classroom morale, and it can be entered as a moderator variable into correlational analysis with other ability and achievement tests. Children who do very poorly on this test, it can be suspected, are likely not to put out their maximum effort on ability tests given in a group situation and therefore their scores are not likely to reflect their 'true' level of ability.

Eysenck Personality Inventory-Junior. The EPI-Junior is the children's form of the EPI for adults. It is a questionnaire designed to measure the two factors of personality which have been found to account for most of the variance in the personality domain-Extraversion and Neuroticism. The Extraversion (E) scale represents the continuum of social extraversion-introversion. High scores reflect sociability, outgoingness and carefreeness. The Neuroticism (N) scale reflects emotional instability, anxiety proneness, and the tendency to develop neurotic symptoms under stress. The Lie (L) scale is merely a validity detector consisting of a number of items which are very rarely answered in the keyed direction by the vast majority of subjects.

The EPI scales were included in the present study as a control variable because previous studies had shown the E and N scales to predict a small but significant part of the variance in scholastic performance. Because of the reading level required by the EPI, it was not given below the fourth grade.

Student Self-Report. This 21-item self-support inventory was composed mainly of items in the self concept inventory used by James Coleman in his study, *Equality of Educational Opportunity*. It reveals the student's attitudes towards school, towards himself as a student, and other attitudes affecting motivation and self-esteem. The questionnaire was administered by the classroom teachers to grades four to eight. Because of the reading level required, it was not administered below grade four.

Background Information
The Home Index. This is a 24-item questionnaire about the home environment, devised by Harrison Gough (1949). It is a sensitive composite index of the socioeconomic level of the child's family. Factor analysis of past data by Gough has shown that the 24 items fall into four categories, each of which can be scored as a separate scale. Part I (Items 6, 7, 8, 9, 10, 15, 16, 23) reflects primarily the educational level of the parents. Part II (Items 1, 2, 3, 4, 5, 13, 20, 24) reflects material possessions in the home. Part III (Items 17, 18, 21, 22) reflects degree of parental participation in middle or upper-middle class social and civic activities. Part IV (Items 11 and 19) relates to formal exposure to music and other arts.

Output Variables
Scholastic Achievement
Stanford Achievement Tests. Scholastic achievement was assessed by means of the so-called 'partial battery' of the Stanford Achievement Tests, consisting of the following sub-tests: Word Meaning, Paragraph Meaning, Spelling, Word Study Skills, Language (grammar), Arithmetic Computation, Arithmetic Concepts, and Arithmetic Applications. The Stanford Achievement battery was administered to grades one to eight.

Distinction between Aptitude and Achievement
Can we justify the separation of our tests into two categories, ability or aptitude tests versus scholastic achievement tests, and then regard the former as *input* and the latter as *output*? Do not intelligence or aptitude tests also measure learning or achievement? The answer to this question is far from simple, but I believe there are at least six kinds of evidence which justify a psychological distinction between intelligence tests and achievement tests.
(1) *Breadth of learning sampled.* The most obvious difference between tests of intelligence and of achievement is the breadth of the domains sampled by the tests. Achievement tests sample very narrowly from the most specifically taught skills in the traditional curriculum, emphasizing particularly the three Rs. The skills or learning sampled

by an intelligence test, on the other hand, represent achievements of a much broader nature. Intelligence test items are sampled from such a very wide range of potential experiences that the idea of teaching intelligence, as compared with teaching, say, reading or arithmetic, is practically nonsensical. In a culturally more or less homogeneous population the broader-based measure called 'intelligence' is more generally representative of the individual's learning capacities and is more stable over time than the more specific acquisitions of knowledge and skill classed as scholastic achievement.

(2) *Equivalence of Diverse Tests.* One of the most impressive characteristics of intelligence tests is the great diversity of means by which essentially the same ability (or abilities) can be measured. Tests having very diverse forms, such as vocabulary, block designs, matrices, number series, 'odd-man out', figure copying, verbal analogies, and other kinds of problems can all serve as intelligence tests yielding more or less equivalent results because of their high intercorrelations. All these types of tests have high loadings on the g factor, which, as Wechsler (1958, p. 121) has said, '. . . involves broad mental organization; it is independent of the modality or contextual structure from which it is elicited; g cannot be exclusively identified with any single intellectual ability and for this reason cannot be described in concrete operational terms.' We can accurately define g only in terms of certain mathematical operations: in Wechsler's words 'g is a measure of a collective communality which necessarily emerges from the intercorrelation of any broad sample of mental abilities' (p. 123). Assessment of scholastic achievement, on the other hand, depends upon tests of narrowly specific acquired skills – reading, spelling, arithmetic operations, and the like. The forms by means of which one can test any one of these scholastic skills are very limited indeed. This is not to say that there is not a general factor common to all tests of scholastic achievement, but this general factor common to all the tests seems to be quite indistinguishable from the g factor of intelligence tests.

(3) *Heritability of Intelligence and Scholastic Achievement.* Another characteristic which distinguishes intelligence tests from achievement tests is the difference between the heritability values generally found for intelligence and achievement measures. Heritability is a technical term in quantitative genetics referring to the proportion of test score variance (or any phenotypic variance) attributable to genetic factors. Determinations of the heritability of intelligence test scores range from about ·60 to ·90, with average values around ·70 to ·80 (Jensen, 1969a). This means that some 70 to 80 per cent of the variance in IQs in the European and North American Caucasian population in which these studies have been made is attributable to

genetic variance, and only 20 to 30 per cent is attributable to non-genetic or environmental variability. The best evidence now available shows a somewhat different picture for measures of scholastic achievement, which on the average have much lower heritability. A review of all twin studies in which heritability was determined by the same methods for intelligence tests and for achievement tests shows an average heritability of ·80 for the former and of only ·40 for the latter (Jensen, 1967). It is likely that scholastic measures increase in heritability with increasing grade level and that the simpler skills such as reading, spelling, and mechanical arithmetic have lower heritability than the more complex processes such as reading comprehension and arithmetic applications. The reason is quite easy to understand. Simple circumscribed skills can be more easily taught, drilled, and assessed and the degree of their mastery for any individual will be largely a function of the amount of time he spends in being taught and in practising the skill. Thus children with quite different learning abilities can be shaped up to perform more or less equally in these elemental skills.

(4) *Maturational Aspects of Intelligence.* An important characteristic of the best intelligence test items is that they clearly fall along an age scale. Items are thus 'naturally' ordered in difficulty. The Figure Copying Test is a good example. Ability to succeed on a more difficult item in the age scale is not functionally dependent upon success on previous items in the sense that the easier item is a pre-requisite component of the more difficult item. The age differential for some tasks such as figure copying and Piagetian conservation tests is so marked as to suggest that they depend upon the sequential maturation of hierarchical neural processes (Jensen, 1970). Teaching of the skills before the necessary maturation has occurred is often practically impossible, but after the child has reached a certain age successful performance of the skill occurs without any specific training or practice. The items in scholastic achievement tests do not show this characteristic. For successful performance, the subject must have received explicit instruction in the specific subject matter of the test. The teachability of scholastic subjects is much more obvious than the kinds of materials that constitute most intelligence tests and especially non-verbal tests.

Cumulative Deficit and the Progressive Achievement Gap

The concept of 'cumulative deficit' is fundamental in the assessment of majority-minority differences in educational progress. Cumulative deficit is actually an hypothetical concept intended to explain an observable phenomenon which can be called the 'progressive achievement gap' or PAG for short. When two groups show an increasing divergence between their mean scores on tests, there is potential evidence of a PAG. The notion of cumulative deficit attributes the increasing difference between the groups' means to the cumulative effects of scholastic learning such that deficiencies at earlier stages make for greater deficiencies at later stages. If Johnny fails to master addition by the second grade he will be worse off in multiplication in the third grade, and still worse off in division in rhe fourth grade, and so on. Thus the progressive achievement gap between Johnny and those children who adequately learn each prerequisite for the next educational step is seen as a cumulative deficit. There may be other reasons as well for the PAG, such as differential rates of mental maturation, the changing factorial composition of scholastic tasks which means that somewhat different mental abilities are called for at different ages, disillusionment and waning motivation for school work, and so on. Therefore I prefer the term 'progressive achievement gap' because it refers to an observable effect and is neutral with respect to its causes.

Absolute and Relative PAG. When the achievement gap is measured in raw score units or in grade scale or age scale units, it is called *absolute*. For example, we read in the Coleman Report (1966, p. 273) that in the metropolitan areas of the northwest region of the US '. . . the lag of Negro scores (in verbal ability) in terms of years behind grade level is progressively greater. At grade six, the average Negro is approximately one-and-a-half years behind the average white. At grade nine, he is approximately two-and-a-quarter years behind that of the average white. At grade 12, he is approximately three-and-a-quarter years behind the average white.'

When the achievement difference between groups is expressed in standard deviation units, it is called *relative*. That is to say, the difference is relative to the variation within the criterion group. The Coleman Report, referring to the findings quoted above, goes on to state: 'A similar result holds for Negroes in all regions, despite the constant difference in number of standard deviations.' Although the absolute white-Negro difference increases with grade in school, the relative difference does not. The Coleman Report states: 'Thus in one sense it is meaningful to say the Negroes in the metropolitan North-east are the same distance below the whites at these three grades – that is, relative to the dispersion of the whites themselves.' The Report illustrates this in pointing out that at grade six about 15 per cent of whites are one standard deviation, or one-and-a-half years, behind the white average; at grade 12, 15 per cent of the whites are one standard deviation, of three-and-a-quarter years behind the white average.

It is, of course, the absolute progressive achievement gap which is observed by teachers and parents, and it becomes increasingly obvious at each higher grade level. But statistically the proper basis for comparing the achievement differences between various subgroups of the school population is in terms of the relative difference, that is, in standard deviation units, called sigma (σ) units for short.

Cross-Sectional versus Longitudinal PAG. Selective migration, student turnover related to adult employment trends, and other factors contributing to changes in the characteristics of the school population may produce a spurious PAG when this is measured by comparisons between grade levels at a single cross-section in time. The Coleman Report's grade comparisons are cross-sectional. But where there is no reason to suspect systematic regional population changes, cross-sectional data should yield approximately the same picture as longitudinal data, which are obtained by repeated testing of the same children at different grades. Longitudinal data provide the least questionable basis for measuring the PAG. Cross-sectional achievement data can be made less questionable if there are also socioeconomic ratings on the groups being compared. The lack of any grade-to-grade decrement on the socioeconomic index adds weight to the conclusion that the PAG is not an artifact of the population's characteristics differing across grade levels. (This type of control was used in the present study reported in the following section.)

Another way of looking at the PAG is in terms of the percentage of variance in individual achievement scores accounted for by the mean achievement level of schools or districts. If there is an achievement decrement for, say, a minority group across grade levels, and if the decrement is a result of school influences, then we should expect an increasing correlation between individual students' achievement scores and the school averages.

Progressive Achievement Gap in a California School District

We searched for evidence of a PAG in our data in several ways, which can be only briefly summarized here. Separate analyses for each of the achievement tests did not reveal any striking differences in PAG, so the results can be combined without distortion of the essential results.

Mean Sigma Differences. The mean difference in sigma (standard deviation) units, based on the white group, by which Negro and Mexican-American pupils fall below the white group at each grade from one to eight is shown in Table 36. The first three columns show the sample sizes on which the sigma differences are based. The sigma differences (i.e. σ below white mean) for Negroes and Mexican-Americans shown in columns four and five is the average

TABLE 36: *Number of white sigma units by which minority group means fall below the white mean*

Grade	SAMPLE SIZE (N)			STANFORD ACHIEVEMENT TESTS	
	White	*Negro*	*Mexican*	*Negro*	*Mexican*
1	285	218	258	·25	·34
2	229	162	250	·57	·37
3	281	207	241	·83	·68
4	237	189	239	·69	·59
5	242	198	211	·75	·54
6	219	169	218	·84	·69
7	388	262	305	·71	·57
8	356	289	303	·64	·62
Mean				·66	·55

Grade	NON-VERBAL INTELLIGENCE		HOME INDEX (SES)		ADJUSTED ACHIEVEMENT MEANS	
	Negro	*Mexican*	*Negro*	*Mexican*	*Negro*	*Mexican*
1	1·07	·53	—	—	− ·09	·15
2	1·03	·70	—	—	·15	·06
3	0·98	·53	·58	1·13	·11	·05
4	0·95	·48	·38	1·18	·17	·15
5	1·05	·62	·70	1·18	·21	·10
6	1·23	·67	·47	1·36	·09	·02
7	1·13	·72	·71	1·36	·07	·08
8	1·18	·79	·77	1·34	·06	·08
Mean	1·08	·63	·60	1·26	·10	·09

of all the Stanford Achievement Tests given in each grade. Note that there is a reliable and systematic increase in the sigma difference from grade one to grade three, for both Negro and Mexican groups, after which there is no further systematic change in achievement gap. The mean gap over all grades is ·66σ for the Negroes and ·55σ for the Mexicans. By comparison, look at columns six and seven, which show the mean sigma differences for those non-verbal ability tests in our battery which do not depend in any way upon reading skill and the content of which is not taught in school; this is the average sigma difference for the Lorge-Thorndike Non-verbal IQ, Figure Copying, and Raven's Progressive Matrices. We see that the sigma differences show a slight upward trend from the lower to the higher grades. Furthermore, the sigma differences are very significantly larger for the non-verbal intelligence tests than for the scholastic achievement tests in the case of Negroes (1·08σ for non-verbal intelligence *versus* 0·66 for achievement). The Mexicans show only a slight difference between their sigma decrement in non-verbal ability and in scholastic achievement (0·63 *versus* 0·55).

If we can regard these non-verbal tests as indices of extra-scholastic learning ability, it appears then that these Negro children do relatively better in scholastic learning as measured by the Stanford Achievement Tests than in the extra-scholastic learning assessed by the non-verbal battery. In this sense, the Negro pupils, as compared with the Mexican pupils, are 'over-achievers', although the Negroes' absolute level of scholastic performance is 0.11σ below the Mexicans! For the Negro group especially, the school can be regarded as an equalizing influence: Negro pupils are closer to white pupils in scholastic achievement than in non-scholastic non-verbal abilities. The mean Negro-white scholastic achievement difference is only 61 per cent as great as the non-verbal IQ difference. This finding is exactly the opposite of popular belief. The white *versus* Mexican achievement difference is 87 per cent as great as the non-verbal IQ difference.

Is there any systematic grade trend in our indices of socioeconomic status and home environment? Columns eight and nine show the sigma differences below the white group on the composite score of Gough's Home Index, which assesses parental educational and occupational level, physical amenities, cultural advantages, and community involvement. (The Home Index was not used below grade three). There is a slight, but not highly regular, upward trend in these sigma differences for both Negro and Mexican groups, as if the students in the higher grades come from somewhat poorer backgrounds. Despite this, the sigmas for scholastic achievement (unlike the non-verbal ability tests) do not show any systematic increase from grade three to eight. Note also that on the Home Index the Mexicans, on the average, are further below the Negroes than the Negroes are below the whites. Moreover, the percentage of the Mexican children whose parents speak only English at home is 19·7 per cent as compared with 96·5 per cent for white and 98·2 per cent for Negroes. In 14·2 per cent of the Mexican homes Spanish or another foreign language is spoken exclusively, as compared with 1·1 per cent for whites and 0·5 per cent for Negroes.

Covariance Adjustments of Achievement Scores. The next step of our analysis consists of obtaining covariance adjusted means on all the achievement tests, using all the ability tests (Lorge-Thorndike Verbal and Non-Verbal IQ, Figure Copying, Raven's Matrices, Making X's, Listening-Attention, and three memory tests), along with sex and age in months, as the covariance controls. What this procedure shows, in effect, is the mean score on the achievement tests ('output') that would be obtained by the three ethnic groups if they were equated on the ability tests ('input').

Columns 10 and 11 of Table 36 show the sigma difference by

which the Negro and Mexican covariance adjusted mean falls below that of the white group. These differences are quite small for both Negroes and Mexicans (averaging 0·10 and 0·09, respectively), and they show no systematic trend with grade level. In other words, when the minority groups are statistically equated with the majority (white) group on the ability test variables, their achievement, on the average, is less than 0·1 sigma below that of the white group. On an IQ scale that would be equivalent to 1·5 points, a very small difference indeed. The adjusted decrement is statistically significant, however, which raises the question of why it should differ significantly from zero at all. The reason could be actual differences between minority and majority schools in the effectiveness of instruction, or incomplete measurement of all the input variables relevant to scholastic learning, or some lack of what is called homogeneity of regression for the three ethnic groups, which works against the covariance adjustment. We know the latter factor is involved to some extent, and some combination of all of them is most likely involved. But taken all together, the fact that the majority-minority difference in mean adjusted achievement scores is still less than 0·1σ means the direct contribution of the schools to the difference must be even smaller than this, if existent at all. Surely it is of practically negligible magnitude.

When the personality variables (the Junior Eysenck Personality Inventory) and the four scales of the Home Index are also included with the ability variables in obtaining covariance adjusted means, the ethnic differences in scholastic achievement are wiped out almost entirely. Two-thirds of the majority-minority differences (for various achievement sub-tests at various grades) are not significant at the five per cent level and are less than 0·1σ. The adjusted mean differences *between* ethnic groups are smaller than the grade-to-grade sigma differences *within* ethnic groups. From this analysis, then, the school's contribution to ethnic achievement differences must be regarded as nil. If the input variables themselves are strongly influenced by the school to the disadvantage of the minority children, we should expect to find a greater sigma difference for non-verbal IQ at grade eight (age 13) than at kindergarten. In the present study Negroes are 1·11σ below whites in non-verbal IQ in kindergarten as compared with 1·17σ in grades seven and eight – a trivial difference. Mexican children are 0·98σ below whites in non-verbal IQ at kindergarten and ·88σ below at grades seven and eight. Thus the minority children begin school at least as far below the majority children in non-verbal ability as they are by grades seven and eight. The schools have not depressed the ability level of minority children relative to the majority, but neither have they done anything to raise it. Differences in verbal IQ are slightly more likely to reflect the effects of schooling, and we note that in grades seven and eight Negroes are 1·00σ below the white mean and Mexicans are 0·90σ below.

Paired Ethnic Group Differences. The maximum discrimination that we can make between the three ethnic groups in terms of all of our 'input' variables (ability tests, personality inventories, and socio-economic indexes) is achieved by means of the multiple point-biserial correlation coefficient.

Table 37 gives the multiple point-biserial correlations between each ethnic dichotomy and all the 'input' variables – first just the ability tests and second the ability tests plus the personality inventory and socioeconomic index.

Note that the three groups are almost equally discriminable from one another in terms of the multiple correlation, especially after the personality and social background variables are added to the predictors. This is interesting, because it means that the two minority groups, though both are regarded as educationally and socio-economically disadvantaged, actually differ from one another on this composite of all input variables almost as much as each one differs from the majority group. The Negro and Mexican groups each differ from the majority group in a somewhat different way in terms of total pattern of scores, and they differ from one another almost as much. A factor analysis, shown in the next section, helps to reveal the ways in which the three groups differ from one another.

The last three columns in Table 37 show the correlation between

TABLE 37: *Point-biserial multiple correlations for 'input' variables and partial correlation for 'output' with 'input' held constant*

	'Input'			'Input'			'Output'		
				Ability + Personality + Home Index			*Stanford Achievement Minus all 'input' variables*		
	All Ability Tests								
Grade	W–N	W–M	M–N	W–N	W–M	M–N	W–N*	W–M	M–N
11	·49	·28	·29	—	—	—	—	—	—
2	·54	·47	·37	—	—	—	—	—	—
3	·54	·45	·35	·62	·59	·46	·06	·02	·07
4	·48	·38	·41	·55	·60	·55	·15	·07	·09
5	·47	·38	·27	·60	·59	·36	·13	·05	·11
6	·53	·47	·42	·69	·67	·59	·14	·11	·04
7	·52	·42	·26	·68	·70	·45	·09	− ·04	·11
8	·57	·42	·43	·65	·66	·46	·06	− ·02	− ·07
Mean	·52	·41	·36	·63	·64	·48	·11	·05	·07

* The quantized ethnic groups are White = 3, Mexican = 2, Negro = 1, so that for W–N and W–M positive correlations indicate higher achievement scores for the white group, and a positive correlation for M–N indicates higher scores for the Mexican group.

each ethnic dichotomy and the Stanford Achievement Tests, with all the 'input' variables partialled out, i.e., statistically held constant. These correlations represent the average contribution made to the ethnic discrimination by the Stanford Achievement Tests regarded independently of the 'input' variables. It can be seen that these correlations are very small indeed. For the sample sizes used here, correlations of less than 0·10 can be regarded as statistically non-significant at the five per cent level. The proportion of the total variance between the ethnic groups that is accounted for by the achievement tests is represented by the square of the correlation coefficient. Applied to the partial correlations for the Achievement Tests in Table 37, this shows how trifling are the ethnic group achievement differences after the ethnic group differences on the input variables have been controlled.

Factor Analysis of All Variables. A factor analysis (varimax rotation of the principal components having Eigen values greater than one) was carried out at each grade level on all test variables obtained at that grade level plus three others: sex, chronological age in months, and welfare status of the parent (whether receiving welfare aid to dependent children). The latter variable was added to supplement the indices of socioeconomic status (the four scales of Gough's Home Index). Since grades four, five and six had all the measures (27 variables) and the same tests were used at each of these grades, they are the most suitable part of our total sample for factor analytic comparisons. The results are essentially the same at all grade levels, although because the personality inventory and the Home Index were not used in the primary grades, and the Figure Copying Test was not used beyond grade six, not all of the factors that emerged at grades four, five and six come out at one or another of the other grades. Moreover, because of the large number of variables entering into the analysis at grades four to six, more small factors come out which, in a sense, 'purify' the main factors by partialling out other irrelevant and minor sources of variance.

Factor analyses were performed first on the three ethnic groups separately to determine if essentially the same varimax factors emerged in each group. They did. All three groups yield the same factors, with only small differences in the loadings of various tests. This finding justifies combining all three groups for an overall factor analysis of the total student sample at each grade level. This was done. Eight factors with Eigen values greater than one emerged at grades four, five and six, accounting respectively for 67 per cent, 66 per cent and 70 per cent of the total variance.

The eight principal components were rotated to approximate simple structure by the varimax criterion. In grades four, five and

H

six four substantial and clear-cut factors emerged. The remaining factors serve mainly to pull out irrelevant variance from the main factors. The four main factors that emerge are:

FACTOR I: *Scholastic Achievement and Verbal Intelligence*

VARIABLES	FACTOR LOADING		
	Gr. 4	Gr. 5	Gr. 6
Lorge–Thorndike Verbal IQ	·75	·75	·85
Word Meaning	·83	·69	·82
Paragraph Meaning	·83	·77	·89
Spelling	·82	·77	·81
Language	·82	·79	·86
Arithmetic Computation	·64	·58	·65
Arithmetic Concepts	·73	·69	·83
Arithmetic Applications	·77	·71	·85

FACTOR II: NON-VERBAL INTELLIGENCE

VARIABLES	FACTOR LOADING		
	Gr. 4	Gr. 5	Gr. 6
Lorge–Thorndike Non-verbal IQ	·61	·57	·32
Raven's Progressive Matrices	·75	·75	·55
Figure Copying	·69	·68	·41

FACTOR III: *Rote Memory Ability*

VARIABLES	FACTOR LOADING		
	Gr. 4	Gr. 5	Gr. 6
Memory Span – Immediate Recall	·85	·81	·77
Memory Span – Repeated Series	·85	·81	·86
Memory Span – Delayed Recall	·83	·79	·74

FACTOR IV: SOCIOECONOMIC STATUS

VARIABLES *Home Index:*	FACTOR LOADING		
	Gr. 4	Gr. 5	Gr. 6
1. Parental Education and Occupation	·75	·74	·77
2. Physical Amenities	·69	·77	·72
3. Community Participation	·66	·76	·75
4. Cultural Advantages	·66	·59	·66
Receives Welfare Aid to Dependent Children	− ·40	− ·34	− ·46

The remaining four minor factors are: (1) Speed, motivation, persistence as defined principally by the Making X's Test, (2) Neuroticism, (3) Extraversion, (4) Age in months. These variables, having their largest loadings on separate factors, are in effect partialled out of the major factors. The four major factors listed above are orthogonal, i.e. uncorrelated with one another, and each one is thus viewed as a 'pure' measure of the particular factor in the sense that the effects of all the other factors are held constant.

Ethnic Group Comparisons of Factor Scores. The final step was to obtain factor scores for every student on each of these four main factors. For the total sample, within each grade, these factor scores are represented on a T-score scale, i.e. they have an overall mean of 50 and a standard deviation of 10.

The ethnic group differences in Factor I do not show any systematic increase from grade four to six, thus lending no support to the existence of a cumulative deficit in the minority groups. Analysis of variance was performed on the factor scores and Scheffé's method of contrasts was used for testing the statistical significance of the differences between the means of the various ethnic groups at each grade level. The results of these significance tests are shown in Table 38. We see that in Factor I (Verbal IQ and Scholastic Achievement) both minority groups are significantly below the majority group, and Negroes are significantly below the Mexican group except in grade six, where the difference is in the same direction but falls short of significance.

On Factor II (Non-verbal Intelligence) Negroes fall significantly

TABLE 38: *The significance of ethnic group differences in mean factor scores, by Scheffé's method of contrasts*

		FACTORS			
		I	II	III	IV
Contrasts (Means)	Grade	Verbal IQ and Achievement	Non-Verbal Intelligence	Memory	Socioeconomic Status
Negro–White	4	− **	− **	− NS	− NS
	5	− **	− **	+ NS	− **
	6	− **	− **	− NS	− NS
Mexican–White	4	− **	− NS	− *	− **
	5	− **	− NS	− NS	− **
	6	− **	+ NS	− NS	− **
Mexican–Negro	4	+ *	+ **	− *	− **
	5	+ **	+ *	− *	− **
	6	+ NS	+ **	− NS	− **

* p < 0·05   NS = Not Significant
** p < 0·01

below whites and Mexicans at all grades, and the differences between Mexicans and white are non-significant at all grades. It should be remembered that this non-verbal intelligence factor represents that part of the variance in the non-verbal tests which is not common to the verbal IQ and achievement tests or to the memory tests. The Mexican-white difference is significant on that part of the ability tests variance which has most in common with scholastic achievement and is represented in Factor I.

Factor III (Rote Memory) shows no significant differences between the Negro and white groups; the Mexican group is significantly below the white at grade four and below the Negro at grades four and five. This finding is consistent with the findings of other studies that mean differences between groups of lower and middle socioeconomic status are smallest on tests of short-term memory and rote learning (Jensen, 1968b).

Factor IV (socioeconomic status) shows relatively small differences between the Negro and white groups, while the Mexican group is significantly below the other two. Again, it should be realized that we are dealing here with 'pure' factor scores which are independent of all the other variables. Thus Factor IV shows us the relative standing of the three ethnic groups in socioeconomic status when all the other variables are held constant. What these results indicate is that Negro and white children statistically equated for intelligence, achievement, and memory ability differ very little in socioeconomic status as measured by our indices, but that Mexican children, when equated on all other variables with white children or with Negro children, show a comparatively much poorer background than either the white or Negro groups. On the present measures, at least, the Mexicans must be regarded as much more environmentally disadvantaged than the Negroes, and this takes no account of the Mexican's bilingual problem. In view of this it is quite interesting that Mexican pupils on the average significantly exceed the Negro pupils in both verbal and non-verbal intelligence measures and in scholastic achievement.

Equality of Educational Opportunity: Uniformity or Diversity of Instruction?

The results of our analysis thus far fail to support the hypothesis that the schools have discriminated unfavourably against minority pupils. When minority pupils are statistically equated with majority children for background and ability factors over which the schools have little or no control, the minority children perform scholastically about as well as the majority children. The notion that poor scholastic achievement is partly a result of the pupil's ethnic minority status *per se*, implying discriminatory schooling, is thus thoroughly falsified by the present study. This does not imply that the same results would be obtained in every other school system in the country. Where true educational inequalities between majority and minority pupils exist, we should expect the present type of analyses to reveal these inequalities, and it would be surprisingif they were not found in some school systems which provide markedly inferior educational facilities for minority pupils. It should be noted, on the other hand, that the present study was conducted in a school district which had taken pains to equalize educational facilities in schools that serve predominantly majority or predominantly minority populations. The success of this equalization is evinced in the results of the present analyses.

16. Institutional Effects on the Academic Behaviour of High School Students

EDWARD L. McDILL
EDMUND D. MEYERS and
LEO C. RIGSBY

IN THE past decade an impressive array of research has been accumulated suggesting that the environment of educational institutions is important in shaping the educational aspirations, orientations, and achievement of individual students.

In reviewing the literature pertaining to 'contextual', 'climate', or 'institutional' effects on students' academic behaviour at the high school level, however, one is struck by the tendency to focus on educational or occupational aspirations as the dependent variable and the average socioeconomic composition of the school as the measure of school context. We lack systematic studies of high schools which use rigorous measures of achievement as the dependent variable and direct indicators of the normative influence of different school climates. Even the few intensive analyses of the high school as a social microcosm, concentrate on the student society, and ignore the teacher-colleague group and the degree of social integration of the two components in the school society.

The present study involves two innovations. First, a standardized measure of achievement is available for students in a national sample of 20 high schools whose overall academic performance and climates show considerable variation. Second, a number of pedagogical and social dimensions of school environment based on data obtained from both students and teachers are used as measures of school climate. Also, the methodology minimizes the likelihood of obtaining spurious contextual or climate effects.

The objective of this exploratory investigation is to assess the *relative* influence on achievement of (1) the socioeconomic context of the school and (2) a number of normative dimensions of school climate, while controlling relevant personal variables.

Method

The Sample
Data were obtained in 20 public, co-educational high schools in 1964 and 1965 from three sources:

(1) self-administered questionnaires to 20,345 students;

(2) two academic tests from *Project Talent* administered to the student bodies – one measuring aptitude for abstract reasoning and the other measuring achievement in mathematics;

(3) self-administered questionnaires to the faculty of each school – a total of 1,029 teachers.

The schools were selected in a non-random manner from seven regions of the US. The institutions varied in academic performance and demographic and social contexts, and the schools vary with respect to socioeconomic and community characteristics as well.

Measures of School Climate

As noted above, the analysis is contextual: students are characterized by a number of aspects of the school they attend and then a determination is made of how their achievement varies while controlling relevant personal and background characteristics such as scholastic ability, family SES, year-in-school, and sex.

The procedure used in developing measures of school climate is a modified version of Selvin's and Hagstrom's (1963) formulation for classifying formal groups according to many variables in order to assess group effects on the behaviour of members. Thirty-nine aggregative characteristics of the schools, based on data from both students' and teachers' questionnaires, were factor analysed and estimates of factor scores were computed for schools on each factor, permitting the results of the factor analysis to be transformed into measures of various dimensions of school climate for subsequent use in the multivariate analysis.

A list of the 39 global characteristics – all of which treat the subject as an informant, not respondent, are presented in Table 39. Twenty-three of these variables are from students' questionnaires and 16 from teachers'. The first 27 variables are scales constructed from two or more true-false items (except variable 20, a single-item indicator) which were adapted from the College Characteristics Index (Pace and Stern, 1958), and the High School Characteristics Index (Stern, 1963). Variables one to 13 are based on students' reports of both faculty and peer behaviour, and variables 14–27 are teachers' perceptions of students' and colleagues' behaviour. The remaining 12 variables are single-item indicators of school climate, . ten of which are drawn from students' questionnaires and two from questionnaires administered to teachers.

Six factors explain more than 80 per cent of the variance for 28 of the variables and more than 60 per cent for 38 of them. Thus, it is concluded that these six constructs summarize with a relatively high degree of precision the information contained in the original 39 variables.

The six factors were interpreted using the variables which have significant loadings in Table 39. Space limitations permit only a brief description of them.

Factor I. Academic Emulation

This factor is statistically more important than any other. Eleven of the 13 variables which load on it deal with topics reflecting the general academic and intellectual tone of the school environment. A school having a high positive score on this factor could be appropriately described as valuing academic excellence.

Factor II. Student Perception of Intellectualism-Estheticism

This construct is composed of nine variables which, with one exception, are 'press' scales based on students' perceptions of the environment. Only one of the nine deals specifically with achievement-competition, whereas four of them measure teacher and student pressures for intellectualism. A school with a high positive score on this factor has a climate stressing an intrinsic value on the acquisition of knowledge.

Factor III. Cohesive and Egalitarian Estheticism

This factor measures the extent to which the student social system emphasizes intellectual criteria for status (variable 37) as opposed to the ascribed criteria of family background (variable 32). It also taps the degree of social integration (variable 31) among students. Variables six and 17 have opposite loadings on this factor, indicating that schools in which the faculty have a theoretical rather than practical orientation (FP for Vocationalism) are the ones in which the student bodies value such topics as art, music, and literature. Thus a school with a high positive score has a student body which is more cohesive, more egalitarian, and more committed to intellectual matters than a school with a low score.

Factor IV. Scientism

Schools having a high positive score on this construct show a scientific emphasis. Of the first four factors, it is the most conceptually pure. Four of the five variables with significant loadings on it deal solely with the degree of scientific ferment in the school.

Factor V. Humanistic Excellence

This factor is also subject-matter specific, dealing primarily with faculty and student pressures toward creating and maintaining

TABLE 39: Rotated varimax factor matrix and communalities[a]

Variable Numbers and Descriptions[b]	FACTORS						h²
Press Scales from Students' Questionnaire:	I	II	III	IV	V	VI	
1. FP[c] for Scientism				.901			.918
2. SP[d] for Scientism				.735			.847
3. SP for Social Conformity		−.517				−.722	.865
4. SP for Aestheticism					.574		.759
5. FP for Humanism		.569			.621		.846
6. FP for Vocationalism			−.676				.745
7. FP for Enthusiasm		.935					.927
8. FP for Supportiveness		.832					.803
9. FP for Independence		.823					.945
10. SP for Intellectualism		.672					.840
11. SP for Competition-Achievement	.853						.929
12. FP for Intellectualism	.948						.978
13. FP for Competition-Achievement	.830						.932
Press Scales from Teachers' Questionnaire:	I	II	III	IV	V	VI	
14. FP for Scientism				.883			.803
15. SP for Scientism				.756			.911
16. SP for Social Conformity						−.736	.837
17. SP for Aestheticism			.526		.700		.895
18. FP for Humanism					.905		.913
19. FP for Vocationalism[e]	.510						.669
20. FP for Enthusiasm							.761
21. FP for Supportiveness[f]	.751						.136
22. FP for Independence				.628			.760
23. FP for Academic Autonomy					.870		.818
24. SP for Intellectualism	.544				.514		.932
25. SP for Competition-Achievement	.748				.536		.946

	I	II	III	IV	V	VI	h[a]
26. FP[c] for Intellectualism	.673	.483					.838
27. FP for Competition-Achievement	.641						.699
Single Items from Students' Questionnaire:							
28. Importance to students to achieve high grades	.910						.918
29. Satisfying to students to work hard on studies	.893						.879
30. Extent to which students admire brightness	.849						.814
31. Degree of social cohesion among students			.789				.823
32. Importance of family background for high social status			−.684				.785
33. Importance of being a leader in activities for high school status	−.893					−.614	.825
34. Importance of car or clothes for high social status						.607	.858
35. Importance of high grades for high social status						−.765	.809
36. Importance of being an athlete or cheerleader for high social status						.731	.792
37. Importance of knowledge of intellectual matters for high social status			.597				.936
Single Items from Teachers' Questionnaire:							
38. Dedication of teachers to developing students' intellectual skills	.627						.680
39. Dedication of teachers to importance of homework	.694						.617
Proportion of Total Variance	.223	.170	−.087	.122	.124	−.094	

a Only loadings significant at the .05 level (.483 or greater) are included.

b The values for Variables 1–27 for a given school are median school scores on the 'press' scales. The values for Variables 28–31 for a given school are percentages of students answering the items in the direction indicated. The values for Variables 32–37 for a given school are median ranks of these six items relative to each other. Finally, the values for 38–39 for a given school are percentages of teachers answering the items in the direction indicated.

c Abbreviation for Faculty Press.

d Abbreviation for Student Press.

e Variable has no significant loadings. Its highest loadings are −.407, −.416, and −.454 on Factors I, III, and V, respectively. Its only significant loading is .861 on Factor VII, which was not retained in the analysis because it is a unique factor having only one variable, Number 21, with a significant loading.

f Variable does not have a significant loading on any of the six factors.

student interest in art, humanities, social studies, and current social issues.

Factor VI. *Academically Oriented Student Status System*

In contrast to the first five factors, this one deals strictly with the social systemic aspects of school climate. Specifically, Factor VI isolates some criteria for prestige among student peers. Schools with high positive scores on it have student bodies which socially reward intellectualism and academic performance more than schools with low scores. Furthermore, high-scoring schools place less stress on participation in extra-curricular activities than do low-scoring schools.

The Measure *of Socioeconomic Context of School*

The indicator of the socioeconomic composition of schools is the proportion of students whose fathers had at least 'some college'. These percentages vary considerably from 10·8 to 80·6.

Measures of Individual Level Attributes

As noted earlier, two academic tests – Abstract Reasoning and Mathematics Achievement – are used in this analysis as measures of ability and achievement, respectively. The AR Test is a 15 item, multiple-choice instrument designed to measure the ability to determine inductively logical relationships among the elements of diagrams.

The MATH test, a 24 item, multiple-choice exam, was designed to measure achievement in mathematics through the ninth-grade level.

Since there were systematic sex and year-in-school differences in performance on the two tests, raw scores were standardized for each sex and grade category, making it unnecessary to statistically control these two variables in the analysis.

Finally, father's education is used as the indicator of the socioeconomic status of the respondent.

The Statistical Procedure

Researchers concerned with separating 'contextual' effects from 'individual' effects have been plagued with the problem of obtaining spurious results. What appear to be contextual effects may actually be statistical artifacts. Tannenbaum and Bachman (1964) have demonstrated that such spurious contextual effects are frequently obtained because the categories of the individual level variable are imprecise; consequently, they contaminate contextual effects and lead to specious findings. Likewise, if the categories of the contextual variable are imprecise, they can contaminate individual effects.

Tannenbaum and Bachman suggest two strategies to minimize this problem, and we followed both. First, use as many categories as feasible on the individual level variables. For both ability level and father's education four categories are employed. This appears to result in precise measurement of these characteristics while providing a large number of cases in each category, which is important for obtaining reliable estimates of effects of independent variables on math achievement.

Measures of the socioeconomic context of the school and the six dimensions of school climate were obtained by ranking the schools on each characteristic and then dichotomizing them at the median.

Tannenbaum's and Bachman's second strategy for minimizing spurious contextual effects is to employ multiple regression techniques which provide a thorough analysis of the relative effects of contextual and individual attributes. The statistical procedure employed here has been shown by Boyle (1966) to coincide formally with multiple regression analysis for dichotomies. It is a slightly modified version of Coleman's (1964) stochastic model developed for the multivariate analysis of attribute data. The model can be used to estimate the effects of polytomous independent attributes, either ordered or unordered, on dichotomous dependent attributes. For the multivariate case, the effect parameter for each independent attribute is an estimate of the proportion of variation in the dichotomous dependent attribute explained by that particular independent attribute while the effects of other independent attributes are controlled.

Results

Table 40 presents the zero-order effects of SES context of the school and of the six climate dimensions (obtained from factor scores) on students' math achievement. These data show an effect in the expected direction of SES context and each of the six dimensions of school climate on maths performance. In terms of relative effects, each of the climate dimensions except Factor IV is more strongly related to achievement than is SES context; the first dimension has over twice the explanatory power.

A vast array of research evidence shows that the two most powerful predictors of academic performance are family SES and intelligence, and our study is no exception (see Table 41). Both factors have important effects, but ability has substantially more explanatory power. Each of these variables is more strongly related to math achievement than any of the contextual or climate variables in Table 40. Thus, it becomes necessary to re-examine the effects of SES context and climate dimensions on achievement with ability and

TABLE 40: *Proportion of students with high scores on mathematics test by school rankings on SES context and six dimensions of school climate*

INDEPENDENT ATTRIBUTES	CATEGORIES ON INDEPENDENT ATTRIBUTES		UNWEIGHTED ESTIMATES OF EFFECT[a]
	Low	High	
SES Context			
Proportion with High Scores	·473	·564	·091
Number of Cases	(9,591)	(9,508)	
Factor I – Academic emulation			
Proportion with High Scores	·420	·621	·201
Number of Cases	(9,773)	(9,326)	
Factor II – Intellectualism – Aestheticism			
Proportion with High Scores	·439	·585	·146
Number of Cases	(8,801)	(10,298)	
Factor III – Cohesive and Egalitarian Aestheticism			
Proportion with High Scores	·452	·578	·126
Number of Cases	(9,087)	(10,012)	
Factor IV – Scientism			
Proportion with High Scores	·474	·558	·084
Number of Cases	(9,065)	(10,034)	
Factor V – Humanistic Excellence			
Proportion with High Scores	·454	·573	·119
Number of Cases	(8,857)	(10,242)	
Factor VI – Academically Oriented Status System			
Proportion with High Scores	·462	·577	·115
Number of Cases	(9,780)	(9,319)	

[a] All effect parameters are significant at the ·01 level.

family SES simultaneously controlled, since the results of Table 40 could be a function of uncontrolled variation in these two personal attributes. The relevant data for determining whether the effects of SES context and climate dimensions persist with these two individual level attributes controlled are summarized in Table 42.

As we can see in Table 42, the effect of socioeconomic composition of the school almost completely disappears. Thus, the putative influence of SES context seems primarily due to family background and scholastic ability of students.

Although controlling scholastic ability and family background reduces the effects of the educational and social school climates, each of the six retains some of its original explanatory power.

Table 43 gives (1) the effects of SES context on math performance with each climate dimension, ability, and father's education controlled and (2) the effects of each climate dimension on maths

TABLE 41: *Proportion of students with high scores on mathematics test by ability and father's education*

INDIVIDUAL ATTRIBUTES	CATEGORIES FOR INDIVIDUAL ATTRIBUTES				UNWEIGHTED ESTIMATES OF EFFECT STANDARDIZED TO DICHOTOMOUS FORM[a]
	Low			High	
	1	2	3	4	
Ability Level (AR Scores)					
Proportion with High Scores	·253	·516	·618	·778	·350
Number of Cases	(6,037)	(4,362)	(4,080)	(4,620)	
Father's Education					
Proportion with High Scores	·369	·473	·590	·685	·211
Number of Cases	(5,018)	(4,909)	(2,769)	(5,603)	

a All effect parameters are significant at the ·01 level.

performance with SES context, ability, and father's education controlled. Not only does holding constant SES context *not* reduce the relation between each climate dimension and math performance after the effects of father's education and ability are removed, but the effects of each climate dimension slightly increase while those of SES context become negative. A plausible statistical explanation of this paradox is presented by McNemar (1962) in his description of 'suppressant' variables. The application of this concept to the

TABLE 42: *Summary effects of contextual SES and climate dimensions on maths performance with ability and family background held constant*

INDEPENDENT ATTRIBUTES	CONTROLLED ATTRIBUTES[a]	WEIGHTED EFFECT ESTIMATES OF INDEPENDENT ATTRIBUTES[b]
Contextual SES	Ability level and father's education	·006[c]
Factor I	Ability level and father's education	·112
Factor II	Ability level and father's education	·077
Factor III	Ability level and father's education	·054
Factor IV	Ability level and father's education	·042
Factor V	Ability level and father's education	·048
Factor VI	Ability level and father's education	·057

a Scholastic ability and family background have approximately constant effects with each of the seven measures of school environment. The effects of ability range from ·317 to ·327 and those for father's education from ·130 to ·152.

b All effect parameters are significant at the ·01 level unless otherwise noted.

c Not significant at the ·05 level.

TABLE 43: *Summary effects of contextual SES on maths performance with climate dimensions, family background, and ability controlled; and summary effects of climate dimensions on maths performance with contextual SES, family background, and ability controlled*[a]

CLIMATE DIMENSIONS	WEIGHTED EFFECT ESTIMATES OF CLIMATE DIMENSIONS[b]	WEIGHTED EFFECT ESTIMATES OF SES CONTEXT[c]
Factor I	·127	− ·042
Factor II	·079	− ·013[e]
Factor III	·065	− ·025
Factor IV	·042	− ·003[e]
Factor V	·060	− ·025
Factor VI	·063	− ·018[d]

[a] All effect parameters are significant at the ·01 level unless otherwise noted. The independent effects of ability and family background are comparable to those reported in footnote ([a]) of Table 42.

[b] The parameters in this column represent the effects of each climate dimension on the dependent attribute with SES context, father's education, and ability simultaneously controlled.

[c] The parameters in this column represent the effects of SES context with a given climate dimension, father's education, and ability simultaneously controlled.

[d] Significant at the ·05 level.

[e] Not significant at the ·05 level.

present problem is as follows: the very slight increase in the effects of the climate dimensions on maths achievement is accounted for by the fact that a variable – SES context of the school – which has almost no relationship to maths scores (when father's education and ability are controlled), influences the relationships between the climate dimensions and the dependent attribute so that they are slightly enhanced. This is because the suppressant variable, in spite of its relationship with an independent variable, has some variation in it that correlates negatively with the criterion. This variation prevents the independent variable (i.e. a particular climate dimension) from correlating as highly with the criterion (i.e. maths performance) as would be the case if the effects of the suppressant variable were removed. Guilford (1965), in his discussion of suppressant or 'suppressor' variables, stresses that the suppressor variable may acquire a negative regression weight. In Table 43 SES context has a negative effect parameter in all six instances.

A crucial question remains unanswered by the data in Tables 42 and 43: does the prevalent climate of the school exert an influence on the achievement level of students independent of their internalized academic orientations? As stated by Blau (1960), in his formulation of structural effects, in order to isolate a structural (or

TABLE 44: *Items in the scale of personal orientation toward intellectualism-achievement*

ITEMS	PERCENTAGE[a]	r[b]	'INTELLECTUAL' RESPONSES
How respondent would use a free hour in school: (1) course; (2) athletics; (3) club or activities; (4) study hall for studying; (5) study hall not for studying.	43·3	·48	1, 4
Rank assigned to 'learning as much as possible in school' among a list of four alternatives.	53·2	·46	1, 2
How respondent would like to be remembered in school: (1) brilliant student; (2) athletic star (boys) or leader in activities (girls); (3) most popular.	33·8	·74	1
How important to respondent to receive good grades: (1) extremely important; (2) important; (3) not important.	33·9	·70	1
How satisfying to respondent to work hard on studies: (1) extremely satisfying; (2) satisfying; (3) not satisfying; (4) unpleasant.	21·9	·76	1
How much respondent admires students who are bright: (1) very much; (2) a little; (3) not at all.	61·8	·59	1

Scale Reliability[c] = ·59

a Percentages are those of a random 10 per cent sample (N = 2,053) of students in each school answering each item in the keyed or 'Intellectual' direction shown in right column of the table.

b The coefficients represent the item-total score correlation which is Phi as a proportion of its maximum value.

c Scale reliability estimate was obtained from the Kuder–Richardson Formula 20.

contextual) effect, one must demonstrate a relation between the group level attribute and a dependent variable at the individual level while the closely related characteristic for individuals is held constant.

In the present analysis, students' individual academic orientations are measured by a summated six-item binary rating scale. The relevant summary statistics for the scale are found in Table 44.

Table 45 presents the summary effects for each of the six climate dimensions with scholastic ability, family SES, and personal intellectual values simultaneously controlled. The data in this table reveal that although intellectual commitment makes a positive contribution to students' achievement above that accounted for by scholastic ability and family background (see footnote a of the table), each of the climate dimensions continues to exert an effect in the expected direction. In fact, the first dimension has an independent effect only slightly lower than that of father's education (·110 *versus* ·119). The fact that the first dimension has more effect than the other five would seem to be explicable in terms of its being the most comprehensive indicator of the academic quality of the school.

None of the six dimensions accounts for a large proportion of variation in maths achievement. However, they are of substantive importance in light of the fact that they make some contribution toward explaining achievement beyond that jointly explained by three variables which systematically have been shown in previous research to be highly correlated with academic performance – ability, father's education, and academic values.

Discussion

The results of this study indicate that, overall, student achievement is not attributable to the social class context of the school. Achievement is also not a function of a number of formal school characteristics deriving from the economic resources of the community; namely, average size of math and science classes, homogeneous grouping of students by ability, annual starting salary for teachers, and average per-pupil expenditure.

However, the results strongly suggest that the individual student's academic behaviour is influenced not only by the motivating force of his home environment, scholastic ability, and academic values,

TABLE 45: *Summary effects of climate dimensions on maths performance with ability, family background, and academic values held constant*

INDEPENDENT ATTRIBUTES	CONTROLLED ATTRIBUTES[a]	WEIGHTED EFFECT ESTIMATES OF INDEPENDENT ATTRIBUTES[b]
Factor I	Ability level, father's education and academic values	·110
Factor II	Ability level, father's education and academic values	·072
Factor III	Ability level, father's education and academic values	·048
Factor IV	Ability level, father's education and academic values	·033
Factor V	Ability level, father's education and academic values	·042
Factor VI	Ability level, father's education and academic values	·046

[a] Scholastic ability, family background, and academic values have approximately constant effects with each of the six dimensions of school climate. The effects of ability vary from ·299 to ·309; those of father's education from ·119 to ·138; and those of academic values from ·135 to ·137.

[b] All effect parameters are significant at the ·01 level.

but also by the social pressures applied by other participants in the school setting. More specifically, the findings lead to the tentative conclusion that in those schools where academic competition, intellectualism and subject-matter competence are emphasized and rewarded by faculty and student bodies, individual students tend to conform to the scholastic norms of the majority and achieve at a higher level. Although the present findings are limited in generality, because of the nature of the sample, they provide a direct assessment of the effects of the normative climates of high schools on the academic performance of students – evidence which has been lacking in earlier contextual studies. Furthermore, they are highly consistent with two findings from a 1965 national survey of the availability of educational opportunities for individuals of different racial and ethnic backgrounds conducted by the us Office of Education in 4,000 public schools (Coleman *et al.* 1967).

(1) Variations in the facilities and curriculums of the schools account for relatively little variation in pupil achievement insofar as this is measured by standard tests.

(2) A pupil's achievement is strongly related to the educational aspirations of the other students in the school.

The content and structure of the relations among the variables comprising the climate dimensions employed here will hopefully provide a focus for further research on high school climates and lead to a clear understanding of what types of educational environments are most conducive to high motivation and achievement by students of varying backgrounds.

17. Educational Environment and Student Achievement

JOHN P. KEEVES

INFORMATION WAS gathered in this investigation on the components of three educational environments, the home, the classroom, and the peer group, which were expected to influence the mathematics and science achievement and attitudes of students at the lower secondary school level.

In Figure 26 a paradigm has been given, showing the influence of the components of the educational environment on change in both achievement and attitudes. The components have been labelled sequentially to indicate that, in general, a component earlier in the sequence influenced all items that followed it.

Exceptions to this sequencing rule were that the practices of the home and classroom did not influence the structure and attitudes of the peer group. While the structural dimensions of the classroom and the peer group were assumed not to influence the attitudes of the home, reverse influences could occur. Not all causal links that were hypothesized have been shown in Figure 26 and only the main relationships have been given in order to simplify the diagram.

The Components of the Educational Environment

Each of the components of the educational environment shown in the paradigm was represented by a specific variable, selected from the many variables that were employed in this investigation. The variables chosen and the reasons for the choice made have been given below.

1. *The Structural Dimension of the Home*

Five variables were selected as being the most important associated with the structural dimension of the home.
a. Level of father's education;
b. father's occupation;
c. mother's occupation before marriage;
d. stated religious affiliation;
e. number of children in family.

FIGURE 26: *A path diagram for the educational environment*

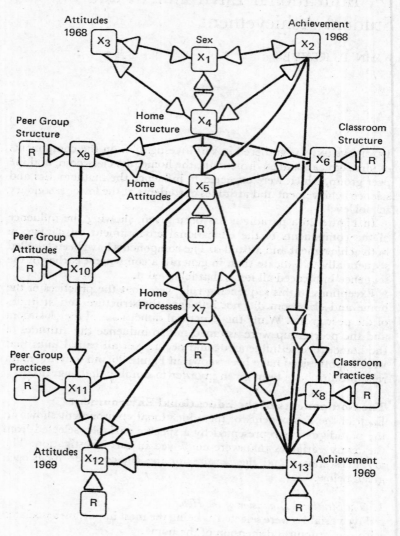

A single new variable, the first principal component, was derived from these five variables, and it has been interpreted as the cultural level of the home.

2. *The Attitudinal Dimension of the Home*

Five variables were used to characterize the attitudinal dimension of the home, and all five were found to be important.
a. The father's attitudes towards the child's present education;
b. the mother's attitudes towards the child's present education;
c. the father's ambitions for the child's future education and occupation;
d. the mother's ambitions for the child's future education and occupation;
e. the parents' hopes and aspirations for themselves.

To represent the attitudinal dimension of the home a single new variable, the first principal component, was derived from these five variables.

3. *The Process Dimension of the Home*

The data on the process dimension of the home were limited to the four characteristics, assessed in 1969, that were considered likely to influence performance at Form I level.
a. parents report favourable relations between home and school;
b. use of books and library facilities;
c. provision of help with formal school work;
d. arrangements made for tackling home assignments.

These four variables involving the practices of the home were represented by a single new variable, the first principal component of the set of measures.

4. *The Structural Dimension of the Classroom*

The following variables were selected as the important variables of the structural dimension of the two types of classroom.

Mathematics
a. Teacher is a mathematics specialist;
b. number of mathematics lectures attended by teacher in 1969;
c. number of students in the class;
d. number of teachers teaching the class regularly;
e. the average occupational status of the class.

Science
a. Teacher is a science specialist;
b. number of science lectures attended by teacher in 1969;
c. number of students in the class;
d. number of periods per week in a laboratory;

3. the average occupational status of the class.

For each of these two sets of variables a new variable was constructed, the first principal component, to represent the structural dimension of the mathematics and science classrooms.

5. *The Process Dimension of the Classroom*

Attempts were made to derive composite measures of the process dimension of the environments of the mathematics and science classrooms that were significantly related to achievement and attitudes in mathematics and science. However, the eight process variables that were constructed were largely independent of one another and did not yield a suitable compound variables. Under these circumstances it was decided to use one of the eight process variables, interaction with individual, which had been found to be significantly related to achievement, attitudes and attentiveness in both mathematics and science. This variable involving the interaction between the teacher and the individual student had been assessed largely from the replies given by the teacher to questions of whether he considered that the student was working to capacity, and whether he mainly commended or rebuked the student. The number of praise statements entered in the student's workbook was also used as a characteristic for this variable. The strength of this measure was probably due to the fact that assessments were made for each student in the sample as an individual, and not from measurements relating to the general classroom environment in which the student worked.

6. *The Structural Dimension of the Peer Group*

In order to assess the effects of the peer group on the individual student, it was decided to examine the influence of the characteristics of the three named best friends of the student. The average occupational status of the fathers of the group of friends was used as a measure of the structural dimension of the peer group in which the individual spent his leisure time.

7. *The Attitudinal Dimension of the Peer Group*

The average level of education expected by the three best friends of the student was employed as a measure of the attitudes towards education of the group of friends with whom the individual worked and played.

8. *The Process Dimension of the Peer Group*

After attempting to combine the three process variables that had been used to assess this dimension of the educational environment of the peer group, it was decided to use only one variable to represent this dimension. A measure of participation in mathematics and science activities by the friends was used to indicate the practices of the group of peers with whom the individual spent his leisure hours.

The variables selected to characterize the components of the educational environments of the home, the classroom and the peer group were, in general, significantly correlated with both initial and final achievement test scores in mathematics and science and with attitudes towards these subjects. In Table 46 the intercorrelations among these variables have been given. Since the hypothesized path model was recursive, the path coefficients could be estimated by a series of regression analyses with the variables expressed in standard firm. To identify path coefficients which were significant, step-wise multiple regression was used with the 10 per cent level of significance ($F=2 \cdot 75$) for the entry and removal of variables. In this way the paradigm was tested with empirical data and causal paths in the model which were not significant were deleted.

Achievement and Attitude towards Mathematics

In Figure 27 the results of the path analyses for the causal relationships between components of the educational environment and performance in mathematics have been presented and the estimates of the path coefficients have been shown.

The major factor influencing final achievement was initial achievement, but both the attitudes of the home and the initial attitudes of the student to mathematics made a small but statistically significant contribution. In addition, the structural characteristics of the classroom and the interaction between the teacher and the student made contributions. The results of the analysis for attitudes towards mathematics showed that initial attitudes of liking mathematics helped to determine final attitudes, but performance in mathematics did not make a significant contribution. The sex of the student was also found to be important, with boys forming more favourable attitudes. In addition, both the participation by the friends of the student in mathematics and science activities in their leisure time, and the interaction between the teacher and the student had significant effects on the attitudes towards mathematics expressed by the student. The influences of other components of the educational environment must not be rejected, since in many cases they may have acted indirectly to influence outcomes through other variables included in the path model.

Achievement and Attitudes towards Science

Figure 28 gives the results of the analyses examining the causal

TABLE 46: *Intercorrelations among environmental measures and achievement and attitudes*

N = 215	1	2	3	4	5	6	7	8	9	10	11	12	13
1. Sex of Student (boy, 1; girl, 2)		*	*	*	-20	*	*	22	*	*	-30	*	-15
2. Achievement, 1968	18a		20	43	52	54	59	21	42	51	*	83	15
3. Attitudes	25	13		*	14	45	33	*	16	48	*	26	45
4. Structure of Home, 1968	*	35	*		67	63	40	*	53	52	*	45	*
5. Attitudes of Home, 1968	20	49	19	67		63	39	26	57	43	*	56	14
6. Practices of Home, 1969	*	48	16	45	63		*	14	39	44	*	51	*
7. Structure of Classroom, 1969	13	54	13	42	44	33		*	39	17	*	63	19
8. Interaction with Individual, 1969	*	18	18	*	*	22	*		*	60	*	23	*
9. Status of Three Friends, 1969	*	35	14	53	57	39	36	14		22	*	44	*
10. Educational Expectations, 1969	30	43	22	48	52	43	57	*	60		22	46	25
11. Maths/Science Activities, 1969	*	*	*	*	*	*	*	*	37	46		*	25
12. Achievement, 1969	16	76	20	40	55	53	57	23	37	30	*		39
13. Attitudes, 1969	24	31	21	20	28	25	14	24	21	30	32	39	

Correlations for mathematics have been recorded in the upper triangle, and correlations for science in the lower triangle.

a Decimal points omitted.

* Indicates $r \leqslant 0.13$, $p > 0.05$

FIGURE 27: *Path diagram for performance in mathematics*

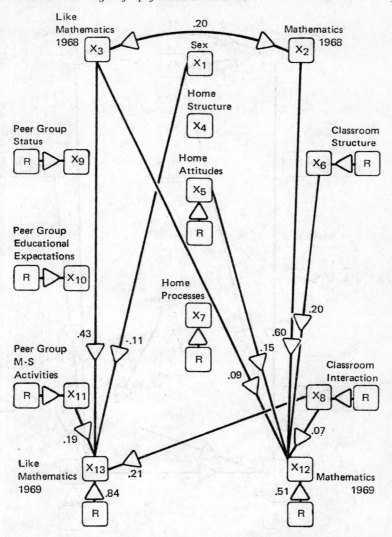

connections between the components of the educational environments of the home, the classroom, and the peer group and both achievement and attitudes to science. The factors that influenced final achievement in science were initial achievement in science and both the attitudes and practices of the home. In addition, the

FIGURE 28: *Path diagram for performance in science*

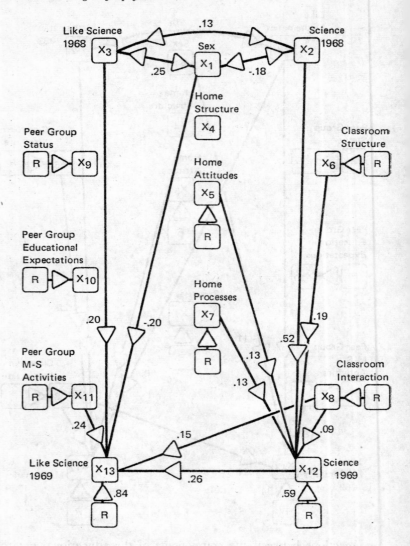

structural characteristics of the classroom and the interaction between the teacher and student also made contributions. In many respects, the factors influencing achievement in science were similar to those reported for mathematics. The major difference was that the variable, initial attitudes towards mathematics, was found to be important, and in the analyses for science the variable, attitudes towards school and school learning, was unlikely to have the same strength as would a measure of interests and attitudes towards science. However, in the analysis for performance in science, the practices of the home were influential, suggesting that the outcomes of the home practices aiding school learning differed according to the nature of the subject.

Attitudes of liking science at the end of the first year of secondary schooling were found to be influenced by similar variables to those that affected attitudes towards mathematics, except that achievement in science made a substantial contribution. This may have arisen from the fact that initial attitudes towards science were not assessed, and a proxy measure of attitudes to school and school learning was employed, which although statistically significant was not likely to have carried the same weight. As in the case of attitudes towards mathematics the interaction between the teacher and the student was important, as was the participation by the student's friends in mathematics and science activities and the sex of the student.

Variance considerations

When initial achievement in mathematics was used alone to predict final achievement in mathematics, a correlation of 0·83 was found, and this variable accounted for 68·4 per cent of the variation in the final achievement scores. However, when the significant variables characterizing the components of the educational environments of the home, the classroom and the peer group were included in the prediction equation these variables together accounted for a further 5·2 per cent of the variation in the mathematics achievement test scores. At the same time the standardized partial regression co-efficient for initial achievement in mathematics had fallen from an original correlation of 0·83 to a value of 0·60. Initial achievement was related to the treatment conditions in the home, the classroom and the peer group, and part of its apparent contribution arose from its connections with the treatment variables. While the path (standardized partial regression) coefficients gave a clear indication of the relative importance of the variables included in the analyses, it was also profitable to examine the contributions of each different component to variation in the criterion measures.

TABLE 47: *Variance accounted for by variables included in the path analysis models*

CRITERION MEASURES:	MATHEMATICS 1969		SCIENCE 1969		LIKE MATHEMATICS 1969		LIKE SCIENCE 1969	
PREDICTOR MEASURES	100bª/c	Stage Variance	100bª/c	Stage Variance	100bª/c	Stage Variance	100bª/c	Stage Variance
1. Performance								
Achievement, 1968		68·4		57·4		20·2		4·3
Attitudes 1968		·8						
Achievement 1969								12·3
2. Sex								
Home	1·5		1·7		·9		3·1	
Classroom	3·0		3·2		3·9		2·1	
Peer group		5·2		8·3	3·1	9·2	5·1	13·3
Variance within Stage 2 — Separate	4·5		4·9		7·9		10·2	
Variance within Stage 2 — Joint	·7		3·4		1·3		3·1	
Total Variance		74·4		65·7		29·2		29·9

In Table 47 the percentages of variance accounted for by the variables included in the path analysis models to predict final achievement and attitudes have been presented. In the first stage of the analyses the initial achievement and attitude measures were included in the regression equation, and in the second stage the variables characterizing the home, classroom, peer group, and the sex of the student were introduced. For each of the variables entered at the second stage the percentage of the total variance each would account for, if it were entered last into the regression equation, was calculated. In addition, the separate contributions of the variables entered into the analyses at the second stage, as well as their joint contributions, were calculated. These estimates of the proportion of variance accounted for provide a further indication of the relative importance of the variables.

In all four analyses the variables included at the second stage made a distinct although not large contribution to the total variance. The home variables accounted for variation in the final achievement measures but not in the final attitude measures. On the other hand the peer group variables accounted for variation in the attitude but not the achievement scores. The classroom variables made relatively large contributions to accounting for variation in both achievement and attitudes; but the sex of the student influenced only the attitudes, making a small contribution to attitudes towards mathematics and a more substantial one to attitudes towards science. These were the separate contributions of the variables; they also acted jointly, and in each analysis they together made a further contribution to accounting for variation in the final achievement or attitude scores. It should be noted that for all analyses, but particularly for the attitudes, there were substantial proportions of the variance unexplained.

Producing Change in the Performance Cycle

In the preceding analyses the major forces of the educational environments of the home, the classroom and the peer group that produced change in achievement and attitudes were identified. These forces were influential in modifying the performance cycle and so in causing change in level of performance. However, not all of the factors involved would appear to be malleable or open to deliberate modification. It is consequently important to distinguish between, for example, the status level of the classroom, which could prove difficult to alter, and the attitudes and practices of the home which if changed by educational counselling could have beneficial effects on the student's performance at school.

The attitudes and aspirations of the parents for the student, while dependent on past performance, influenced level of achievement in both mathematics and science. If in cases where the parental attitudes were low, both the father and the mother could be encouraged to take a greater interest in their child's education and to hold a higher level of expectation for him, the evidence from this inquiry suggested there would be gains in achievement. The practices of the home, including relationships between the home and the school, the use made of books and library facilities, and the arrangements and practices associated with school work at home, were found to have an effect on achievement in science, but not a significant effect on achievement in mathematics, when other variables were taken into account. If the level of these practices associated with the home could be raised for some students, then my evidence suggests that gains in achievement would be made in certain subjects at least.

The structural characteristics of the classroom were found to influence achievement in both mathematics and science, and while the variable employed for this component of the environment included characteristics of the teacher, it also included the average occupational status level of the class and the size of the class. The evidence from other sections of this investigation suggested that if a science class was taught by a teacher who was a specialist in his subject and who attended lectures in his subject to keep himself in touch with the work he was teaching, then the achievement of a student in science would be raised. Likewise in mathematics, if the class was taught by a regular teacher who did not have to spend long hours in preparation, then level of achievement would also increase. These characteristics of teachers of mathematics and science can be changed, and the evidence indicates that specific changes, for example, increased training and more effective planning of the school timetable, can have beneficial effects. Reducing class size, which is a commonly heard cry of teachers' organizations, would not appear to have the advantages for achievement in mathematics and science at this grade level that have been claimed.

The variable used in these analyses for the process dimension of the classroom environment was a measure of the interaction between the teacher and the student, and it was found to influence achievement and attitudes towards both mathematics and science. This measure of interaction with the individual student must be regarded as a reciprocated relationship between the teacher and the student. The evidence from this investigation suggests that in science classrooms interaction with the individual was influenced by the past performance of the student and by the status characteristics of his home. However, interaction with the individual was also strongly influenced, particularly as far as mathematics teachers were concerned, by the practices of the home.

If the student does the tasks required of him, works to capacity in the classroom and does not require reprimand then a high level of personal affiliation with the teacher is created which in turn leads to a higher level of performance by the student. Change in this relationship between the teacher and the student can be brought about by both teachers and students.

The activities engaged in by the students' peers were found to influence attitudes towards both mathematics and science, and these attitudes affected the level of achievement of the student. Certain changes in the characteristics of the peer group in which the student spent his leisure would, from the evidence of this inquiry, influence attitudes towards schooling.

These comments draw attention to components of the educational environment that can be changed, and whose modification can be expected to lead to higher performance in mathematics and science at the lower secondary school level. While these findings are necessarily limited to mathematics and science, the factors discussed above may have similar effects on subjects other than these.

Furthermore, the factors which when modified in certain directions would produce gains in achievement and the development of more favourable attitudes are not necessarily restricted to those identified in this chapter. There is a complex net of forces operating, and some factors which are amenable to modification may have indirect effects on performance at school, acting through components shown above to be influential.

18. Social Environment and Cognitive Development: Toward a generalized Causal Analysis

HERBERT J. WALBERG and
KEVIN MARJORIBANKS

Introduction

From an extensive review of longitudinal research on human development, Bloom (1964) constructed a mathematical model of human growth which, in the past decade, has helped to reorientate research related to cognitive development. The model states that $I_2 = I_1 + f(E_{2-1})$, where I represents measures of a characteristic at two points in time, and where E represents the relevant characteristics of the intervening environment. From the model Bloom hypothesized that measures of I_1 and comprehensive measures of E_{2-1} would account for nearly 100 per cent of the variance in I_2 at any period of development, and that variations in the environment have their greatest quantitative effect on a characteristic at its most rapid period of change and least effect on the characteristic during the least rapid period of change. Thus the model implied the necessity of having available refined environmental measures if accurate predictions and explanations of cognitive growth were to be made. As a result, a substantial amount of research was generated which examined environmental correlates of cognitive development which in turn influenced the growth of research into early childhood and compensatory education.

In the present study the relations between reading achievement, measured at two points in time, and the intervening home environment of three samples of English children are analysed in an examination of the Bloom model. From the analysis it is suggested that the existing Bloom paradigm requires modification, and a generalized causal model of cognitive growth is proposed.

The Bloom Model

Underlying the Bloom model of development is the 'Overlap Hypothesis' proposed by Anderson (1939), that in longitudinal studies of characteristics such as cognitive ability, the correlation between the characteristic at one age and the characteristic at another age may be thought of as a correlation between a part and a whole which includes the part. For example, the correlation between intelligence at age three and intelligence at age 18 may be seen as the correlation between intelligence at age three and intelligence at age three plus the gain in intelligence from age three to age 18. From an application of the Overlap Hypothesis to longitudinal data of intelligence test scores, Anderson and Bloom proposed that the trajectory of the scores becomes more stable and less subject to environmental influences as the child grows older. However, more recent investigations of the same longitudinal data suggest that misleading gain scores were used in the previous research and that the environment makes a small and steady, rather than diminishing, contribution to the growth of intelligence. Moreover, it has been pointed out that the Overlap Hypothesis does not take into account the possibility of genetically programmed effects occuring through-out the development of intelligence analagous to adolescent growth spurts and sexual maturation (see Cronback and Snow, 1974).

Although the challenges to the Overlap Hypothesis and thus to the Bloom model may call into question Bloom's emphasis on the influence of early environments on cognitive development, his paradigm did lead directly to the development of significant research on learning environments in the home. However, the research, which has already been described in section three of the present text and which is summarized in Table 48, was cross-sectional in design with no measures of prior characteristics being employed; thus the research did not directly test Bloom's hypothesis of longitudinal development. In his own work, Bloom (1964) inferred environmental effects, especially powerful early effects without having environmental measures available and thus he did not really test his own model. Instead he examined Anderson's hypothesis of the relation of the initial status of a characteristic to gain scores in the characteristic. But as Thorndike (1966) suggests, in a review of Bloom's work, 'the study of change is one of the trickiest areas in which to work if the one must use the fallible instruments that are psychometrician's tools'. However, the real Bloom model is con-cerned with predicting final status from initial status, and the intervening environment. Therefore the application of the model is not restricted by the limitations surrounding the use of gain scores.

A direct test of the Bloom model was made by Hanson (1971) who used Fels Research Institute data on 50 boys and 60 girls from 60 white middle-class families. IQ scores at two ages were analysed in relation to prior IQ and environmental characteristics during the intervening periods. The investigation did not support the hypothesis

TABLE 48: *Summary of studies related to the learning environment of the home which were generated from Bloom's research*

STUDY	CRITERION VARIABLE	VARIANCE ASSOCIATED WITH ENVIRONMENT	
		R^2	R_1^2
Dave (1963)	word knowledge	·62	·71
	reading	·53	·62
	arithmetic problem-solving	·50	·59
	language	·47	·58
	word discrimination	·48	·55
	spelling	·37	·40
	arithmetic computation	·31	·34
Wolf (1964)	global IQ score	·48	·55
Marjoribanks (1972)	verbal	·50	·59
	number	·50	·64
	spatial	·07	·09
	reasoning	·16	·19
Weiss (1969)	achievement motivation		
	boys	·31	·69
	girls	·26	·49
	self esteem		
	boys	·38	·64
	girls	·28	·62

R_1^2 indicates the percentage of variance accounted for by the environment, after accounting for predictor and criterion errors of measurement.

that the environment has a greater impact on younger children. The variances accounted for by the regression model were 45 and 51 per cent for five-and-a-half and nine-and-a-half-year-olds respectively. When corrected for predictor and criterion errors of measurement, the corresponding figures are 57 and 77 per cent.

Direct tests of the Bloom model have also been made in classroom studies of cognitive, affective, and behavioural performance. In a series of multivariate studies of physics test scores and intervening classroom environments it was shown (Walberg, 1972) that about 75 per cent (80 per cent corrected for criterion errors of measurement) of the post test variance could be explained by the initial test scores and the learning environment measures.

Two recent longitudinal studies examined the simultaneous effects of school and home environments on educational achievement. From a sample of 231 12-year-old boys and girls from schools in the Australian Capital Territory, Keeves (1972) obtained measures of academic achievement from tests given one year apart, as well as assessments of intervening home, peer group and classroom environments. The pre-test and environment measures accounted for 74 per cent of the post-test achievement in mathematics and 66 per cent in science (both uncorrected for measurement error). In a similar analysis using three samples of English schoolchildren (described below), Peaker (1971) accounted for 57, 67 and 63 per cent of the uncorrected variance in educational achievement of children finishing primary school and those in first and fourth year of secondary schools, respectively. These investigations did not report the reliabilities of all variables which are necessary for attenuation corrections.

Path Analysis

Keeves and Peaker are among the first to use path analysis in research analysing environmental correlates of cognitive performance. Path analysis is a graphical technique (Figure 29) for hypothesizing a network of causal relations among a set of variables. The example in Figure 29 (which has been examined above) employs single-headed arrows to portray possible causal effects, while double-headed arrows indicate possible correlated causal variables. The broken lines show distal measures hypothesized to be mediated through more proximal variables. That is, it is proposed that family social status and the number of children in the family are superfluous explanatory variables when comprehensive measures of home environment are taken into account. The reason for including the inverse of sibsize is explained in the sixth reading in the present book.

FIGURE 29: *Path analysis diagram*

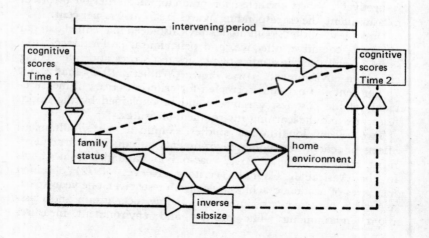

Once a network such as that presented in Figure 29, is constructed, it may be tested using regression analysis (Cohen, 1968; Darlington, 1968; Blalock and Blalock, 1968; Borgatta, 1971). Causality may be inferred from regression under several assumptions:

1. All variables which might affect the dependent variable are either included in the regression equation or are uncorrelated with the variables which are included.
2. Terms are included in the regression equation to handle any curvilinear or interactive effects.
3. The dependent variable has no effect on the independent variable.

These assumptions are rarely met completely, but regression can be useful in experimentally uncontrolled research. Violations of the first assumption mean that a partial and possibly misleading picture of causal relations is drawn. However, the path-guided regression analysis may provoke research that includes other hypothesized variables in subsequent equations. It may also be shown either that hypothesized variables are not correlated with the independent variables or that they add no additional explanation of the variance and are thus unparsimonious or are mediated by (share common variance with) independent variables already in the model. The second assumption may be met by including products of the independent variables to account for interactions and squares or other mathematical forms of the variables to account for curvilinearity; even though Keeves, Peaker and nearly all social scientists employing path-guided regressions have not done so. The third assumption requires judgement; relevant prior events may often be presumed to cause subsequent events rather than vice versa, and common sense can be helpful in provisionally denying reversed causality.

A fourth assumption of causal regressions, only now becoming fully appreciated, is that the dependent and independent variables are measured without error. This assumption is highly questionable in social science research. Bock (1972) has pointed out that in physical science, the measuring instruments and objects measured are relatively fixed, and errors are mostly attributable to experimentally uncontrolled conditions. In biological science neither the objects nor conditions are fixed, and both contribute to error. In social science even the instruments are variable: for example, a prior administration of an alienation scale or a political attitude schedule may affect scores on a second administration because some subjects remember the contents of the scales and their prior responses. Causal relations in social science research may thus appear weak not because they are weak, but because both causes and effects are unreliably measured. Fortunately, measurement and test theory provides formulae for correcting relations attenuated by measurement error. Given the unreliability of the variables, the formulae provide estimates of relations between variables measured without error (Cronbach *et al.* 1972). In the following investigation, path analysis, as presented in Figure 29, is used to test the Bloom model by examining the relation between the environment and reading achievement scores. An attempt is made, within the constraints of the available data, to satisfy the assumptions of path analysis which have been discussed.

The Sample

The data used in the analysis were collected in 1964 as part of the Plowden (1967) study of primary schoolchildren in England, and then collected in 1968 as part of a follow-up study. In the initial investigation, the sampling procedure had two stages. First a stratified random sample was taken from all types of maintained primary schools in England. The schools were divided into three size strata; those with 26 to 50 pupils, 51 to 200 pupils, and schools with 201 and more pupils. Within these strata the schools were classified into four types: infants only, junior schools with an infants section, junior without infants, and all-age schools. From official government statistics an estimation was made of the pupil population, for each of the 12 cells of the sample frame, for England as a whole. It was decided that approximately 3,500 children would be surveyed in the initial study, and as a result a theoretical sample of 3,500 was distributed between the 12 cells in the sample frame. The distribution among the cells was in proportion to the estimated populations. From the theoretical distributions of the sample, the number and type of schools required for the study was determined. Eventually 173 primary schools were selected; 66 infants only, 54 junior without infants, 46 junior with infants, and seven all-age schools.

In the second stage of the sampling procedure, a systematic sample of children was selected from the 173 schools in such a way that from the junior with infants schools and from the all-age schools, children of three age-levels could be chosen. These three age-levels were defined as top infants, bottom juniors and top juniors. From the junior-only schools, two age-levels were chosen and only top infants could be selected from infants-only schools. From the schools in the largest size stratum, 12 children per age group were selected; from schools in the 51-200 size group eight children per age group were chosen; and in the smallest size stratum four children were selected from each age group. In total, 3,349 children's names were selected.

From the selected sample, children who had parents teaching in the sampled schools were withdrawn, and when more than one child in a family was selected, one child was picked at random as the subject for the study. For these reasons, 112 children were deleted from the original sample, leaving an interview sample of 3,237 which was distributed approximately equally between boys and girls. Of the interview sample, 87 parents refused to be interviewed, and 58 parents could not be contacted, leaving a final interview sample for the first survey of 3,092 with 1,023 top juniors (average age, 11), 1,016 bottom juniors (average age, eight), and 1,053 top infants (average age, seven).

In 1968 the three cohorts were surveyed again. During the intervening four years, each cohort had moved up so that in 1968 the senior group (average age 15) was in the fourth year of secondary school, the middle group (average age, 12) in the first year of secondary school, and the junior group (average age, 11) in the last year of the primary school. It was not possible to trace all the original members of the cohorts. The number of children with complete records for both surveys is 2,350 or 76 per cent of the 1964 sample.

In both surveys, in 1964 and 1968, a structured interview schedule was used to gather information about the home environment and the socioeconomic status of the families of the children in the sample. The parents were interviewed in their homes by government social survey interviewers and in 96 per cent of the cases it was the child's natural mother who was interviewed. Although the interviewers were instructed to make every effort to interview the mother on her own, in 43 per cent of the interviews in 1964 at least one other person, generally a child, was present for part or whole of the interview. In 17 per cent of the interviews the father was present. On average, the interviews lasted for an hour, with a quarter of them lasting for approximately one-and-a-half hours. From the home interview surveys, indices were constructed which assessed the literacy of the home, parental aspirations for the child, and parental interest in education. The items that were used to assess each of the environmental indices are presented in Table 49.

Although the indices are not as conceptually comprehensive as those in the studies of Dave, Wolf, Weiss and Marjoribanks, they are much more refined than the measures of the home environment that are generally used in large scale studies (e.g. Flanagan, 1962; Coleman, 1966; Husén, 1967).

For the present study a single measure of the intervening home environment was constructed by taking the means of the two assessments of each of the environmental indices. Then a single environment score was developed from an equally weighted composite of the three means. Similarly, an index of family status was

TABLE 49: *Environmental indices and their related environment items*

ENVIRONMENTAL INDICES	ENVIRONMENT ITEMS
Literacy of the home	Whether: the father or mother belong to a library, the mother reads, the father reads, the child reads at home, the child has library books at home; and the number of books in the home.
Parental aspirations for the child	Whether: a particular type of secondary school was desired, further education was wanted for the child, parents wanted child to take A-level examinations; the type of job desired for the child; preferred age for the child to leave school.
Parental interest in education	Whether the parents: played with the child in the evenings, did things with the child at weekends, took an interest in school, had visited the school; whether the father helped with caring for the child in the home; how many hours a week the husband spent away from the home.

obtained for the analysis by calculating the means of the 1964 and 1968 measures of father occupation, family income and father education and then computing an equally weighted composite of the three means. The intervening sibsize influence was assessed in the same manner. The Spearman-Brown estimated internal consistency reliability of the final equally-weighted home environment index averaged 0·6 and ranged from ·53 for first-year secondary school girls to ·65 for fourth-year secondary boys.

In a review of the original cross-sectional Plowden research, Glennerster (1969) questioned the assumed direction of causality between home environment and cognitive development. For example, it was pointed out that while parental interest in the child may foster academic achievement, the child's ability may increase parental aspirations. Such a problem of interpretation is less critical for the present longitudinal data since initial reading achievement may be entered first in regression models and environment may be entered second so as to determine the variance in home environment, independent of initial reading achievement, associated with final achievement. The ordering of the variables in Peaker's longitudinal analysis of the Plowden data and of the follow-up data collected on the 'Plowden children' has also been criticized (see Acland, 1973). In the Peaker analysis the predictor variables were entered into regression equations in four stages: Time 1 (1964) environment variables, Time 1 reading scores, type of secondary school, and Time 2 (1968) environmental variables. Thus it is not surprising that the variables of the first three stages account for a disproportionately large percentage of the variance in the 1968 achievement scores. As Acland suggests, the Peaker approach implies that the initial achievement variables and the first stage environment variables belong to a single category with the result that the influence of early environment on later achievement is highly inflated. However, if the initial reading scores are defined as control variables and the environment variables are defined as independent variables, then the effect of early environment on later achievement scores would be greatly reduced.

In addition to the deficiencies of the analysis that have been pointed out, Peaker apparently ignored the possibilities of non-linearity, interaction, and attenuation attributable to unreliability. For example, (a) increments to the quality of the home environment may produce diminishing returns on achievement after a certain point; (b) more stimulating environments may be more beneficial to initially poorly achieving children; and (c) the weight of environment in the equations may be under-estimated since it is measured less reliably than initial achievement. An effort was made in the present study to take account of these kinds of possibilities by entering the products and quadratics of all the independent variables that are shown in Figure 29, and correcting the final equations for attenuation due to measurement errors of independent and dependent variables.

Results and Discussion
The first set of results, which are presented in Table 50, were obtained from a series of multiple regression models. In the first analysis the criterion was initial 1964 reading achievement scores with the 1964 family status and inverse of sibsize as the predictors. The results indicate initial reading is significantly but moderately associated with concurrent family status and inverse of sibsize, with the associations being weaker in the younger samples.

In the second analysis (see Table 50) the 1964 family status and sibsize variables explain statistically significant variance in the intervening home environment, but leave from 65 to 81 per cent of the variance in environment unexplained (47 to 71 per cent when corrected for errors in measuring the environment). Both sets of results imply that while children from higher social status families and those from small sibships tend to score higher on the reading tests and to reside in stimulating homes, there are many exceptions. Thus, insofar as reading achievement predicts adult social status, there appears to be an opportunity for social ascendancy of children in lower status families particularly if the sibship is small.

The longitudinal analyses in Table 51 show that large amounts of

TABLE 50: *Cross-sectional regressions*

SAMPLES	Statistic	INITIAL READING EQUATION Family status	Inverse sibsize	R²	INTERVENING ENVIRONMENT EQUATION Family status	Inverse sibsize	R²
Fourth-year	b	·510**	5·802**	·132**	·794**	3·516**	·286**
boys	e	·083	1·313		·067	1·059	
	R^2_1	·086**	·045**		·265**	·021**	
Fourth-year	b	·556**	5·261**	·160**	·783**	4·130**	·304**
girls	e	·075	1·258		·063	1·064	
	R^2_1	·121**	·038**		·276**	·027**	
First-year	b	·744**	5·764**	·130**	·896**	2·261*	·347**
boys	e	·122	1·766		·065	1·023	
	R^2_1	·104**	·025**		·338**	·009*	
First-year	b	·658**	2·398	·098**	·728**	4·516**	·295**
girls	e	·109	1·707		·065	1·013	
	R^2_1	·092**	·005		·255**	·014**	
Primary	b	·588**	− ·715	·061**	·667**	2·727**	·260**
boys	e	·111	1·876		·059	·993	
	R^2_1	·061**	·000		·245**	·014**	
Primary	b	·511**	3·075	·074**	·559**	·653	·189**
girls	e	·100	1·685		·059	·998	
	R^2_1	·066**	·008		·188**	·001	

Note: The statistics in the rows are the raw regression weights (b), their standard errors (e), and the increment in variance explained with the addition of each variable (R^2_1). Relationships significant at the ·05 and ·01 level are indicated respectively with one and two asterisks.

variance in final reading achievement are accounted for by the initial reading scores and the intervening home environment: the major portion of the variance is explained by prior achievement, but the additional variance associated with environment is significant in all cases. In three samples, the product of initial reading and intervening environment adds significantly to the equations, and in four samples the quadratic form of initial reading makes a significant contribution. The other products and quadratics were not significant in more than one sample. In two samples the addition of the product and quadratic terms reduces the regression weight for the linear form of environment because the linear, quadratic, and product terms are highly correlated, and each cannot be accurately estimated when they are all in the same equation. The significant product term suggests the possibility that initial achievement and the intervening environment may interact, that is the possibility of an 'aptitude-treatment interaction'. However, skewness indices revealed slight departures from normality in the reading test scores for the present

TABLE 51: *Longitudinal regressions*

SAMPLES	STATISTIC	A INITIAL READING	B INTERVENING ENVIRONMENT	INTERV. FAMILY STATUS	INTERV. INVERSE SIBSIZE	AB	A^2	R^2	R^2_c
Fourth-year boys	b	1.365**	.320**	−.042	−.496	−.005	−.011*		
	e	.150	.123	.063	.860	.006	.005		
	R^2_1	.722**	.019**	.005	.002	.044**	.031*	.750**	
	R^2_{1c}	.854	.027						.875
Fourth-year girls	b	1.617**	.412**	−.035	−.017	−.007	−.017*		
	e	.174	.145	.069	1.002	.008	.007		
	R^2_1	.676**	.028**	.009	.000	.085**	.004*	.771**	
	R^2_{1c}	.799	.047						.840
First-year boys	b	.383**	.074**	.272**	1.023	.000	.007		
	e	.112	.100	.079	1.008	.005	.004		
	R^2_1	.617**	.014**	.011**	.001	.001	.003	.649**	
	R^2_{1c}	.731	.010						.735
First-year girls	b	.122	.160	.156	1.007	.001	.013**		
	e	.118	.121	.071	.961	.006	.004		
	R^2_1	.591**	.035**	.004*	.002	.005*	.132**	.648**	
	R^2_{1c}	.699	.002						.696
Primary boys	b	.182	.265**	.096	2.068*	−.001	.007		
	e	.134	.099	.071	1.041	.006	.004		
	R^2_1	.388**	.051**	.001	.006**	.000	.005	.451**	
	R^2_{1c}	.479	.083						.558
Primary girls	b	−.073	.165	.071	1.561	.002	.019**		
	e	.143	.116	.065	1.003	.006	.004		
	R^2_1	.357**	.029**	.001	.003	.004	.014**	.408	
	R^2_{1c}	.440	.046						483

Note: The statistics in the rows for each population are in order: the unstandardized regression weight (b), its standard error (e), the incremental variance explained by each variable (R^2), and the same statistic for the first two independent variables corrected for measurement error of the two variables and the criterion. The figures in the last column are estimates of variances accounted for in the population with the same correction. Relationships significant at the ·05 and ·01 levels are indicated respectively with one and two asterisks.

samples; moreover the indices for initial and final reading tests had opposite signs for the samples in question. Scattergrams and response surfaces (see Figure 30) showed that the product and quadratic terms merely adjust the equation weights for these slightly non-normal distributions. The final reading test for the fourth-year groups, for example, is slightly left or negatively skewed, indicating a low 'ceiling' for the test; that is, in effect, those with highest 'True' achievement are not well discriminated from the next highest group due to the test's limitations. Thus, the results of high initial reading scores and high levels of stimulation and particularly their combination, may falsely appear to be cases of slightly diminishing returns (Figure 30).

The increments in variance associated with inverse Sibsize and

FIGURE 30: *Regression surface for fourth-year boys*

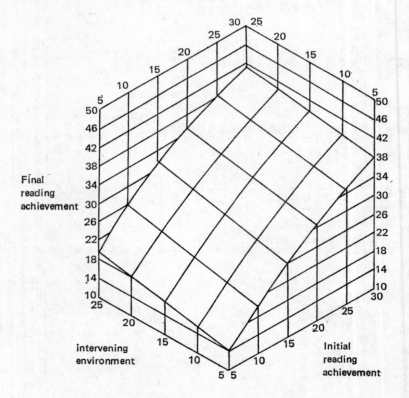

family status are comparatively very small and significant in only one and two samples respectively. These very small increments are the apparent direct effects of these variables on final reading achievement that are unmediated by the home environment. More comprehensive measures of the home environment are likely to mediate completely these effects.

Table 51 shows that the estimated accountable population variances in final reading achievement corrected for errors of measurement are substantial. They are considerably higher than the corresponding uncorrected variances and far higher than the concurrent corrected variances accounted for by status and sibsize (see Table 50). The variance in final reading achievement explained by initial reading achievement is from 18 to 23 per cent higher than the raw estimates when corrected for measurement error. Corrected estimates of variance in final reading achievement accounted for by environment are about 50 per cent higher in the primary and fourth-year groups. The dotted lines in Figure 30 show the regression slopes of final reading achievement on environment, corrected for measurement error in both variables for fourth-year boys scoring high (above ·5 standard deviations higher than the mean) medium, and low (below −·5 standard deviations below the mean) on initial reading. The corrected slopes indicate how uncorrected regression can underestimate environmental effects when there are substantial errors in measuring the environment. On the other hand, the corrected environmental slopes in all cases are far smaller than the uncorrected initial reading achievement slopes; and in the case of the first-year secondary groups the corrected environmental slopes are smaller than uncorrected environmental slopes because the correction raises the already high correlation of initial achievement and intervening environment.

The corrected variances are higher in older groups and higher for boys than girls. The increasing predictability with age and for boys is attributable to the higher correlations of initial and final reading with age and in the samples of boys. Environment has a small significant, positive association with final reading, independent of initial reading in all samples, and the magnitude of its effect is not dependent on sex nor is it consistently stronger in younger groups as hypothesized by Anderson and Bloom. The results do not provide support for the proposition that the influences of the home environment on reading achievement are greater in the early years of schooling than in the secondary stage of education.

Conclusion

The Anderson Overlap Hypothesis and the Bloom model of

cognitive development have provoked a substantial amount of research in the last decade. All the studies, including the present one, may be criticized for a variety of reasons, several of which were mentioned in a previous section. The most common and obvious fault of many of the studies is the use of data collected at a single point in time to infer cognitive growth over time. However, some of the later work has employed longitudinal data. Keeves and Peaker have used path analysis to guide their regressions towards causal inferences; and Keeves, in collection measurements not only of the home but of peer and school environments, has come closest to meeting the first assumption of path analysis regarding the inclusiveness of the set of causal variables. For example, a limitation of the present study is that no measures of the school, neighbourhood or peer group were included.

In future work it can be hoped that measurement of both social environment and cognitive growth will be improved. Both characteristics are multivariate, and it is likely to be found that different environments and parts of environments will produce different effects on a variety of growth measures and will produce different effects on different individual characteristics depending on the pattern of their initial states. Some of these apparent effects may be attributable to skewed observations, as seems to be the case in the Plowden longitudinal data. However, for subsequent research the following equation, which is constructed from the model that Bloom developed and from the results of the present study, might be estimated.

$$I_{j,t_2} = \sum b_j I_{j,t_1}^* + \sum b_k E_{k,t_{1\text{-}2}}^* + \sum b_k E_{k,t_{1\text{-}2}}^* + \sum b_{jk}(I_{j,t_1}^*)(E_{k,t_{1\text{-}2}}^*)$$

where I_j, t_2 is a given individual characteristic, the first term on the right hand side of the model is a weighted composite of a number of antecedent individual characteristics (the asterisk indicates the characteristics are in the optimal mathematical form; for example, linear, quadratic, or logarithmic, for prediction); the second term is a similar intervening environmental composite, and the last term is the weighted composite of products of antecedent characteristics and environment. Research based on the proposed generalized model would allow for the multiplicity of possible causes in the two domains, and the possibility that initial characteristics interact with environment measures, determining later characteristics. The equation does not take into account the possibilities of genetically programmed factors analogous to sexual maturation effects or the adolescent height spurts that may hasten or impede cognitive growth (Wilson, 1972). Nor does it explicitly consider the absorption of early environments that produce unobservable propensities which are latent until later developmental stages; but only recently have these effects been claimed, and they are still controversial (McCall, 1970; McCall *et al.*, 1972).

The results of the present study suggest that adolescents may benefit as much as younger children from a stimulating home environment. Moreover, the larger amounts of variance explained by initial achievement in reading in comparison with that explained by the intervening four-year environments should be a reason for patience rather than pessimism among parents and educators. A stimulating home environment for several years is likely to lead to some enhancement of cognitive ability. If the environmental stimulation in the home and peer group were to be co-ordinated with school environments and sustained throughout infancy, childhood and adolescence, then substantial cognitive gains might be achieved.

By analysing the longitudinal development of human characteristics and by emphasizing the need for more refined measures of learning environments, Bloom provided the necessary impetus for studies of environmental influences on cognitive growth. In the present study an attempt has been made to build upon the model provided by Bloom and suggest a modified paradigm which might be used to guide future research in environmental social psychology.

References

ACLAND, H. (1973). Review of Peaker, G. F. (1971). *The Plowden Children Four Years Later*. Slough: NFER. In *Harvard Educ. Rev.*, **43**, 296–8.

ALLIN SMITH, W. and GRIMES, J. W. (1961). 'Compulsivity, anxiety, and school achievement', *Merrill-Palmer Quarterly*, **7**, 247–71.

ANASTASI, A. (1956). 'Intelligence and family size', *Psychol. Bull.*, **53**, 187–209.

ANDERSON, G. J. (1968). 'Effects of classroom social climate on individual learning'. Unpublished doctoral dissertation, Harvard University.

ANDERSON, G. J. (1970). 'Effects of classroom social climate on individual learning', *Amer. Educ. Res. J.*, **7**, 135–52.

ANDERSON, G. J. (1971). 'The assessment of learning environments: a manual for the Learning Environment Inventory and the My Class Inventory'. Atlantic Institute of Education, Halifax, Nova Scotia.

ANDERSON, G. J. and WALBERG, H. J. (1968). 'Classroom climate and group learning', *Internat. J. Educ. Sci.* **2**, 175–80.

ANDERSON, G. J. and WALBERG, H. J. (1972). 'Class size and the social environment of learning: a mixed replication and extension', *Alberta J. Educ. Res.*, **18**, 227–86.

ANDERSON, G. J., WALBERG, H. J. and WELCH, W. W. (1969). 'Curriculum effects on the social climate of learning: a new representation of discriminant functions', *Amer. Educ. Res. J.*, **6**, 315–28.

ANDERSON, H. H. (1939). 'The measurement of domination and of socially integrative behaviour in teachers' contacts of children', *Child Develop*, **10**, 73–89.

ANDERSON, H. H. and BREWER, H. M. (1945). 'Studies of teachers' classroom personalities: I. Communicative and socially integrative behaviour of kindergarten teachers', *Applied Psychol. Monograph*, No. 6.

ANDERSON, H. H. and BREWER, J. E. (1946). 'Studies of teachers' classroom personalities: II. Effects of teachers' dominative and integrative contacts on children's classroom behaviour', *Applied Psychol. Monograph*, No. 8.

ANDERSON, J. E. (1939). 'The limitations of Infant and Preschool Tests in the Measurement of Intelligence', *J. Psychol.*, **8**, 351–79.

ANDERSON, R. H. and RITCHER, C. (1969). 'Pupil progress', in EBEL, R. L. (Ed.). *Encyclopedia of Educ. Res.* New York: Macmillan.

ANTHONY, B. C. M. (1967). 'The identification and measurement of classroom environmental process variables related to academic achievement'. Unpublished doctoral dissertation, University of Chicago.

ARGYRIS, C. (1964). *Integrating the Individual and the Organization*. New York: Wiley.

ASTIN, A. W. (1962). ' "Productivity" of undergraduate institutions', *Science*, **136**, 129–35.

ASTIN, A. W. (1963a). 'Differential college effects on the motivation of talented students to obtain the PhD degree', *J. of Educ. Psychol.*, **54**, 63–71.

ASTIN, A. W. (1963b). 'Undergraduate institutions and the production of scientists', *Science*, **141**, 334–8.

ASTIN, A. W. (1965a). 'Effects of different college environments on the vocational choices of high aptitude students', *J. Counsel. Psychol.*, **12**, 28–34.

ASTIN, A. W. (1965b). *Who Goes Where to College?* Chicago: Science Research Associates.

ASTIN, A. W. (1968a). *The College Environment.* Washington: American Council on Education.

ASTIN, A. W. (1968b). 'Undergraduate achievement and institutional "excellence"', *Science*, **161**, 661–8.

ASTIN, A. and HOLLAND, J. (1961). 'The environmental assessment technique: a way to measure college environments', *J. of Educ. Psychol.*, **52**, 308–16.

ASTIN, A. W. and PANOS, R. J. (1966). 'A national research data bank for higher education', *Educ. Record*, **47**, 5–17.

ASTIN, A. W. and PANOS, R. J. (1969). *The Educational and Vocational Development of College Students.* Washington, D.C.; American Council on Education.

ASTIN, A. W. and PANOS, R. J. (1971). 'Evaluation of educational programs', Chapter 20 in forthcoming revision of THORNDIKE, R. L. (Ed.), *Educ. Meas.* Washington, D.C.: American Council on Education.

AUSUBEL, D. P. (1968). *Educational Psychology: A Cognitive View.* New York: Holt, Rinehart and Winston.

BARKER, R. G. (1968). *Ecological Psychology.* Stanford: Stanford University Press.

BARKER, R. G. and GUMP, P. V. (1964). *Big School, Small School.* Stanford: Stanford University Press.

BARR, A. S. (1929). *Characteristic Differences in the Teaching Performance of Good and Poor Teachers of the Social Studies.* Bloomington, Indiana: Public School.

BARTH, R. S. (1970). 'Open Education: Assumptions about learning and knowledge'. Unpublished doctoral dissertation, Harvard University.

BAR-YAM, M. (1969). 'The interaction of student characteristics with instructional strategies: a study of students' performance and attitude in an innovative high school course'. Unpublished doctoral dissertation, Harvard University.

BAYLEY, N. (1965). 'Comparisons of mental and motor test scores for ages 1–15 months by sex, birth order, race, geographical location and education of parents', *Child Develop.*, **36**, 379–411.

BEREITER, C. (1965). 'Academic instruction and preschool children', in: *Language Programs for the Disadvantaged.* National Council of Teachers of English.

BEREITER, C. and ENGLEMAN, S. (1966). *Teaching Disadvantaged Children in the Preschool.* Englewood Cliffs: Prentice-Hall.

BERNSTEIN, B. (1961). 'Social structure, language and learning', *Educ. Res.*, **3**, 163–76.

BIDDLE, J. (1964). 'The integration of teacher effectiveness research', in BIDDLE, B. J. and ELLANA, W. J. (Eds.), *Contemporary Research on Teacher Effectiveness.* New York: Holt, Rinehart and Winston.

BIDWELL, C. (1965). 'The school as a formal organization', in MARCH, J. G. (Ed.) *Handbook of Organizations.* Chicago: Rand McNally.

BLALOCK, H. M. and BLALOCK, A. B. (Eds.) (1968). *Methodology in Social Research.* London: McGraw Hill.

BLAU, P. H. (1960). 'Structural effects', *American Sociological Review*, **25**, 178–93.

BLOCK, J. *et al.* (1951). 'Testing for the existence of psychometric patterns', *J. Abnormal Social Psychol.*, **46**, 356–9.

BLOOM, B. S. (Ed.) (1956). *Taxonomy of Educational Objectives: Cognitive Domain.* New York: Longmans, Green.

BLOOM, B. S. (1964). *Stability and Change in Human Characteristics.* New York: Wiley.

BLOOM, B. S. (1966). 'Twenty-five years of educational research', *Amer. Educ. Res. J.*, **3**, 211–21.

BOCK, R. D. (1966). 'Contributions of multivariate experimental designs to educational research', in CATTELL, R. B. (Ed.) *Multivariate Exper. Psychol.* Chicago: Rand-McNally.

BOCK, R. D. (1972). Review of CRONBACH, L. J., GLESER, G. C., NANDA, H. and RAJARATWAM, N. (1972). *The Dependability of Behavioral Measures*. New York: Wiley. In *Science*, **178**, 1275–6.

BOCK, R. D. and HAGGARD, E. A. (1968). 'The use of multivariate analysis in behavioral research', in WHITLA, D. K. (Ed.). *Handbook of Meas. and Assess. in the Behavioral Sciences*. Reading, Mass.: Addison-Wesley.

BOCK, R. D. and VANDENBERG, S. G. (1968). 'Components of heritable variation in mental test scores', in: VANDENBERG, S. G. (Ed.) *Progress in Human Behavior Genetics*. Baltimore: Johns Hopkins Press.

BORGATTA, E. F. (Ed.). (1971). *Sociol. Methodol.* London: Jossey-Bass.

BORUCH, R. F. and CREAGER, J. A. (1970). Investigation of Measurement Error in Educational Survey Research. (Proposal submitted to the Office of Education.)

BOTTENBERG, R. A. and WARD, J. H. (1963). *Applied Multiple Linear Regression.* Texas: Personnel Research Laboratory.

BOWLES, S. and LEWIN, H. M. (1968). 'The determinants of scholastic achievement – an appraisal of some recent evidence', *J. Human Resources*, **3**, 3–24.

BOYLE, R. P. (1966). 'The effect of the high school on students' aspirations', *Amer. J. Sociol.*, **71**, 628–39.

BRACHT, G. H. and GLASS, G. V. (1968). 'The external validity of experiments', *Amer. Educ. Res. J.*, **5**, 437–74.

BURKHEAD, J., FOX, T.G. and HOLLAND, J. W. (1967). *Input and Output in Large-City High Schools*. Syracuse: University Press.

BURKS, B. S. (1928). 'The relative influence of nature and nurture upon mental development', *National Society for the Study of Education Yearbook*. **27**, 219–316.

BURT, C. (1937). *The Backward Child*. London: University of London Press.

BURT, C. (1955). 'The evidence for the concept of intelligence', *Brit. J. Educ. Psychol.*, **25**, 158–77.

BURT, C. (1957). 'The distribution of intelligence', *Brit. J. Psychol.*, **48**, 161–75.

BURT, C. L. (1958). 'The inheritance of mental ability', *Amer. Psychol.*, **13**, 1–15.

BURT, C. (1961). 'Intelligence and social mobility', *British J. Statis. Psychol.*, **14**, 3–24.

BURT, C. (1961). 'The gifted child', *Brit. J. Statis. Psychol.*, **14**, 123–39.

BURT, C. (1963). 'Is intelligence distributed normally?' *Brit. J. Statis. Psychol.*, **16**, 175–90.

BURT, C. (1966). 'The genetic determination of differences in intelligence: A study of monozygotic twins reared together and apart', *Brit. J. Psycho.*, **57**, 137–53.

BURT, C. and HOWARD, M. (1956). 'The multifactorial theory of inheritance and its application to intelligence', *Brit. J. Statis. Psychol.*, **9**, 95–131.

BUSSIS, A. M. and CHITTENDEN, E. A. (1970). *Analysis of an Approach to Open Education*. Princeton: Educational Testing Service.

CALLIS, R. (1963). Counseling. *Rev. Educ. Res.*, **33**, 179–87.

CAMPBELL, D. T. and STANLEY, J. D. (1963). 'Experimental and quasi-experimental designs for research on teaching', in GAGE, N. L. (Ed.). *Handbook for Research on Teaching*. Chicago: Rand McNally.

CARTER, C. O. (1970). *Human Heredity*. Harmondsworth: Penguin.

CARTWRIGHT, D. and ZANDER, A. (1968). *Group Dynamics: Research and Theory* (3rd ed.). Evanston, Illinois: Row, Peterson.

CATTELL, R. B. (1963). 'Theory of fluid and crystallized intelligence: a critical experiment', *J. Educ. Psychol.*, **54**, 1–22.

CATTELL, R. B. and BUTCHER, H. J. (1968). *The Prediction of Achievement and Creativity.* New York: Bobbs-Merrill.

CICIRELLI, V. G. (1967). 'Sibling configuration, creativity, IQ and academic achievement', *Child Develop.*, **38**, 481–90.

COHEN, J. (1968). 'Multiple regression as a general data-analytic system', *Psychol. Bull.*, **70**, 426–43.

COLEMAN, J. S. (1964). *Introduction to Mathematical Sociology*. London: Free Press of Glencoe.

COLEMAN, J. S. *et al.* (1966). *Equality of Educational Opportunity*. Washington, D.C.: US Department of Health, Education, and Welfare.

CORAH, N. L. *et al.* (1965). 'Effects of perinatal anoxia after seven years', *Psychol. Monographs*, **79**, Whole No. 596.

CREAGER, J. A. (1970). 'On methods for analysis and interpretation of input and treatment effects on education outcomes'. American Council on Education (mimeo).

CREAGER, J. A. and BORUCH, R. F. (1970). 'Orthogonal analysis of linear composite variance, *Proceedings, 77th Annual Convention*. American Psychological Association.

CREAGER, J. A., ASTIN, A. W., BAYER, A. E. and BORUCH, R. F. (1968). 'National norms for entering college freshmen – fall 1968'. ACE Research Report 3 (1).

CREAGER, J. A., ASTIN, A. W., BAYER, A. E., BORUCH, R. F. and DREW, D. E. (1969). 'National norms for entering college freshmen – fall 1969'. ACE Research Report 4 (7).

CRONBACH, L. J. (1957). 'The two disciplines of scientific psychology', *Amer. Psychol.*, **12**, 671–84.

CRONBACH, L. J., GLESER, G. C., NANDA, H. and RAJARATWAM, N. (1972). *The Dependability of Behavioral Measures*. New York: Wiley.

CRONBACH, L. J. and SNOW, R. E. (1974). *Aptitudes and Instructional Methods*. New York: Appleton.

CROWNE, D. P. and MARLOWE, D. (1964). *The Approval Motive*. New York: Wiley.

DARLINGTON, R. B. (1968). Multiple regression in psychological research in practice. *Psychol. Bull.*, **69**, 161–82.

DARLINGTON, R. B., WEINBERG, S. L. and WALBERG, H. J. (1973). 'Canonical variate analysis and related techniques', *Rev. Educ. Res.*, **43**, 433–54.

DAVE, R. H. (1963). 'The identification and measurement of environmental process variables that are related to educational achievement'. Unpublished doctoral dissertation, University of Chicago.

DEUTSCH, M. (1962). 'Social and psychological perspective for the facilitation of the development of the preschool child'. Prepared for the Arden House Conference on Preschool Enrichment of Socially Disadvantaged Children (mimeo).

DEUTSCH, M., KATZ, I. and JENSEN, A. R. (1968). *Social Class, Race and Psychological Development*. New York: Holt, Rinehart and Winston.

DOUGLAS, J. W. B. (1968). *All Our Future*. London: Peter Davies.

DREGER, R. M. and MILLER, K. S. (1960). 'Comparative psychological studies of negroes and whites in the United States', *Psychol. Bull.*, **57**, 361–402.

DUNCAN, O. D. (1966). 'Path analysis: sociological examples', *Amer. J. Sociol.*, **72**, 1–16.

DYER, H. S. (1968). 'School factors and educational opportunity', *Harvard Educational Review*, **38**, 38–56.

DYER, P. B. A. (1967). 'Home environment and achievement in Trinidad'. Unpublished doctoral dissertation, University of Alberta.

EDWARDS, D. W. (1971). 'The development of questionnaire method of measuring exploration preferences', in FELDMAN, M. J. (Ed.). *Studies in Psychotherapy and behavior change: 2. Theory and Research in Community Mental Health*. Buffalo: State University of New York at Buffalo.

EICHENWALD, H. (1966). 'Mental retardation', *Science*. **153**, 1,290–6.

EKSTROM, R. B. (1961). 'Experimental studies of homogeneous groupings: a critical review', *School Rev.*, **69**, 216–26.

ELLIS, N. R. (Ed.) (1963). *Handbook of Mental Deficiency*. New York: McGraw-Hill.

ENDLER, N. and HUNT, J. (1968). 'S-R inventories of hostility and comparisons of the proportions of variance from persons, responses, and situations for hospitality and anxiousness', *J. of Personality and Social Psychol.*, **9**, 309–15.

ENTWISTLE, D. R. (1966). *Word Associations of Young Children*. Baltimore: Johns Hopkins Press.

ERLENMEYER-KIMLING, L. and JARVIK, L. F. (1963). 'Genetics and intelligence: a review', *Science*, **142**, 1, 477–9.

EYSENCK, H. J. (1971). *Race, Intelligence and Education*. London: Temple Smith.

EYSENCK, H. J. and COOKSON, D. (1969). 'Personality in primary school children: 3-family background, *Brit. J. Educ. Psychol.*, **40**, 117–31.

FARQUHAR, W. W. (1963). 'Motivation factors related to academic achievement: final report of cooperative research project', No. 846. Michigan: Office of Research and Publications.

FELDMAN, D. (1973). 'Problems in the analysis of patterns of abilities, *Child Develop.*, **44**, 12–18.

FELDMAN, K. A. and NEWCOMB, T. M. (1969). *The Impact of College on Students*. San Francisco: Jossey-Bass.

FERGUSON, G. A. (1954). 'On learning and human ability', *Canadian J. Psychol.*, **8**, 95–112.

FERGUSON, G. A. (1956). 'On transfer and the abilities of man,' *Canadian J. Psychol.*, **10**, 121–31.

FINCH, F. H. and NEMZEK, C. L. (1940). 'Attendance and achievement in secondary school', *J. Educ. Res.*, **34**, 119–26.

FLANAGAN, J. C. *et al.* (1962). *Project Talent*. University of Pittsburgh.

FLANDERS, N. A. (1965). 'Some relationships among teacher influence, pupil attitudes and achievement'. U.S. Office of Education Cooperative Research Monograph 12.

FRASER, E. (1965). *Home Environment and the School*. London: University of London Press.

FROST, J. L. and HAWKES, G. R. (1966). *The Disadvantaged Child*. New York: Houghton Mifflin.

GAGE, N. L. (1963). *Handbook of Research on Teaching*. Chicago: Rand McNally.

GARDNER, D. and CASS, J. E. (1965). *The Role of Teacher in the Infant and Nursery School*. Oxford: Pergamon.

GERST, M. and MOOS, R. (1972). 'The psychological environment of university student residences', in MITCHELL, W. A. (Ed.), *Environmental Design: Research and Practice*. Los Angeles: University of California.

GLASS, G. V. (1968). 'Educational Piltdown men', *Phi Delta Kappan*, **34**, 148–51.

GLASS, G. V. and HAKSTIAN, R. A. (1969). 'Measures of association in comparative experiments', *Amer. Educ. Res. J.*, **6**, 403–14.

GLENNERSTER, H. (1969). 'The Plowden Research', *Royal Stat. Soc. J.*, Series A, **132**, 194–204.

GOODMAN, S. M. (1959). *The Assessment of School Quality*. Albany: New York State Education Department.

GORDON, M. M. (1964). *Assimilation in American Life*. New York: Oxford University Press.

GOUGH, H. G. (1949). 'A short social status inventory', *J. Educ. Psychol.*, **40**, 52–6.

GRAHAM, F. K. (1962). 'Development three years after perinatal anoxia and other potentially damaging newborn experiences', *Psychol. Monographs*, **78**, Whole No. 522.

GRAY, S. W. and KLAUS, R. A. (1965). 'An experimental preschool program for culturally deprived children', *Child Develop.*, **36**, 887–98.

GREENHOUSE, S. W. and GEISSER, S. (1959). 'On methods in the analysis of profile data', *Psychometrika*, **24**, 95–112.

GROBMAN, A. B. (1969). *The Changing classroom: the role of the Biological Sciences Curriculum Study.* New York: Doubleday.

GUILFORD, J. P. (1965). *Fundamental statistics in Psychology and Education.* New York: McGraw-Hill.

HANSON, R. A. (1971). 'The Development of verbal intelligence: a longitudinal study'. Unpublished doctoral dissertation. University of Chicago.

HAYS, W. L. (1963). *Statistics.* New York: Holt, Rinehart and Winston.

HEATHERS, G. (1969). 'Grouping', in EBEL, R. L. (Ed.), *Encyclopedia of Educ. Res.* New York: Macmillan.

HEMPHILL, J. K. (1956). *Group Dimensions: A Manual for their Measurement.* Columbus: Ohio State University.

HERRIOTT, R. E. (1963). 'Some social determinants of educational aspiration', *Harvard Education Review*, **33**, 157–77.

HESS, R. D. (1964). 'Educability and rehabilitation: the future of the welfare class', *Marriage and Family Living*, **24**, 422–9.

HESS, R. D. and SHIPMAN, V. (1965). 'Early blocks to children's learning', *Children*, **12**, 189–94.

HOLLAND, J. L. (1957). 'Undergraduate origins of American scientists, *Science*, **126**, 433–7.

HOLLAND, J. L. (1959). 'Determinants of college choice', *College and University*, **35**, 11–28.

HONZIK, M. P. (1957). 'Developmental studies of parent-child resemblance in intelligence', *Child Develop.*, **28**, 215–28.

HOTELLING, H. (1933). 'The most predictable criterion', *J. Educ. Psychol.*, **26**, 139–43.

HOTELLING, H. (1936). 'Relations between two sets of variates', *Biometrika*, **28**, 321–77.

HOYT, D. P. (1959). 'Size of high school and college grades', *Personnel and Guidance Journal*, **37**, 569–73.

HOYT, D. P. (1965). *The Relationship between College Grades and Adult Achievement.* Iowa City: American College Testing Program.

HUNTLEY, R. M. C. (1966). 'Heritability of intelligence', in MEADE, J. E. and PARKES, A. S. (Eds.), *Genetic and Environmental Factors in Human Ability.* Edinburgh: Oliver and Boyd.

HUSEN, I. (1967). *International Study of Achievement in Mathematics.* London: Wiley.

ILG, F. L. and AMES, L. B. (1964). *School Readiness: Behaviour Tests used at the Gessell Institute.* New York: Harper and Row.

JENSEN, A. R. (1961). 'Learning abilities in Mexican-American and Anglo-American children', *California J. Educ.*, **12**, 147–59.

JENSEN, A. R. (1963). 'Learning abilities in retarded, average, and gifted children', *Merrill-Palmer Quarterly*, **9**, 123–40.

JENSEN, A. R. (1965). 'Rote learning in retarded adults and normal children', *Amer. J. Mental Defic.*, **69**, 828–34.

JENSEN, A. R. (1966a). 'Verbal mediation and education and educational potential', *Psychol. in the Schools*, **3**, 99–109.

JENSEN, A. R. (1966). 'Social class and perceptual learning', *Mental Hygiene*, **50**, 226–39.

JENSEN, A. R. (1967). 'Estimation of the limits of heritability of traits by comparison of monozygotic and dizygotic twins', *Proceedings of the National Academy of Sciences*, **58**, 149–57.

JENSEN, A. R. (1968a). 'Social class, race, and genetics: implications for education', *Amer. Educ. Res. J.*, **5**, 1–42.

JENSEN, A. R. (1968b). 'Patterns of mental ability and socioeconomic status', *Proceedings of the National Academy of Sciences*, **60**, 1330–7.

JENSEN, A. R. (1968a). 'Social class and verbal learning', in DEUTSCH, M., JENSEN, A. R. and KATZ, I. (Eds.), *Social Class, Race, and Psychological Development*. New York: Holt, Rinehart and Winston.

JENSEN, A. R. (1969). 'How much can we boost IQ and scholastic achievement?' *Harvard Educ. Rev.*, **39**, 1–123.

JENSEN, A. R. (1969b). 'Intelligence, learning ability, and socioeconomic status', *J. Special Educ.*, **3**, 23–35.

JENSEN, A. R. (1970a). 'A theory of primary and secondary mental retardation', in ELLIS, N. R. (Ed.), *International Review of Research in Mental Retardation*, Vol. IV. New York: Academic Press.

JENSEN, A. R. (1970b). 'Hierarchial theories of mental ability', in DOCKRELL, B. (Ed.), *On Intelligence*. London: Methuen.

JENSEN, A. R. and ROHWER, W. D. (1963). 'Verbal mediation in paired-associate and serial learning', *J. Verbal Learn. and Verbal Behavior*, **1**, 346–52.

JENSEN, A. R. and ROHWER, W. D. (1965). 'Syntactical mediation of serial and paired-associate learning as a function of age', *Child Develop.*, **36**, 601–8.

JENSEN, A. R. and ROHWER, W. D. (1970a). 'Mental retardation, mental age, and learning rate', *J. Educ. Psychol.*, **59**, 402–3.

JENSEN, A. R. and ROHWER, W. D. (1970b). 'An experimental analysis of learning abilities in culturally disadvantaged children'. Final Report, Office of Economic Opportunity. Contract No. OEO 2404.

JOHN, V. P. (1962). 'The intellectual development of slum children. Paper presented at American Orthopsychiatric Association'.

KAISER, H. F. (1960). 'Directional statistical hypotheses', *Psychol. Rev.*, **67**, 160–7.

KATZ, D. and KAHN, R. L. (1966). *The Social Psychology of Organizations*. New York: Wiley.

KAUFMAN, B. (1965). *Up the down Staircase*. Englewood Cliffs, N.J.: Prentice-Hall.

KEEVES, J. P. (1972). *Educational Environment and Student Achievement*. Stockholm: Almquist and Wiksell.

KELLAGHAN, T. and MACNAMARRA, J. (1972). Family correlates of verbal reasoning ability. *Develop. Psych.*, **7**, 49–53.

KELLY, J. G. (1966). 'Ecological constraints on mental health services', *Amer. Psychol.*, **21**, 535–9.

KELLY, J. G. (1967). 'Naturalistic observations and theory confirmation: an example', *Human Develop.*, **10**, 212–22.

KENNEDY, W. A., DE RIET, V. and WHITE, J. C. (1963). 'A normative sample of intelligence and achievement of Negro elementary school children in the southeastern United States', *Monographs Society Research in Child Development*, **28**, No. 6.

KENNETT, K. F. and CROPLEY, A. J. (1970). 'Intelligence, family size and socioeconomic status', *J. of Biosocial Sci.*, **2**, 227–36.

KNAPP, R. H. and GOODRICH, H. B. (1952). 'Origins of American Scientists: A study made under the direction of a committee of the faculty of Wesleyan University.' Chicago: University of Chicago Press.

KNAPP, R. H. and GREENBAUM, J. H. (1953). *The younger American Scholar: his collegiate origins*. Chicago: University of Chicago Press.

KUHN, T. S. (1962). *The Structure of Scientific Revolutions*. Chicago: University of Chicago Press.

LEAHY, A. M. (1935). 'Nature-nurture and intelligence', *Genetic Psychol. Monographs*, **17**, 237–308.

LESSER, G. et al. (1964). 'Mental abilities of children in different social and cultural groups'. New York: Cooperative Research Project, No. 1635.

LEWIN, K. (1965). *Field Theory in Social Science*. New York: Harper and Row.

LICHTENWALNER, J. S. and MAXWELL, J. W. (1969). 'The relationship of birth order and socioeconomic status to the creativity of preschool children', *Child Develop.*, **40,** 1241–7.

LINDQUIST, E. F. (1953). *Design and analysis of experiments in Psychology and Education.* Boston: Houghton-Mifflin.

McCALL, R. B. (1970). 'Intelligence Quotient Pattern over age: comparisons among siblings and parent-child pairs', *Science*, **170,** 644–8.

McCALL, R. B., WACHS, T. D. and WILSON, R. S. (1972). 'Similarity in developmental profile among related pairs of human infants', *Science*, **178,** 1004–7.

McCARTHY, D. (1946). 'Language development in children', in CARMICHAEL, L. (Ed.), *Manual of Child Psychol.* New York: Wiley.

McDILL, E. L., MEYERS, E. D. and RIGSBY, L. C. (1969). 'Educational climates of high schools – their effects and sources', *Sociol. of Educ.*, **74,** 567–86.

McGURK, F. C. J. (1956). 'A scientist's report on race differences', in HUMPHREY, H. H. (Ed.), *School Desegregation: Documents and Commentaries.* New York: Thomas Y. Crowell. 1964.

McNEMAR, Q. (1962). *Psychological Statistics.* New York: Wiley.

MAGUIRE, T. O., GOETZ, E. and MANOS, J. (1972). 'Evaluation activities of the IPI Project Year 2: the evaluation of two instruments for assessing classroom climate for primary grades'. Alberta Human Resources Research Council.

MARKLAND, S. (1963). 'Scholastic attainments as related to size and homogeneity of classes', *Educ. Res.*, **6,** 63–7.

MARJORIBANKS, K. (1971). 'The learning environment of the home: an instrument', *Australian and N.Z. J. Sociol.*, **7,** 69–77.

MARJORIBANKS, K. (1972a). 'Ethnic and Environmental Influences on Mental Abilities', *Amer. J. Sociol.*, **78,** 323–37.

MARJORIBANKS, K. (1972b). 'Ethnicity and Learning Patterns: A Replication and an Explanation', *Sociology*, **6,** 417–31.

MARJORIBANKS, K. and WALBERG, H. J. (1974). 'Family environment: sibling constellation variables and social class', *J. Biosocial Sci.* (in press).

MARJORIBANKS, K. and WALBERG, H. J. (1974). 'Social class, family size and cognitive performance', in *Proceedings of Biennial Conference of the International Society for the Study of Behavioral Development.* University of Michigan.

MARJORIBANKS, K., WALBERG, H. J. and BARGEN, M. (1974). 'Mental abilities: social class and sibling constellation correlates', *Brit. J. of Soc. and Clinical Psychol.* (in press).

MAXWELL, J. (1969). 'Intelligence, education and fertility: a comparison between the 1932 and 1947 Scottish surveys', *J. Biosocial Sci.*, **1,** 247–71.

MENNE, J. W. (1967). 'Techniques for evaluating the college environment', *J. Educ. Meas.*, **4,** 219–25.

MICHAEL, J. A. (1966). 'On neighbourhood context and college plans', *Amer. Sociol. Rev.*, **31,** 706–7.

MITZEL, H. E. and RABINOWITZ, W. (1953). 'Assessing social emotional climate in the classroom by Withall's technique', *Psychological Monographs*, **63,** No. 368.

MOLLENKOPF, W. G. and MELVILLE, S. D. (1956). *A study of secondary school characteristics as related to test scores.* Research Bulletin 56–6. Princeton: Educational Testing Service.

MOOS, R. (1968). 'The assessment of the social climates of correctional institutions', *J. Res. in Crime and Delinquency*, **5,** 174–88.

MOOS, R. (1969). 'Sources of variance in response to questionnaires and in behaviour', *J. Abnorm. Psychol.*, **74,** 405–12.

MOOS, R. (1971). 'Revision of the ward atmosphere scales: technical report.' Unpublished manuscript, Social Ecology Laboratory, Stanford University.

Moos, R. (1972). 'Assessment of the psychosocial environments of community-oriented psychiatric treatment programs', *J. Abnor. Psychol.*, **79**, 9–18.

Moos, R. (1974). 'A model for the facilitation and evaluation of social change', *J. Applied Behavioral Sci.* (in press).

Moos, R. and Houts, P. (1968). 'Assessment of the social-atmospheres of psychiatric wards', *J. Abnorm. Psychol.*, **73**, 595–604.

Moos, R. and Otto, J. (1972). 'The community-oriented programs environment scale: A methodology for the facilitation and evaluation of social change', *Community Mental Health J.*, **8**, 28–37.

Mosteller, F. and Moynihan, D. P. (Eds.) (1972). *On Equality of Educational Opportunity*. New York: Random House.

Murray, C. (1967). 'The effects of ordinal position on measured intelligence and peer group acceptance in adolescence', *Brit. J. of Soc. and Clinical Psychol.* **10**, 221–7.

Murray, H. (1938). *Explorations in Personality*. New York: Oxford University Press.

Newman, H. H., Freeman, F. N. and Holzinger, K. J. (1937). *Twins: A Study of Heredity and Environment*. Chicago: University of Chicago Press.

Nisbet, J. D. (1953). 'Family environment and intelligence, *Eugenics Rev.*, **45**, 31–40.

Nisbet, J. D. and Entwistle, N. J. (1967). 'Intelligence and family size, 1949–1965', *Brit. J. Educ. Psychol.*, **37**, 188–93.

Nunnally, J. C. (1967). *Psychometric Theory*. New York: McGraw-Hill.

Oldman, D., Bytheway, B. and Horobin, G. (1971). 'Family structure and educational achievment', *J. of Biosocial Sci.*, *Supplement* **3**, 81–91.

Osler, S. F. and Cooke, R. E. (1965). *The Biological Basis of Mental Retardation*. Baltimore: Johns Hopkins Press.

Otto, W. (1969). *The Wisconsin Prototypic System of Reading Skill Development: An Interim report*. Madison: Wisconsin Research and Development Center for Cognitive Learning.

Pace, C. R. (1960). 'Five college environments', *College Board Rev.*, **41**, 24–8.

Pace, C. R. (1963). *College and University Environmental Scales*. Princeton: Educational Testing Service.

Pace, C. R. (1966). 'Comparisons of CUES results from different groups of reporters'. College Entrance Examination Board, Report No. 1. University of California, Los Angeles.

Pace, C. R. (1969). *College and University Environment Scales Technical Manual*. Princeton: Educational Testing Service.

Pace, C. R. (1970). 'Differences in campus atmosphere', in Miles, M. and Charters, W. (Eds.), *Learning in Social Settings*. Boston: Allyn and Bacon.

Pace, R. and Stern, G. C. (1958). 'An approach to the measurement of psychological characteristics of college environments', *J. of Educ. Psychol.*, **49**, 269–77.

Panos, R. J., Astin, A. W. and Creager, J. A. (1967). 'National norms for entering college freshmen – fall 1967', *ACE Research Report*, 2 (7).

Pasamanick, B. and Knobloch, H. (1966). 'Retrospective studies on the epidemiology of reproductive causality: old and new?', *Merrill-Palmer Quarterly*, **12**, 7–26.

Peaker, G. F. (1971). *The Plowden Children Four Years Later*. Slough: NFER.

Pearson, K. (1903). 'On the inheritance of the mental and moral characters in man, and its comparison with the inheritance of physical characters', *J. Anthropology Institute*, **33**, 179–237.

Pervin, L. L. (1968). 'Performance satisfaction as a function of individual environment fit', *Psychol. Bull.*, **69**, 56–68.

PIERCE, W. D., TRICKETT, E. I. and MOOS, R. H. (1972). 'Changing ward atmosphere through staff discussion of the perceived environment', *Archives of General Psychiatry*, **26**, 35–41.

PLOWDEN, B. *et al.* (1967). *Children and their Primary Schools*. London: HMSO.

POOLE, A. and KUHN, A. (1973). 'Family size and ordinal position: correlates of academic success', *J. of Biosocial Sci.*, **5**, 51–9.

RACKHAM, J. (1968). 'Technology, control, and organization', in PYM, D. (Ed.), *Industrial Society*. Harmondsworth: Penguin.

RAMAYYA, D. P. (1971). 'A comparative study of achievement skills, personality variables and classroom climate in graded and non-graded programs'. Unpublished doctoral dissertation, University of Utah.

RAPIER, J. L. (1966). 'The learning abilities of normal and retarded children as a function of social class'. Unpublished doctoral dissertation, University of California, Berkeley.

RATHBONE, C. H. (1970). 'Open Education and the Teacher'. Unpublished doctoral dissertation, Harvard University.

RAUSCH, H. C., DITTMAN, A. T. and TAYLOR, T. T. (1959). 'Person, setting, and change in social interaction', *Human Relations*, **12**, 361–78.

RECORD, R. G., McKEOWN, T. and EDWARDS, J. H. (1969). 'The relation of measured intelligence to birth order and maternal age', *Annals of Human Genetics*, **33**, 61–9.

RICHARDS, J. M. (1966). 'A simple analytic model for college effects', *School Rev.*, **74**, 308–92.

ROMBERG, T. A. and HARVEY, J. G. (1969). *Developing Mathematical Processes: Background and Projections*. Madison: Wisconsin Research and Development Centre for Cognitive Learning.

SARASON, S. B., LEVINE, M., GOLDENBERG, I. I., CHERLIN, D. L. and BENNETT, E. M. (1966). *Psychology in Community Settings: Clinical, Educational, Vocational, Social Aspects*. New York: Wiley.

SCHRAMM, W. (1962). 'Learning from instructional television', *Rev. Educ. Res.*, **32**, 156–67.

SCHULTZ, R. E. (1966). 'The control of "error" in educational experimentation', *School Rev.*, **74**, 150–8.

SEARS, P. S. and SHERMAN, V. S. (1964). *In Pursuit of Self Esteem*. Belmont, California: Wadsworth.

SELVIN, H. C. and HAGSTROM, W. O. (1963). 'The empirical classification of formal groups', *Amer. Sociol. Rev.*, **28**, 399–411.

SEWELL, W. H. (1964). 'Community of residence and college plans', *Amer. Sociol. Rev.*, **29**, 24–38.

SEWELL, W. H. and ORENSTEIN, A. M. (1965). 'Community of residence and occupational choice', *Amer. J. Sociol.*, **70**, 551–63.

SHAYCROFT, M. F. (1967). *The High School Years: Growth in Cognitive Skills*. Pittsburgh: University of Pittsburgh.

SHUEY, A. M. (1966). *The Testing of Negro Intelligence*. New York: Social Science Press.

SILBERMAN, C. E. (1970). *Crisis in the Classroom*. New York: Random House.

SKEELS, H. M. (1966). 'Adult status of children with contrasting early life experiences: a follow-up study', *Child Develop. Monographs*, **31**, No. 3, Serial No. 105.

SKEELS, H. M. and DYE, H. B. (1939). 'A study of the effects of differential stimulation on mentally retarded children', *Proceedings and Addresses of the American Association of Mental Deficiency*, **44**, 114–36.

SKODAK, M. and SKEELS, H. M. (1949). 'A final follow-up study of one hundred adopted children', *J. Genetic Psychol.*, **75**, 85–125.

STEPHENS, J. M. (1968). *The Process of Schooling: A Psychological Examination.* New York: Holt, Rinehart and Winston.

STERN, G. C. (1963). 'High school characteristics index', in *Scoring Instructions and College Norms.* Syracuse: Syracuse University.

STERN, G. (1970). *People in Contest: Measuring Person-Environment Congruence in Education and Industry.* New York: Wiley.

STODOLSKY, S. S. and LESSER, G. S. (1967). 'Learning Patterns in the disadvantaged, *Harvard Educ. Rev.*, **37**, 564–93.

STRANG, R. (1937). *Behavior and Background of students in college and secondary school.* New York: Harper and Row.

TANNENBAUM, A. S. and BACHMAN, J. G. (1964). 'Structural versus individual effects', *Amer. J. Sociol.*, **69**, 585–95.

THOMAS, J. A. (1962). 'Efficiency in education: a study of the relationship between selected inputs and mean test scores'. Unpublished doctoral dissertation. Stanford University.

THORNDIKE, R. L. (1951). 'Community variables as predictors of intelligence and academic achievement', *J. Educ. Psychol.*, **42**, 321–38.

THORNDIKE, R. L. (1966). 'Intellectual status and intellectual growth', *J. Educ. Psychol.*, **57**, 121–7.

TRICKETT, E. J. and Moos, R. H. (1970). 'Generality and specificity of student reactions in high school classrooms', *Adolescence*, **5**, 373–90.

TRICKETT, E. J. and TODD, D. M. (1972). 'Assessment of the high school culture: an ecological perspective', *Theory Into Practice*, **11**' 28–37.

TRICKETT, E. J., KELLY, J. G. and TODD, D. M. (1972). 'The social environment of the high school: Guidelines for individual change and organizational redevelopment', in GOLANN, S. E. and EISENDORFER, D. (Eds.), *Community Psychology and Mental Health*. New York: Appleton.

TUCKER, L. R., DAMARIN, F. and MESSICK, S. (1966). 'A base-free measure of change', *Psychometrika*, **31**, 457–73.

TURNER, R. H. (1964). *The Social Context of Ambition.* San Francisco: Chandler.

TYLER, L. E. (1965). *The Psychology of Human Differences.* New York: Appleton-Century-Crofts.

VERNON, P. E. (1969). *Intelligence and Cultural Environment.* London: Methuen.

WALBERG, H. J. (1968a). 'Structural and effective aspects of classroom climate', *Psychol. in the Schools*, **5**, 247–53.

WALBERG, H. J. (1968b). 'Can educational research contribute to the practice of teaching?', *J. of Social Work*, 6, 77–85.

WALBERG, H. J. (1968c). 'Teacher personality and classroom climate', *Psychol. in the Schools*, **5**, 163–9.

WALBERG, H. J. (1969a). 'Predicting class learning. A multivariate approach to the class as a social system', *Amer. Educ. Res. J.*, **4**, 529–42.

WALBERG, H. J. (1969b). 'Social environment as a mediator of classroom learning', *J. Educ. Psychol.*, **60**, 443–8.

WALBERG, H. J. (1969c). 'Class size and the social environment of learning', *Human Relations*, **22**, 465–75.

WALBERG, H. J. (1970a). 'A model for research on instruction', *School Review*, **78**, 185–200.

WALBERG, H. J. (1970b). 'An evaluation of an urban-suburban bussing program: student achievement and perception of class learning environments'. Boston, Mass. Metropolitan Council on Educational Opportunity.

WALBERG, H. J. (1971). 'Models for optimizing and individualizing school learning', *Interchange*, **3**, 15–27.

WALBERG, H. J. (1972). 'Social environment and individual learning: a test of the Bloom model', *J. Educ. Psychol.*, **63**, 69–73.

WALBERG, H. J. and AHLGREN, A. (1970). 'Predictors of the Social Environment of Learning', *Amer. Educ. Res. J.*, **7**, 153–68.

WALBERG, H. J. and ANDERSON, G. J. (1968). 'Classroom climate and individual learning', *J. Educ. Psychol.* **59**, 414–9.

WALBERG, H. J. and ANDERSON, G. J. (1972). 'Properties of the achieving urban classes, *J. Educ. Psychol.*, 381–5.

WALBERG, H. J. and MARJORIBANKS, K. (1973). 'Differential mental abilities and home environment: a canonical analysis', *Develop. Psychol.*, **9**.

WALBERG, H. J. and THOMAS, S. C. (1971). 'Characteristics of Open Education: Toward an Operational Definition'. Newton, Massachusetts: TDR Associates.

WALBERG, H. J., HOUSE, E. R. and STEELE, J. M. (1973). 'Grade level, cognition, and effect: a cross-section of classroom perceptions', *J. Educ. Psychol.*, **64, 2,** 142–6.

WALBERG, H. J., SORINSON, J. and FISCHBACH, T. (1972). 'Ecological correlates of ambience in the learning environment', *Amer. Educ. Res. J.*, **9**, 139–48.

WALBERG, H. J., STEELE, J. M. and HOUSE, E. R. (1974). 'Subject matter areas and cognitive press', *J. Educ. Psychol.* (in press).

WALLEN, N. E. and TRAVERS, R. M. W. (1963). 'Analysis and investigation of teaching methods', in GAGE, N. L. (Ed.), *Handbook of Research on Teaching*. Chicago: McNally.

WECHSLER, D. (1958). *The Measurement and Appraisal of Adult Intelligence* (4th ed.). Baltimore: Williams and Wilkins.

WEISS, J. (1969). 'The identification and measurement of home environmental factors related to achievement motivation and self esteem'. Unpublished doctoral dissertation, University of Chicago.

WELCH, W. W. and WALBERG, H. J. (1972). 'A national experiment in curriculum evaluation', *Amer. Educ. Res. J.*, **9**, 373–83.

WELCH, W. W., WALBERG, H. J. and WATSON, F. G. (1970). *Evaluation Strategy, Implementation, and Results: A Case Study of Harvard Project Physics*. Cambridge, Mass: Harvard University.

WERTS, C. E. (1968). 'Path analysis: testimonial of a proselyte', *Amer. J. Sociol.*, **73,** 509–12.

WERTS, C. E. and WATLEY, D. J. (1969). 'A student's dilemma: big fish – little pond or little fish – big pond', *J. Counsel. Psychol.*, **16,** 14–19.

WHITEHEAD, A. N. (1929). *The Aims of Education*. New York: Macmillan.

WILSON, A. B. (1967). 'Educational consequences of segregation in a California community', *Racial Isolation in the Public Schools*, Appendices, Vol II, p. 185. Washington, D.C.: US Commission on Civil Rights.

WILSON, R. S. (1972). 'Twins: Early Mental Development', *Science*, **175,** 914–7.

WISEMAN, S. (1964). *Education and Environment*. Manchester: Manchester University Press.

WITHALL, J. (1949). 'Development of a technique for the measurement of socio-emotional climate in classrooms', *J. Exper. Educ.*, **17,** 347–61.

WITHALL, J. (1951). 'The development of a climate index', *J. Educ. Res.*, **45,** 93–9.

WOLF, R. M. (1964). 'The identification and measurement of environmental process variables related to intelligence'. Unpublished doctoral dissertion, University of Chicago.

ZIGLER, E. (1967). 'Familial mental retardation: a continuing dilemma', *Science*, 155, 292-8.